ROYAL HISTORICAL SOCIETY

STUDIES IN HISTORY

New Series

SAMUEL RAWSON GARDINER AND THE IDEA OF HISTORY

This series is supported by annual subventions from the Economic History Society and from the Past and Present Society

SAMUEL RAWSON GARDINER AND THE IDEA OF HISTORY

Mark Nixon

THE ROYAL HISTORICAL SOCIETY
THE BOYDELL PRESS

First published 2010

A Royal Historical Society publication
Published by The Boydell Press
an imprint of Boydell & Brewer Ltd
PO Box 9, Woodbridge, Suffolk IP12 3DF, UK
and of Boydell & Brewer Inc.
668 Mt Hope Avenue, Rochester, NY 14620, USA
website: www.boydellandbrewer.com

ISBN 978–0–86193–310–5

ISSN 0269–2244

A CIP catalogue record for this book is available
from the British Library

The publisher has no responsibility for the continued existence or accuracy of
URLs for external or third-party internet websites referred to in this book,
and does not guarantee that any content on such websites is,
or will remain, accurate or appropriate.

Papers used by Boydell & Brewer Ltd are natural, recyclable products
made from wood grown in sustainable forests

Printed in Great Britain by
CPI Antony Rowe, Chippenham and Eastbourne

FOR NANCY-MAY MATTHEWS

'life is short and Gardiner is long'

Guernsey Jones, 1901

Contents

Acknowledgements

It would not have been possible to carry out this research without the financial assistance of the Student Awards Agency for Scotland, the Arts and Humanities Research Board (as was), and the Faculty of Arts of Stirling University. St Deiniol's Library, Hawarden, gave me two fellowships, each of one month's duration, in order to stay and conduct research there, for which I would like to thank the Warden and the Trustees. The Institute of Historical Research awarded me a Scouloudi History Research Fellowship for 2003–4, which was of inestimable assistance in the final stages.

The staff of the following libraries cannot be thanked enough: Stirling University Library, the National Library of Scotland, the Mitchell Library, St Deiniol's Library, the British Library, London University Library, Edinburgh University Library, Glasgow University Library, Newcastle University Library, the Bodleian Library, Oxford, and Cambridge University Library. I must offer particular acknowledgement to Gordon Willis at Stirling University Library, for arranging for me to take out, on long-term loan, Gardiner's *History* on top of my standard borrowing allowance. The staff of that library do an excellent job, often in the face of difficult circumstances. Two other libraries should also receive special mention. Glasgow's Mitchell Library is perhaps Britain's finest public institution, as wonderful and unique as the city itself. St Deiniol's Library is Britain's best-kept academic secret, offering a combined working and social environment unparalleled in my experience. My fondest thanks go to the Librarian, Patsy Williams (and her assistant librarians of the past decade), Greg Morris, Karen Parry, and the Warden, Peter Francis. In addition to these libraries, I must also thank the staff of the relevant archives, special collections and manuscripts divisions of the following institutions: King's College, Cambridge; City University, London; King's College London; University College London; University of London Library; All Souls' College, Oxford; Christ Church, Oxford; Jesus College, Oxford; Merton College, Oxford; the University of Reading; the University of Calgary; the Huntington Library, San Marino, CA; and the University of Pennsylvania. Many thanks also to the Warden and Fellows of Merton College, Oxford, for permission to reproduce the portrait photograph (MCPh/A13/4) on the cover.

A number of individuals have helped with specific elements of my research, and I would like to thank the following for taking the time to respond to my various requests for information, suggested reading, and their thoughts on my ideas: Daniel Breazeale, John Drakakis, David Fahey, Tim Grass, David Killingray, Timothy Lang, John Morrill, Myron Noonkester and Adrian Streete. Fiona Chalamanda helped me with translating some

German passages, Stephen Penn with some Latin. Just because the material that Joe Bray helped me with has been excised (for reasons of space and balance only) does not mean that I do not appreciate his help – quite the opposite. Conversations with Jonathan Wild have been particularly inspirational and formative for my developing ideas. Helen Dingwall, Jane Garnett and Richard Whiting offered judicious comments on early drafts of this book, for which I am grateful. Finally, the two anonymous readers appointed by the RHS and Arthur Burns as editorial advisor offered extremely helpful comments and a great deal of support; without them, rather obviously, this book would never have come to fruition.

Early versions of parts of this book were given as papers on a number of occasions. In addition to offering my gratitude to those present who offered comments and questions, I would like to offer particular thanks to Peter Yeandle for the invitation to speak at Histfest VII, Lancaster, in the summer of 2003 and to James Knowles for the invitation to speak at the Caroline Drama Symposium organised by him on behalf of the Scottish Institute for Northern Renaissance Studies, held at Stirling in April 2004. The members of the Modern British History Seminar of the Institute of Historical Research have been an inspiration, and offered keen, yet kind, criticism when I spoke to them in February 2004. I must also express my heartfelt gratitude to those who have spoken at or attended the History of Ideas seminar series that it was my pleasure to co-ordinate at Stirling.

David Bebbington guided my early development as a researcher with more tolerance, critical acumen and liberal learning than anyone has any right to expect. For ten years I was, off and on, a student of the history department at Stirling University, and built up a series of debts – in particular to Jim Smyth, Emma Macleod, Bob McKean, George Peden and Mike Rapport, and, of course, to the office staff: Linda Bradley, Margaret Hendry and Annabelle Hopkins. The inhabitants of B19 were highly supportive; Neil Forsyth, Alison Kennedy and Ross Christie had their ears bent more than most. The environment at St Deiniol's is highly conducive to work, but the friendship of Anne Isba and Neslihan Senoçak has ensured that my visits have been extremely pleasurable as well as productive. Roland Quinault has been more helpful than he probably realises. Without the support of my parents, Ro and Allan Drowley, this book would never have been completed. I cannot even begin to give due recognition to the ways in which Bethan Benwell has supported me throughout this process. Nancy-May Matthews, one of a number of members of my family who have shared my fascination with the past, offered financial help with the building up of my personal Gardiner library. Unfortunately she passed away during the period in which the manuscript was being prepared and will never see the result; for this reason, I dedicate the book to her memory.

Mark Nixon
April 2010

Abbreviations

CR	*Contemporary Review*
DN	*Daily News*
DNB	*Dictionary of national biography*
EB	*Encyclopædia Britannica* (9th edn)
EHR	*English Historical Review*
ER	*Edinburgh Review*
FR	*Fortnightly Review*
HJ	*Historical Journal*
ILN	*Illustrated London News*
NBR	*North British Review*
NQ	*Notes and Queries*
PMG	*Pall Mall Gazette*
QR	*Quarterly Review*
RH	*Revue historique*
TLS	*Times Literary Supplement*

Editorial Note

The following abbreviations are used throughout for Gardiner's principal writings:

CD	*The constitutional documents of the puritan revolution, 1625–1660*, 3rd edn, Oxford 1906
C&P	*History of the Commonwealth and Protectorate, 1649–1660: with a supplementary chapter*, London 1902
CPH	*Cromwell's place in history: founded on six lectures delivered in the University of Oxford*, London 1898
GCW	*History of the Great Civil War, 1642–1649*, London 1893
HoE	*History of England, from the accession of James I to the outbreak of the Civil War*, London 1883–4
OC	*Oliver Cromwell*, London 1900

In the cases of the *History of England*, the *History of the Great Civil War*, and the *History of the Commonwealth and Protectorate*, these are the octavo 'Cabinet editions' published by Longmans. In each case, they are revised editions of earlier works. They are, however, the editions which are most readily found in libraries and, indeed, were the editions which were most widely read. They have been chosen as the principal editions for study in this book for ease of reference for the reader, but also in recognition of the fact that it is with these editions that Gardiner reached his audience and influenced developing thought on seventeenth-century British history.

The appropriate section of the Gardiner bibliography provided as an appendix to this book may be consulted for the publication details of the different editions. Nevertheless, a short bibliographical explanation is required. The ten-volume *History of England* (1883–4) reprints five separate titles, each of which originally appeared as two-volume editions between 1863 and 1882. They were revised for the 'Cabinet edition', but to different degrees. The last set saw little more than the correction of printing errors; the first set, which had first appeared twenty years earlier, underwent significant revision, although the outline argument and the essential details are almost untouched. The opening chapter, for instance, in which Gardiner offered an 'Historical Retrospect' from 'England before the Conquest' to 'The last years of Elizabeth' was clearly considered by him to be in the main superfluous in 1883, although many of the later chapters are untouched by revision of any kind. Similarly, the *History of the Great Civil War* is more revised than the *History of the Commonwealth and Protectorate*, although again neither is greatly changed and neither see any substantial changes to the structure or the argument. The main changes were in physical form. The *History of the Great Civil War* had originally appeared in three volumes; the 'Cabinet edition' appeared in four. The uncompleted *History of the Commonwealth and Protectorate* had appeared in three volumes by the time of Gardiner's death in 1902, reaching 1656. After his death, the first chapter of the proposed fourth volume was published in a matching binding, and then incorporated into the fourth volume of the 'Cabinet edition'.

Although the 'Cabinet editions' are the principal editions chosen for this study, it is sometimes necessary to refer to the original editions, in which cases the full relevant reference is given.

As the eighteen volumes covering the period 1603 to 1656 were intended by Gardiner as a continuous narrative history, they have been treated throughout this book as a single entity, as indeed they have been by most scholars since their publication. On those occasions when the present author wishes to refer to the *History of England*, the *History of the Great Civil War* and the *History of the Commonwealth and Protectorate* in this way, the phrase 'the *History*' is used. This applies only to the main text; footnotes will, of course, make it clear to which of these three titularly distinct works reference is being made.

For the volume of biography entitled *Oliver Cromwell*, the Longmans, Green & Company's 1900 octavo edition has been preferred to Goupil & Company's 1899 first edition in folio. Goupil's version was part of a series of lavishly illustrated biographies of British statesmen published in limited numbers (1,475 copies on standard-issue paper, and 350 on 'Japanese paper'). These volumes have become highly collectable and are rarely to be found in public or university libraries, unlike the Longmans edition. Aside from the deletion from the Longmans edition of the preface in which the owners of the originals of the images reproduced were thanked, the present author is unaware of any verbal difference between the two editions.

Similarly, the third edition of the *Constitutional documents* has been selected for ease of reference, being the edition which has rarely, if ever, been out of print since its first appearance in 1906 (Oxford/Clarendon kept it in print until the 1990s; it is currently available in a print-on-demand edition from Kessinger Publishing). As the second edition of 1899 had an enlarged compass (beginning in 1625 rather than 1628) and also saw the addition of a few more documents, Gardiner added a small amount of material to the introductory chapter and restructured its sections, whilst leaving unchanged its essentials and its conclusions (although a few further points of clarification were added and a few sentences removed). Only minor corrections were made in the text of the introduction for the third edition; however, the pagination is different, and it is for this reason that it is necessary to specify the edition.

To avoid repetition, Gardiner's name has been deleted from all references to his writings. All volume and page references for articles in the *Dictionary of national biography* refer to the 1921 Oxford University Press reprint. Act, scene and line numbers given for Shakespeare references are taken from the most recent relevant 'Arden' edition, currently published by International Thomson Publishing Services. Note also that, according to the former style, book titles and quotations use Thirty Years' War, but that, according to modern style, the form Thirty Years War is used in the body of the text.

Introduction

During 2002 a major television series entitled 'The Civil War' was broadcast by the BBC. In the opening episode the presenter, Tristram Hunt, introduced the topic while sitting on a beach. Apparently playing with a couple of pieces of driftwood and a piece of string that he had found on his stage, Hunt began his narrative with the assertion that what has traditionally been called 'the English Civil War' was neither a single event nor a specifically English event, and should be thought of, rather, as 'the British Civil Wars'. Moreover, he opined, they should be recognised as a part of a wider European conflagration. And then, with a flourish, he dramatically stabbed the driftwood – now lashed together into the form of a crucifix – into the sand and declared that the wars in Britain and the wider European conflict were all about religion.[1] Visually, the image was striking, and the effect on the viewer was to suggest the newness of this vision of the events of the 1640s. Indeed, his introduction to the subject did present to the audience many elements of the current ruling orthodoxy in early Stuart studies – or, at least, set up the principal counter-argument to the previous prevailing orthodoxy, that of the Marxist historians of the 1960s and 1970s who, following Christopher Hill, talked of an 'English Revolution' caused by, and constitutive of, a particular social order.[2] Hunt's account, however, was not new – in a few short sentences, he had summarised the analysis provided by the first great historian of the period, the Victorian Samuel Rawson Gardiner.

Although he has not been the subject of any large-scale study, Gardiner, by dint of his reputation amongst his peers, his huge industry within historical studies and his magisterial works, has received the attention of a number of commentators on late nineteenth-century historiography and seventeenth-century studies. They offer a confusing number of different characterisations of the man and his work. Labels suggested by such work include nonconformist,[3]

1 'The Civil War', episode 1, 'The Breakdown', BBC2, 7 Jan. 2002.

2 The 'Revisionist' School is, of course, a complex, many-headed beast (as, indeed, was the Marxist School), and some scholars have questioned the centrality of religion to the conflict, stressing instead the actions, ambitions, squabbles and so on of high political actors at the Stuart court. However, all agree that the social theory of the 'Revolution' must be rejected, and that the conflict encapsulates a series of British wars: R. Cust and A. Hughes 'Introduction', to R. Cust and A. Hughes (eds), *The English Civil War*, London 1997.

3 M. G. Finlayson, *Historians, puritanism, and the English Revolution: the religious factor in English politics before and after the Interregnum*, Toronto 1983, 26; R. Howell, 'Who needs another Cromwell? Nineteenth-century images of Oliver Cromwell', in R. C. Richardson (ed.), *Images of Oliver Cromwell: essays for and by Roger Howell Jr*, Manchester 1993, 28.

positivist,[4] liberal nationalist,[5] crypto-imperialist,[6] partisan Gladstonian Liberal[7] or 'Victorian Liberal',[8] a non-partisan[9] and honest truth-teller,[10] a constitutional evolutionist,[11] an early part of the 'anti-Whig reaction',[12] Whig,[13] 'whiggish'[14] or 'broadly Whig',[15] chronicler,[16] anachronistic,[17] authoritative[18] and 'nearly infallible',[19] and hopelessly fallible.[20]

4 N. Tyacke, 'An unnoticed work of Samuel Rawson Gardiner', *Bulletin of the Institute of Historical Research* xlvii (1974), 244–5.

5 T. Lang, *The Victorians and the Stuart heritage: interpretations of a discordant past*, Cambridge 1995, 151–2, 155, 161, 163.

6 M. Noonkester, 'Liberalism in imperialism: S. R. Gardiner confronts English hegemony in Ireland', unpubl. paper, Southern Conference on British Studies, Fort Worth, Tx, 5 Nov. 1999, 7.

7 J. S. A. Adamson, 'Eminent Victorians: S. R. Gardiner and the Liberal as hero', *HJ* xxxiii (1990), 641–57.

8 R. C. Richardson, 'Cromwell and the inter-war European dictators', in Richardson, *Images of Oliver Cromwell*, 109.

9 J. R. Hale, *The evolution of British historiography: from Bacon to Namier*, London 1967, 60.

10 A. J. Grant, *English historians*, London 1906, p. lxxii.

11 C. Russell, 'Introduction', to C. Russell (ed.), *The origins of the English Civil War*, London 1973, 4–5.

12 P. M. B. Blaas, *Continuity and anachronism: parliamentary and constitutional development in Whig historiography and in the anti-Whig reaction between 1890 and 1930*, The Hague 1978, 41–3.

13 T. K. Rabb, 'Reflections on the comparison between historians and scientists', in H. Kozicki (ed.), *Developments in modern historiography*, New York 1993, 73. One very recent study of the historiography of the Civil War period has claimed that 'Gardiner produced the definitive Whig narrative of the period': A. MacLachlan, *The rise and fall of revolutionary England: an essay on the fabrication of seventeenth-century history*, Basingstoke 1996, 26. However, one must remain sceptical about the level of understanding of Gardiner attained in a text that throughout its pages calls him 'Samuel Ralston Gardiner'.

14 G. R. Elton, 'Lawrence Stone, The causes of the English Revolution' [review], repr in *Studies in Tudor and Stuart politics and government*, III: *Papers and reviews, 1973–1981*, Cambridge 1983, 475–6; B. H. G. Wormald, *Clarendon: politics, historiography and religion, 1640–1660*, Cambridge 1964, passim, but especially the introduction.

15 R. Cust, *The forced loan and English politics, 1626–1628*, Oxford 1987, 5.

16 H. A. L. Fisher, *Pages from the past*, Oxford 1939, 59.

17 R. G. Usher, *A critical study of the historical method of Samuel Rawson Gardiner with an excursus on the historical conception of the puritan revolution from Clarendon to Gardiner*, St Louis, Wa 1915, passim.

18 A. Fletcher, *The outbreak of the English Civil War*, London, 1985, p. viii. In a similar vein, to others he was 'authoritative … and confident' (W. H. Coates, 'An analysis of major conflicts in seventeenth-century England', in W. A. Aiken and B. D. Henning [eds], *Conflict in Stuart England*, London 1960, 18) and 'scholarly and authoritative' (R. Macgillivray, *Restoration historians and the English Civil War*, The Hague 1974, 48).

19 C. Hill, 'Introduction', to S. R. Gardiner, *History of the Great Civil War*, repr. edn, London 1987, i, p. xxx. It is interesting to note that this is a 'late-Hill' perspective. In an earlier, more radically Marxist, phase, Hill complained of 'the tyranny of Gardiner', in an essay for *Modern Quarterly* i (1938), 91, cited in MacLachlan *Rise and fall*, 242.

20 The essential element in, for instance, the critique of the anonymous correspondent of the *TLS* who signed her/his letters as 'Historian': *TLS*, 25 Sept. 1919, 515; 23 Oct.

It seems almost incredible that such a diverse (and contradictory) set of opinions – and this presents only a selection of the views that have been expressed, by only a small selection of those that have commented on him – could be held with regard to one man. What is it about Gardiner that causes such confusion? One thing becomes clear when one takes the time to read Gardiner's work and analyse it, as is attempted in this book: his historical method in practice appears to bear little relationship to that described by most of the authors of the studies referenced above.

This apparent difficulty in pinning Gardiner down, or failure to evaluate properly the man and his work, is exemplified by Lytton Strachey. Although his series of essays on historians[21] did not include one on Gardiner, Strachey used a characterisation of Gardiner in expounding two of his subjects: Macaulay and Creighton. In the essay on Macaulay, who, Strachey wanted to argue, was a partial and colourful narrator, he wrote:

> What are the qualities that make a historian? Obviously, these three – a capacity for absorbing facts, a capacity for stating them, and a point of view. The two latter are connected, but not necessarily inseparable. The late Professor Samuel Gardiner, for instance, could absorb facts, and he could state them; but he had no point of view; and the result is that his book on the most exciting period of English history resembles nothing so much as a very large heap of sawdust.[22]

Conversely, in his essay on Creighton, who, Strachey wished to argue, was an impartial chronicler of the highest order (not that Strachey had any regard for Creighton's approach), he wrote:

> [Creighton] belonged to … the school of Oxford and Cambridge inquirers, who sought to reconstruct the past solidly and patiently, with nothing but facts to assist them – pure facts, untwisted by political or metaphysical bias and uncoloured by romance. In this attempt Creighton succeeded admirably. He was industrious, exact, clear-headed, and possessed a command over words that was quite sufficient for his purposes. He succeeded more completely than Professor Samuel Gardiner, whose history of the Early Stuarts and the Civil Wars was a contemporary work. Gardiner did his best, but he was not an absolute master of the method. Strive as he would, he could not prevent himself, now and then, from being a little sympathetic to one or other of his personages; sometimes he positively alluded to a physical circumstance; in short, humanity would come creeping in. A mistake! for Professor Gardiner's feelings about mankind are not illuminating; and the result is a slight blur.[23]

1919, 591; 20 Nov. 1919, 674–5; 4 Dec. 1919, 714. Perhaps the first discussion to take this line is H. Craik, *The life of Edward earl of Clarendon, lord high chancellor of England*, London 1911.

21 L. Strachey, *Portraits in miniature and other essays*, London 1931.

22 Ibid. 169–70.

23 Ibid. 208–9.

Although these two characterisations are not exact opposites (Strachey clearly considers Gardiner to be perennially dull), they still contain contradictions. Gardiner acts as the dry-as-dust counterbalance to the partial Macaulay, and as the partial counterbalance to the 'extremely scientific' Creighton. Thus, the historian that 'had no point of view' is also, it is implied, twisted by 'bias'. Unable or unwilling to settle on a final idea of Gardiner, Strachey merely invents new ones to serve each of his purposes.

Although Strachey did not take a final opinion on Gardiner, many have. What is noteworthy about these attempts to 'understand' Gardiner is that they are all based on details extracted from Gardiner's life – they ultimately refer to the context of Gardiner's writing. They have then become hypotheses, the evidence for which, or instances of which, can then be discovered retrospectively in his writings, whether or not they are obviously there. This is the 'contextualist' method of historiographical analysis.

The contextualist accounts of Gardiner revolve around two poles: his 'scientific' methodology and his religio-political connections. Indeed, these are the two issues which have informed most writing on late-Victorian historiography. Theorists of disciplinisation and professionalisation have posited that period as one of a new approach to the study of history, in which the university-based professional, with a suitable training in empirical historical method, took the role of the principal interpreter of the past away from the gentleman-scholar, the 'Man of Letters', whose literary modes were to be replaced by rational exposition.[24] Historians of religion and politics, however, have viewed history-writing as governed principally by religious or political concerns, just as they view the historical process as governed principally by religious or political concerns. This 'ideological' understanding of history-writing is the predominant model for all historians, not just historians of historiography, and certainly not limited to those interested in late nineteenth-century interpretations of the past. It provides a method that is easily understood and easily applied by those who have no special training in, or knowledge of, methods of historical study through the ages, but who need some kind of coverage of the subject in order to carry out the deconstruction of past interpretations of their chosen topic, period or individual that is considered necessary to an adequately discursive historiography. In short, it is the method favoured by historians of every historical phenomenon except History itself.

This in turn leads into another problem of much historiographical analysis – the emphasis on topic rather than historical theory or an individual historian. In addition to the understandable preoccupation of political historians with politics, there is a tendency for the political historian's period

24 The best modern account of disciplinisation is to be found in D. Amigoni, *Victorian biography: intellectuals and the ordering of discourse*, Hemel Hempstead 1993.

of study to act as a focus as s/he studies historiography.[25] This results in a peculiarity of the study of the history of historiography: that most commentators on a given historian are themselves not historians of the period in which the historian under study lived. Rather, they are historians of the period which the earlier historian studied. Thus, virtually all the descriptions of Gardiner to be found have been written by historians of the early seventeenth century rather than of the late nineteenth century. They are preoccupied with what Gardiner got right and what Gardiner got wrong, and the concepts that they use to describe him are without exception treated as bias, that is as those elements of Gardiner's thought which are seen as destructive of a 'seventeenth-century real' – for which, read 'late twentieth- or early twenty-first-century "seventeenth-century real"'. The historian of historiography should be interested, however, in what is constitutive of a 'nineteenth-century "seventeenth-century real"'.

This approach to historiography – seeing its analysis from the point of view of topic rather than historiography or the historian – deepened during the course of the twentieth century under the shadow that has been cast over the study of British historiography by Herbert Butterfield. In *Man on his past* (1955), Butterfield called for an approach to the history of historiography which treated of a historical problem and the ways it has been understood. For him, 'the history of historiography' is potentially stuck in the 'marshy fields of intellectual and social history', those 'vague and indefinite subjects' that he always warned students against attempting.[26] To study historiography from these vantage points entails studying 'the history of the various concepts which the historian has to handle, and the concepts which govern his reconstruction of the past'.[27] To Butterfield that is a minefield, and by studying the treatment of a particular issue instead, he argued, it is possible 'to emancipate us from the tyranny of those superimposed concepts which so often control our historical reconstructions', thus advertising his belief that there is a 'real' against which the historiography can be compared in order to lay bare the ideological assumptions of the historian.[28]

Whether as a result of the calls for such work from Butterfield or from some other imperative, this approach to the history of historiography has become commonplace. Thus in the field of the study of the historiography of the seventeenth century there is, for example, William Lamont's *Puritanism and historical controversy* (1996), R. C. Richardson's *The debate on the English Revolution* (1977, 1988, 1998) and Alistair MacLachlan's *The rise and fall of revolutionary England* (1996). All are valuable studies, but all were written

25 Needless to say, this is not a problem solely of political history; here, historians of politics are acting as an exemplar.

26 H. Butterfield, *Man on his past: the study of the history of historical scholarship*, Cambridge 1955, p. xvi.

27 Ibid. 20.

28 Ibid. 21.

by historians of the seventeenth century rather than historians of historiography, or of the times which their ostensible subjects – the post-seventeenth-century historians – inhabited. However, studies in which historiography is more clearly the principal area of interest to the writer do exist, such as John Kenyon's *The history men* (1983) and Rosemary Jann's *The art and science of Victorian history* (1985). A hybrid of these two main approaches exists in the work of historians interested in how a particular generation sought to understand an aspect or specific period of the past; Timothy Lang's *The Victorians and the Stuart heritage* (1995) is a case in point. Unfortunately, the problems of contextualism noted in the work of historians not specialising in the history of historiography are present in these studies also.

In his book, Kenyon included a chapter section entitled 'The Stuarts: Gardiner to Trevelyan', in which he dedicated ten pages to a close discussion of Gardiner – or at least what at first appears to be a close discussion of Gardiner, but on closer inspection proves itself to be a close reading of Gardiner's critics. There are just five footnote references to Gardiner's own writing – and in each case it was to a passage in the short prefaces which Gardiner provided for each of the volumes of his *History of England*, rather than to the main body of text in those works. The large number of articles and reviews published in various journals were left out of the picture entirely, despite the fact that it is in those that Gardiner made his most explicit comments on the theory and method of history. The impression that the reader gets is that Kenyon's knowledge of Gardiner's work is very limited – and the impression is not dispelled by the analysis that he offers.

That analysis essentially rests on, indeed repeats, the accusations offered by the historian Roland G. Usher in his *A critical study of the historical method of Samuel Rawson Gardiner* (1915). Usher sought to destroy his subject's reputation and, despite the detailed refutation of his charges by Gardiner's widow, friends and other historians, many of his unsubstantiated claims have stuck.[29] The result of Kenyon's use of Usher is that he engages in an apparently comprehensive critical analysis of Gardiner, declaring that he was wrong in much of his detail, perhaps in all of his generalisations, and certainly in his entire conception of the seventeenth century and of historical method. However, he does not offer the reader anything by which to understand Gardiner's method and his selection of detail and construction of generalisations. Thus, Kenyon asserts that 'for all his protestations to the contrary Gardiner had approached the period with his mind made up, and tailored his narrative accordingly',[30] but quite what Gardiner's mind was is left unclear. Certainly Kenyon makes a few suggestions with regard to particular points, for example that Gardiner believed that Charles I was always wrong and

29 Usher's book occasioned a lengthy debate in the letters pages of the *TLS*, in each issue from 25 Sept. to 18 Dec. 1919.

30 J. Kenyon, *The history men: the historical profession in England since the Renaissance*, London 1983, 219.

that his enemies were always right (an inaccurate generalisation of Kenyon's own) but he refuses to offer his readers any insight into what he considers to be the origins of Gardiner's views on Charles and Cromwell.[31] He repeatedly refers to Whiggism or neo-Whiggism, but only in that way that, post-Butterfield, the phrase 'the Whig interpretation' has become an empty signifier and of dubious analytical use.[32] Kenyon also makes the claim that Gardiner eschewed his early Irvingism for Liberalism and Positivism,[33] which is so inaccurate a statement as to be worth nothing. However, even if it were true, he seems to have had no idea why Gardiner may have either eschewed Irvingism or taken up Liberalism or Positivism, or what the historian might have taken from any of them with regard to his understanding of the past or approach to historical theory and method. What Kenyon does offer his readers, however, is biographical detail. Thus, he mentions Gardiner's famed tricycling trips to the battlefields of England, Ireland and Europe, as part of his portrait-painting of the 'positivist'.[34] With little knowledge of Gardiner's texts, Kenyon resorts to what little is known about Gardiner's life in his attempt to understand the historian's work, or perhaps to illustrate what he wished to say about Gardiner's significance – which was that the great Victorian historian was one of the figures of a late nineteenth-century 'scientific' historiography which played an important part in the development of the profession but which failed to understand what their ideological preoccupations added to or subtracted from a 'true' historical account.

Rosemary Jann's *The art and science of Victorian history*, although a considerably more sophisticated work than Kenyon's, suffers from similar problems. Her understanding of Victorian historiography rests on the familiar trope of professionalisation, although she rightly complicates the somewhat simplistic accounts of that process that she had encountered elsewhere, by arguing that – particularly at Oxford and Cambridge – the amateur, literary mode and the professional, scientific mode of historical writing survived hand-in-hand for much longer than has been supposed.[35] However, Jann posits Gardiner as one of those who did come after (theoretically, if not chronologically) the historians in whom she was interested, that is as a more clearly 'scientific' historian. As with Kenyon, direct knowledge of Gardiner's work is not apparent in Jann's text – indeed, she only provides a single quotation from

31 Ibid. 220.

32 In Butterfield's original use of the term, in *The Whig interpretation of history* (1931), it is used in such a way as to incorporate the work of virtually every historian to have gone before Butterfield and certainly all historians interested in the history of the constitution; it has since become a term with an apparently inexhaustible applicability, being used to describe extremely diverse historians, whether Whig or Tory in their personal politics, or whether 'literary' or 'scientific' in their methodology.

33 Kenyon, *The history men*, 222.

34 Ibid. 214.

35 R. Jann, *The art and science of Victorian history*, Columbus, OH 1985, passim, but especially her 'Conclusion: desired presents and re-ordered pasts', 207–14.

Gardiner's work, and that by way of a citation in a quotation taken from the writings of his friend C. H. Firth. And, like Kenyon, she relies on Usher's earlier study. Her apparent failure to read any of Gardiner's work before writing about him may well have contributed to her failure to recognise that Gardiner deserved to stand alongside Maitland and Bury, her two examples from the so-called 'scientific' generation who prove, on closer examination, to be as literary as they are scientific. However, that insight, had she reached it, would also have been made alongside the traditional ideological reading that she provides for her main subjects. In her opening paragraph, Jann states that the 'Victorians plundered the past for the raw stuff of imagination and shaped what they found to their own political, social, and aesthetic ends'.[36] Later, she reminds her readers that she is 'primarily concerned with examining the ways certain nineteenth-century historians negotiated intellectual and moral dilemmas specific to their age',[37] and not how those historians negotiated the intellectual and moral dilemmas of the period that they were studying. For Jann, then, the study of historiography entails merely the tracing of the shaping of the past in the service of contemporary political concerns.

Unsurprisingly, therefore, a scan of the entries in the index to her book reveals precious few references to any theorists of history-writing or philosophers whose influence may be traced in British historiography, particularly foreign theorists: no Hegel, no Fichte, no Kant, no Schleiermacher, no Schelling, no Comte, a single mention of Vico in the main text, one to Herder in the introduction only, a couple of mentions of Schiller, and just two footnote references to Langlois and Seignobos. Philosophy plays little part in Jann's account of the art and science of Victorian historiography. For Gardiner, she provides a short biographical account that offers no analysis of his working methods, alongside a couple of serious misrepresentations. As a scientific historian, in her understanding of that genre, for example, Gardiner 'considered picturesque detail untrustworthy and, even if true, trivial'.[38] Such a conclusion could not be held by any reader of Gardiner's account of a pillow-fight between Fairfax and Cromwell. Moreover, he was willing to incorporate certain stories even when he did not believe them to be true, as long as they could be used to provide a window on a character, such as Cromwell's reported visit to see the corpse of Charles, and his famous line, 'trust in God, and keep your powder dry'.[39] These stories probably are not true, Gardiner wrote, in the sense of 'what really happened', but they were created and freely circulated because they expressed, for their author and the hearers, a truth not stated, because it cannot be adequately represented, in the formal histories. At these moments, Gardiner is a long

36 Ibid. p. xi.
37 Ibid. p. xii.
38 Ibid. 217.
39 See chapter 5 below for a discussion of Gardiner's use of these words.

way from the scientific historian that Jann posited. However, what Jann has learned from Usher's critiques, from the stories of trips to battlefields, of his time spent in the archives, and other biographical details, told her that he was a 'scientific' historian; without paying any attention to his texts, nor having an interest in speculative philosophy, she was unlikely to come to any other conclusion.

Jann's work, despite its expressed concentration on the political uses to which Victorian historiography was put, has as its overall organising principle the idea that late nineteenth-century historiography was of a pronounced 'scientific' nature, in contrast to the literary nature of the work in which she is principally interested. It is this distinction which selects her leading characters and demotes the likes of Gardiner to her 'epilogue'. This trope of 'disciplinisation' is of dubious value when applied to Gardiner in particular, but it might also be considered a somewhat artificially constructed interpretation in general. Indeed, her own conclusions suggest that this may be the case. As a result, it is necessary to keep open the possibility that Gardiner was no scientistic Positivist, but rather a more literary-inclined, less Positivist-inclined historian than he has often been characterised. However, the image of Gardiner the scientist has become something of a given amongst historians. Thus, it is necessary to question how it was that the image was drawn, and how it has gained such wide currency.

Gardiner's friend, disciple and literary executor Charles Harding Firth was one of those who noted, in a short biographical essay,[40] the famed cycle trips to the Civil War battlefields, but, unlike later writers in awe of Gardiner, did not offer any assessment of their success. His ambiguous telling of the story of these trips – which come across as a sort of leisure activity that propitiously helped Gardiner in his work – is not fully admitted as evidence towards his image of Gardiner as a 'scientist'. Recounted at the end of a list of Gardiner's research activities, and immediately prior to a listing of Gardiner's teaching activities (interesting and impressive in their industriousness, in Firth's eyes, but far from being part of Gardiner's great scholarly achievements), they serve to add colour to the description of the working historian – less a research activity, more a domestic form of the Grand Tour with its sites of antiquarian interest: 'His chief recreation was cycling, and in his holidays he familiarised himself with the battle-fields of the English civil war and followed the campaigns of Montrose in Scotland and of Cromwell in Ireland.' One might wonder why Firth, for whom his master was very much the model of the scientific historian, sought to downplay the cycling trips despite their great potential for helping to characterise Gardiner as the great researcher. That research was central to Firth's interests is clear for, while he wrote that '[f]or many years [Gardiner] lived in Gordon Street,

40 C. H. Firth, 'Samuel Rawson Gardiner', in S. Lee (ed.), *The dictionary of national biography: supplement, 1901–1911*, Oxford 1912.

within easy reach of the British Museum and the Record Office', suggesting that his domestic arrangements were organised around his research activities, another writer more interested in Gardiner's religious activities would argue that Gardiner lived in Gordon Street, where he had first moved with a father determined to position himself at the centre of Irvingite activity, to be within easy reach of Gordon Square Central Church (where Gardiner was a deacon) and later All Saints', the Anglican church also on Gordon Square at which he became a communicant after he left the Catholic Apostolic Church. Given this research prism in Firth's writings on Gardiner, why did he not make much of the cycling trips? Gardiner clearly believed in the abiding usefulness of good geographical knowledge for the historian, and was always ready to criticise others for their map-making failings.[41] Certainly, Gardiner was very proud of his 'enquiries on the spot'[42] and he himself, in his preface to the first volume of his study of the Civil War – a preface excised for the 1894 four-volume edition, the standard version read and referenced by historians – made claims to some kind of scientific methodology in these trips. He also, however, expressed his own doubts as to their success:

> I cannot describe battles which I have not seen as if I had; yet, if to describe a battle as if he saw it is no part of the historian's task, he need not therefore turn aside from the duty of describing it with truthfulness, as far as his materials allow him to do so, and I have therefore thought it right to visit the fields on which all the important struggles of the war took place. I am only afraid that I have often given my narrative the appearance of greater accuracy than is attainable, and I must therefore ask my readers to supply a chorus of doubt, and to keep in mind that they read, not an account of that which certainly happened, but of that which appears to me to have happened after such inquiry as I have been able to make.[43]

Indeed, as if to underline the contingent nature of the conclusions drawn from his field trips, on at least one occasion Gardiner had had to admit probable error in reply to the criticisms of others, and on several occasions offered thanks to various individuals for assistance which had saved him from publishing error-laden maps.[44] Recognising this problematic contingency meant that Firth sought to downplay the cycling trips.

However, in the hands of the later disciples of Gardiner, the vision of the tricycling topographer capable of admitting the contingency of his findings was transformed into a model of the scientist at work, an image that could then be transposed into the image of the impartial historian whose commen-

41 On the former point see Gardiner's review of '*Introduction aux études historique*. Par C. V. Langlois et C. Seignobos', *EHR* xiii (Apr. 1898), 327; on the latter point see, ironically, his critique of '*Oliver Cromwell and the rule of the Puritans in England*. By Charles Firth' [review], *EHR* xv (Oct. 1900), 804.

42 GCW i, p. vii.

43 *History of the Great Civil War, 1642–1649*, I: *1642–1644*, London 1886, p. xi.

44 See, for example, GCW, i, pp. vii, xi–xii.

tary on the military aspect of the Civil War should be taken as gospel. Retrospectively, the evidence for such a conclusion was 'found' in Gardiner's writings, both in his discussions of the battles and in his own discussion of his methods, although there was a possible counter-reading available in Gardiner's own words. Was Gardiner a successful 'scientific' historian'? Was he an unsuccessful 'scientific' historian? Did Gardiner hold that a truly 'objective' 'scientific' history was even possible? Alas, the answers to those questions as offered by existing historiographical approaches are formulated away from the published texts and then supported by reference to the writings. Indeed, the passage quoted above has been used both by those seeking to present Gardiner as an impartial, scientific historian, and by those seeking to show that Gardiner was as fallible as the next writer, either by the failure in practice of his methods, or their inherent weaknesses.[45]

This concentration on Gardiner's research as a historian has led, along with the concentration on the political and religious ideological content 'found' in Gardiner, to the neglect of Gardiner as a writer. The Strachey articles make clear their author's belief that Gardiner was no skilled writer, and even Firth, Gardiner's greatest disciple, was critical of his master as a stylist – although his comments are tinged with respect for the elements of Gardiner's work that tended to lead their author into such dryness: 'He sought to interest his readers by his lucid exposition of facts and the justice of his reflections rather than by giving history the charms of fiction.'[46] Similarly,

> Such difficulties are an inevitable result of the conflict between the requirements of the two functions which the historian has to perform. The scientific side of history demands one thing, the artistic another ... [Gardiner's] natural gifts ... lay in a different direction [from Macaulay's], and he wisely devoted himself more to the scientific than to the artistic part of the historian's task.[47]

Gardiner the researcher, and Gardiner the scientist, are both models that are founded on a failure to make a close reading of his works central to a study of his techniques, and further convince the student that a close reading should not be carried out: Gardiner's work in the archives and in mapping battlefields is important and illuminating, but his written work is dull, dreary and unstylish.

'Gardiner the scientist' is a construction based on that provided by his disciples, chief amongst whom was Firth. In a number of articles published

45 For differing uses of the passage see E. M. Hunt, 'Samuel Rawson Gardiner' in H. Ausubel, J. B. Brebner and E. M. Hunt (eds), *Some modern historians of Britain*, New York 1951, 105; Hale *Evolution of British historiography*, 280; and Jann *Art and science*, 217–18. It may be worth noting that Jann does not reference Gardiner directly, but the discussion of him by Firth in an article in the *Quarterly Review* of 1902 in which these words of Gardiner are quoted.

46 Firth, 'Gardiner' (1912), 78.

47 Idem, 'Two Oxford historians: 2. Samuel Rawson Gardiner', *QR* cxcv (1902), 563–5.

upon Gardiner's death, Firth sought to construct a Gardiner whom the reader would be led to see as the consummate professional, scientific historian. For example, in one article in which he raised a comparison with one of the great symbols of German scientific method, a conscious use of symbolism that could scarcely have been missed by any of his readers, Firth said that

> In estimating Gardiner's place amongst historians, the comparison with Ranke suggested in foreign appreciations of his work, inevitably arises in the mind … in more than one respect he resembled the great German scholar. Like Ranke, he endeavoured to see things exactly as they were, and to let the facts speak for themselves; he was like Ranke too in his breadth of view, in his constant sense of the connexion between national and European life, and in the independence and equity of his judgements. As an investigator Gardiner was at least the equal of Ranke.[48]

Using Ranke – a historian whose name connoted rigorous, scientific method to Firth and his contemporaries – as the model, it was possible for Gardiner's disciple to construct an image of the older historian as a scientist and seeker of truth.

This construction of Gardiner as a scientist perhaps had a two-fold impulse. First, the research-oriented Firth described his master as the kind of historian that he himself aspired to be – a scientist. Second, as an Oxford man,[49] Gardiner could be used to represent that university and prove its Modern History School's 'scientific' credentials. Firth was obsessed with the reputation of the University of Oxford and the lack he perceived of real 'scientific' activity to match any reputation in historical studies at Oxford (a reputation that he felt was much more deserved by the universities of Germany, France and the United States), and which often comes across to the reader as a profound insecurity.[50] He may have been given a further jolt by Bury's inaugural lecture on 'The science of history' at Cambridge in the year of Gardiner's death. Whatever the impulse behind Firth's construction of 'Gardiner the scientist', however, one effect is clear: an idea of the master had been constructed that Gardiner's admirers could constantly and uncriti-

[48] Idem, 'Samuel Rawson Gardiner' [obituary], *Proceedings of the British Academy* (1903–4), 300.

[49] Gardiner had been an undergraduate at Christ Church (1848–51), and had held research fellowships at All Souls (1884–92) and Merton (1892–1902). For records of his time at Oxford see Christ Church, dean and chapter archives, i.b.10, fos 130, 133, 136; li.b.5, fo. 136; J. S. G. Simmons, 'All Souls', in M. G. Brock and M. C. Curthoys (eds), *The history of the University of Oxford*, VII: *Nineteenth-century Oxford*, II, Oxford 2000, 218; Merton College archives, college register, 1877–1914, MS 1.5a, 232, 234, 323, 342. William Stubbs, Regius Professor of Modern History at Oxford, described Gardiner in a lecture given in 1884 as 'a man who should be claimed and must be reclaimed for Oxford': *Seventeen lectures on the study of medieval and modern history and kindred subjects*, Oxford 1887, 433.

[50] For a particularly telling insight into his thought on these matters see his *Modern history in Oxford, 1841–1918*, Oxford 1920.

cally refer to in their portrait-painting, and his critics could constantly and uncritically refer to in their reputation-dashing. Firth may say that Gardiner was a master of his own scientific method, and Usher may argue that Gardiner singularly failed to adhere to his own scientific method, but the governing assumption of both interpretations is that Gardiner had a scientific method, the constraints of which he either succeeded or failed to observe.

Such an understanding is clearest in those studies in which Gardiner is characterised according to religious or political labels. For instance, Gardiner's vice-presidency of the Oxford Home Rule League suggests that he was a Gladstonian Liberal, a hypothesis which can then be supported by the 'finding' of Gladstonian Liberal ideology in his published works. However, this approach can also be seen to be at work in those assessments of Gardiner's working methods which one might expect to be centred on Gardiner's writings. In these studies biographical details have also been allowed to create an impression, one that Gardiner's writings can perhaps be used to dispel rather than support. For instance, many writers have commented very favourably on Gardiner's famed tricycle trips to Civil War battlefields, which can be convincingly used to show his use of 'scientific methods' – in this case, his interest in topography and careful mapping – in an attempt to go beyond the weaknesses of partisan first-person accounts and later accounts written by non-combatants; and yet Gardiner himself wrote that one cannot be sure with respect to the recreation of historical events, no matter how careful the research methods used.

Similarly, the use to which Timothy Lang puts Gardiner's religious and political allegiances in his explanation of the historian's work often does not stand up to scrutiny. For example, his insistence that a discipleship of Gladstone led Gardiner to support Irish home rule, and then to use his *History* for the promotion of that political goal, does not appear to fit the chronology of the historian's political development.[51] Here, one can begin to have some insight into the problem of beginning historiographical analysis in the life, rather than the work, of the historian. It is a serious possibility that Gardiner's political views regarding Ireland resulted from his historical study of seventeenth-century Ireland. Certainly, it should be treated as a worthwhile hypothesis, and tested. In order to do that, however, it is necessary first to attempt a deeper analysis of his work. To some extent, this is suggested by Lang's own admission that the 'same liberal nationalism that informed Gardiner's politics shaped his conception of the historian's craft',[52] although clearly, and as these words further suggest, for Lang the cause-effect relationship is one of politics to work. But Gardiner was a writer, and it is in his work that the beginnings of any study of other aspects of his life should be sought.

51 See chapter 2 below.
52 Lang, *Victorians*, 164.

So, what have students of Gardiner's work come to understand of his conception of the historian's task? Unfortunately, similar problems to those that have arisen in attempts to understand Gardiner's writings on the past have often also militated against a sophisticated understanding of Gardiner's approach to historical writing: by focusing on Gardiner's life in history, rather than his actual writings on the subject (distributed and hard to locate as they are), a portrait has been drawn of the research-oriented historian, for whom the writing act was little more than a necessary but untheorised activity appended to the hard work carried out in the literal or metaphorical field.

It is quite clear, therefore, that contextualist accounts fail the analyst of the history of historiography. A new method is required, or, perhaps, an old method re-established. In order to try to formulate such a method, it is necessary to discuss not where different contextualist accounts have gone wrong with regard to Gardiner – although this can be a valuable exercise – but what features are shared by contextualist accounts which illumine the theoretically-flawed and practically-disadvantageous structure of their application to historiographical analysis. The universalising nature of the contextualist analysis – in which the context privileged by the historian is assumed to be of insurmountable power and to influence all that is produced under its auspices – leads to two deep, and linked, structural problems, one in the formulation of the analysis and the other in its practical exposition. In the first case, by offering a model which claims to explain everything without reference to the particular – ironically, a fitting definition of an ideological position – contextualist analysis separates itself from the work that it is intended to illuminate. The life of the historian becomes the focus, and the writings become marginalised. They are revisited only when an adequate hypothesis has been constructed away from the text which can then be applied to, or tested using, the historiography. This in turn disinclines the analyst to carry out an exercise in close reading, for such a practice diverts energy away from the 'correct' practice of studying closely the writer's activities in politics or religion, or within a circle of friends or the family. Unfortunately, this prevents a possible critique of the entire contextualist methodology from opening up within the intellectual vision of the student: close reading tends to bring to the surface those inconsistencies and local conditions that serve to deconstruct any over-arching conception. This suggests a way forward – a close reading of the work of the historian which will seek to understand what informs the text rather than what informs the historian.

The result is somewhat akin to a history of ideas approach, one in which the extremely complex network of intellectual influences that the text suggests to the reader becomes the object of analysis. As well as providing a more speculative, less authoritative account of the work, such a close reading will also promote the discussion of the local issues at work in the text. It recognises the different levels of intellectual influence and operation, and it recognises the different levels at which they inform, and operate within, the text. Thus, a more text-centred approach becomes necessary, that is one in which the textual evidence, rather than the contextual evidence, leads the analysis.

This, however, should not be confused with those literary analyses which, broadly, offer a textualist study lacking any serious attempt to understand the ideas which operate in the mind and work of the historian. A case in point is Hayden White's *Metahistory* (1973), a text which has had an enormous impact on the study of the history of historiography. In *Metahistory* and elsewhere, White's interest is in the narrative structure of historiography and the tropological strategies which the historian uses. Paradoxically, however, the result of his methods has been a withdrawal from the text itself on a par with that experienced in contextualist studies. By denying the deep structure of meaning in the historian's concepts and constructions, or rather by arguing that the deep structure is available to be read at the surface of the text, White offers no need to close read, to analyse at a close level what the historian is doing in his or her text. As a result, despite constant reference to language – as is common in critical-theoretical writers – there is no stylistic analysis of historians' works in any of his writings, no close attention to the operations of language in the text and the linguistic choices made by the historian. As a result, although in itself a literary understanding of historiography, it cannot and does not offer an understanding of the historian's literary understanding of his or her own work. The text just is, or, rather, it exists solely as a textual item, devoid of any productive relations outside of literature itself – it is not made by any constitutive act on the part of the writer or extraliterary discourses.

The method proposed in this book may broadly be characterised as one drawn from the history of ideas. Intellectual history, however, is not without its points of controversy regarding method. In recent years the field has been dominated by the work of a school of study centred around Quentin Skinner and John Pocock. Although their work does have differences, their separate approaches share much and, indeed, they each refer to, and endorse, the work of the other. Thus, although (to use terms introduced by a leading critic of their work) Pocock advocates a 'linguistic contextualism' which assumes that textual production is governed by the linguistic and ideological forms available to the writer, and Skinner embraces a 'social conventionalist' account whereby the text is shaped by that which his or her society allows and offers them,[53] both methods minimise the creative role of the author, assume the unknowability of authorial intention from the text and posit the knowability of sufficient extra-textual evidence (whether linguistic or social) to be able to offer a true account of the meanings which inhere in the text. Both methods are based on the need to engage with the intellectual networks within which writing takes place and thus observe the criterion

[53] M. Bevir, *The logic of the history of ideas*, Cambridge 2001, 32–48.

advocated above as necessary for a method that contrasts with the political contextualism of traditional approaches to historiography. However, in both cases, there is an assumption that an objective understanding of the meaning of a text is possible. Rather than offer a method which seeks a complete and objective reading of a text – a universalising activity – it is preferable to suggest a practice which offers an appreciation of the text which is not driven by the dictates of a fixed method.[54]

John Burrow, although broadly supportive of the Skinner/Pocock school of intellectual history, has suggested that such a method can produce only a partial picture. In the introduction to his *A Liberal descent* (1981), a study of four Victorian historians, he wrote that 'academic readers whose interest is chiefly in the history of social and political thought may find the chapters on individual historians clogged with discussion of their personal traits and with biographical detail ... They would, I think, have missed the point, and the point is not marginal to intellectual history but central to it'.[55] Drawing explicit attention to the work of Skinner and Pocock, Burrow goes on to argue that his method – broadly that described as 'contextualist' – should be used alongside their mode of analysis:

> That understanding a past author or work presupposes attention to his intellectual context is now an orthodoxy of intellectual history and needs no labouring. But contexts also need detailed examination of texts and authors for their fuller illumination. What the essentially classificatory activity of distinguishing forms of discourse or available theoretical languages ideally needs as its complement is a sense of the complex ways in which individuals respond to, assimilate and reshape the materials of their intellectual milieux.[56]

Thus, Burrow advocates the use of a traditional biographical method alongside the political analyses of Pocock and Skinner in order to provide a fuller picture of historians and their historiography.

It is clear that, in the work of all three, the primary point of interest is the context with which it is possible to understand the ideas incorporated into the text. For Pocock the context is linguistic, for Skinner it is intellectual and for Burrow it is biographical, but it is a context, all the same. Why this should be so is explained by their principal focus of interest: politics. While Skinner and Pocock signal this in the titles of their main statements of methodology (respectively, *Visions of politics* and *Politics, language and time*), Burrow declares his central preoccupation in his opening discussion, in which he says that his book is concerned with 'an aspect of nineteenth-century English political thought, approached ... through the study

54 The distinction between method and practice used here is that advanced by P. Feyerabend in *Against method*, 3rd edn, London 1975

55 J. W. Burrow, *A Liberal descent: Victorian historians and the English past*, Cambridge 1981, 4.

56 Ibid. 5.

of historiography'.[57] An analysis of history-writing is being carried out here solely with the idea in mind that it is a useful source for the study of political thought, not that it has its own, independent existence, as a form of literature or discourse worthy of study in its own right. The stress on politics is necessarily contextualist because, by always situating the historian's texts within a discourse (politics) to be understood as the primary discourse, it readily assumes some kind of relationship between the 'text' and the 'context', the form of the latter explaining the content of the former.

Thus, if historiography is to be approached as a subject of interest in its own right, it is necessary to attempt a revision of the kind of work advocated by Pocock, Skinner and Burrow. It is not only inadequate to move to the kind of work which Burrow envisages, in which his own preoccupation with the writer and Pocock's and Skinner's preoccupation with what, discursively, makes the historian, are jointly carried out, it is also inadequate to attempt a synthetic approach in which the two sets of methods are both always in mind, for to do so would import the problems associated with each. Rather than putting forward a method of analysing context in order to understand a text, this book is based on the realisation that a practice is needed in which the essential distinction that has been drawn between text and context must be problematised and re-ordered. Only then is it possible to elucidate historiography – the production of what may be called, to use the traditional terms, texts about contexts – as a discourse in its own right.

In order to attempt to get beyond the limitations of both the contextualist and textualist modes of analysis, this book will attempt to bring together a history of ideas approach which seeks an understanding of the often sophisticated conceptualisations made by the historian and which may not easily be construed by a narrow attention on a simplistic model of ideology, and a close reading which assumes the active and complex construction of meaning and representation in the text. On a theoretical level, this necessitates the treatment of every discourse – whether it is a discourse traditionally referred to as a text or as a context – as merely one of a myriad of contexts which operate as a relatively fluid discursive formation. Crucial here is the acceptance that all such discourses are of equal status, and that none should be privileged in the mind or the practice of the analyst. When the historian selects one of these discourses as his or her focus, it becomes what we might wish to call the text, around which the network of contexts continues to operate on, and be operated upon by, the text. Or, the text is to be viewed in a total context, of which it is itself a part. Thus, the construction of the text as a text becomes a self-conscious act on the part of the historian. As well as teaching the analyst that the chosen discourse should not become a privileged discourse – because one should not privilege that which is tantamount to an operation of subjective choice – this practice also solves many

57 Ibid. 2.

of the problems of the work of Pocock, Skinner and Burrow, for it involves a refusal to reduce one discourse to a subordinate relationship with another, and opens up a wide vista of possibilities regarding the flow of influence within the network of the discursive formation. The simple analysis of one discourse as constitutive of, or constituted by, another should be replaced by the appreciation of a complex network of discourses in which our selection of one such discourse as the focus of analysis does not change its relationship with the rest of the network.

This theoretical approach raises the practical objection that it is impossible to appreciate in their entirety the full series of discourses which operate in society. Thus, the student of historiography must choose those discourses (contexts) which have a close relationship with the chosen discourse (text) as being of more relevance to the understanding of the text. However, this means that it is important that we theorise a system of the selection of discourses to create our field of contexts which can give meaning to our analysis. A fully objective set of criteria is unattainable, for the selection of contexts is as subjective and should be as self-conscious as the selection of the text described above. Nevertheless, cultural theory offers some answers to this conundrum. For example, working within the Centre for Contemporary Cultural Studies, Richard Johnson advanced the concept of 'circuits of culture', in which intersecting 'sites' of cultural process (such as production, consumption and representation) operate. For Johnson, this model is not only theoretically adequate, but practically advantageous: 'Each moment depends upon the others and is indispensable to the whole. Each involves distinctive changes of form, real transformations. If we are practically occupied with one moment and familiar with its forms, the other moments may not exist for us.'[58] In these words it is possible to see the similarities between Johnson's 'circuits of culture' and the theory of a network of contexts. For Johnson, too, his model seeks to solve the problem of methodological preoccupation with only one of the possible sites of meaning within the network, through his refusal to privilege any of the intersecting processes and his concomitant insistence upon treating them as equal elements within the circuit. Cultural Studies offers an early variant of the approach being advanced in this book.

Similar, if not identical, concerns have arisen in the field of discourse analysis. Traditionally, such approaches have treated as unproblematic the distinction between text and context, privileging the former as a site of meaning explicable, at least in part, with a descriptive account of the latter. Recently, however, this position has been placed under sustained critique, and discourse analysts have begun to develop the principle of 'interdiscursivity', in which all discourses are treated as ineluctably related to, and engaged to, other discourses, none of which may be treated as necessarily

[58] R. Johnson, 'The story so far: and other transformations', in D. Punter (ed.), *Introduction to contemporary cultural studies*, London 1986, 284.

central to the full enterprise of analysis. Thus, Michael Meyer has posited a 'hermeneutic circle' in which interpretation requires analysis of all sites of meaning and all relationships between them, whilst always keeping in mind the realisation of the ways in which those sites and their relationships can only be understood within the whole, which is itself only explicable through the parts. Such a method is, according to Meyer, necessarily 'text-reducing', that is it de-privileges what was, in earlier forms of discourse analysis, the centred object of study.[59] Again, similarities with the approach advanced in this book can be seen.

One attempt within discourse analysis to integrate these theoretical preoccupations into practical interpretation is that of Ron Scollon, who focused his work on those points of intersection to which he gave the name a 'nexus of practice'.[60] As this term implies, Scollon's interest was in moments of social action, rather than discourse, and thus his method of 'mediated discourse analysis'[61] appears to have little use for the study of discourses that are not what might be called real-time discourses, that is discourses which can be isolated in time and space. Indeed, this is a problem for much discourse analysis, for, even when the problematisation of the text/context boundary is admitted, a given text is assigned a certain ontological status as a material text under consideration. Thus, Johnson, Meyer and Scollon all deal with the 'real', whereas a history of ideas approach centres on the ideal.

For example, Scollon has presented a method of 'nexus analysis' in which any given text is understood in terms of all those texts with which, at the point of selection, it intersects.[62] However, as Scollon's method is intended to be used for a discernible moment in a discernible place (such as the writing of a letter on a given morning while sitting in a particular café), it does not immediately lend itself to the analysis of a more amorphous sense of a 'discourse', such as one in which all discourses are theoretically treated as contexts rather than, as Scollon suggests, as texts. This problem is compounded by the relative irrecoverability of past constitutive acts compared with the present. Nevertheless, the idea of intersection ('nexus') may be useful, if it is reformulated as an issue of 'adjacency'. It may be objected that all discourses can be adjacent in one way or another – or constitutively adjacent to one discourse which is constitutively adjacent to the chosen discourse, to the point of infinite regress. However, some discourses – politics, religion, philosophy, for example – are more clearly

59 M. Meyer, 'Between theory, method, and politics: positioning of the approaches to CDA', in R. Wodak and M. Meyer (eds), *Methods of critical discourse analysis*, London 2001, 16.

60 R. Scollon and S. W. Scollon, 'Nexus analysis: expanding the circumference of discourse analysis', unpubl. paper, PARC Forum, Paolo Alto, CA, 12 Dec. 2002.

61 R. Scollon, *Mediated discourse as social interaction: a study of news discourse*, Harlow 1998, passim.

62 Ibid.

adjacent to historiography than others, such as medicine or geology. This is not to say, of course, and in accordance with the theory of discursive networks, that historiography may not be influenced by metaphors drawn from medical discourse, or by ideas of time and development as they are discussed by geologists. It does, however, provide a language to describe or explain the selection of discourses to be treated as related contextually to our chosen text. And, again drawing from Scollon, who insists that there must be evidence of the appearance of a particular discourse at the nexus, it suggests that we can only consider discourses which are explicitly referred to in our text, either by direct reference or through the use of borrowed terms. Rather than treat this rule as a methodological principle, however, it may be considered preferable to treat it as practically advantageous; thus, it leaves open the possibility of using relevant material or discourses not explicitly referred to in the text under consideration while also offering a logic of exclusion. Crucially, however, it neither necessitates nor advocates the privileging of any single discourse, such as politics, as having a primary relationship with historiography. Rather, this book will remain open to the possible discussion of any discourse which may, through its appearance in textual evidence, be posited as holding a relationship with the chosen text – the work of Samuel Rawson Gardiner.

Moreover, this book, itself an attempt at a history of ideas approach, will move forward with the assumption that Gardiner was himself, first and foremost, a historian of ideas. He has traditionally been viewed as a historian of politics, but it is a central assertion of this book that such an account places undue limitations on an appreciation of his approach to historical change. This new view of the great historian is, in truth, not new at all, for it is given credibility by Firth's claim that 'Gardiner "did not confine himself to relating facts, but traced the growth of the religious and constitutional ideas which underlay" the greatest political conflict ever known to these islands.'[63] It will be supported in subsequent chapters, in particular in chapter 4, but for practical purposes has to be treated as an underlying assumption throughout the book.

This book is divided into five chapters. The first two will attempt to elucidate Gardiner's theory of the past: chapter 1 consists of an analysis of the philosophical underpinnings of his historiography; chapter 2 attempts to use that knowledge to show how those theories operate in a general conceptualisation of the past. Chapters 3 and 4 provide case studies ('Religion' and 'Politics') of how those theories operate at a more local level. The fifth chapter will attempt a close reading, drawing out some elements of Gardiner's writing of the past, analysing his understanding of the role of writing in historiography, and the possibilities its different genres offer the historian,

[63] This is cited in A. W. Ward, 'Historians, biographers and political orators', in A. W. Ward and A. R. Waller (eds), *The Cambridge history of English literature*, XIV: *The nineteenth century*, III, Cambridge 1916, 14, 88.

and seeking to describe and elucidate Gardiner's use of one fictional genre – drama – in this most realist of nonfictional genres. This last part is, necessarily, highly selective: there is enough material to write many such chapters, and the selection made displays the theoretical preoccupations of its author. It does, however, offer more general conclusions which help to make other features of Gardiner's writing explicable.

Together, these five chapters offer a reassessment of Gardiner which attempts to insert into the study of his works an appreciation of his thought and of his writing, two issues one might expect to find in any historiographical analysis but which are, all too often, forgotten.

1

Theory

If Gardiner's historical practice is to be understood, an attempt to divine his historical theory is essential. However, Gardiner's ideas about history have rarely been mentioned as historians and students of historiography have chosen rather to focus on his political and religious life. In part, this neglect has been occasioned by – or, perhaps, has caused – the concentration on Gardiner's *magnum opus*, the eighteen-volume *History*.[1] In this work, the historian did not explicitly discuss any grand theory of history or, indeed, any other writer's theories regarding the study of the past. However, in his private correspondence, and his reviews of historical works, Gardiner did refer to larger issues of theory and method, and to certain theorists and other writers whose ideas had influenced historical practice in general, and Gardiner's practice in particular. Using these less well-studied sources, this chapter will seek to construct a hypothesis regarding his own theoretical position which can be tested in subsequent chapters focusing on his practice.

The shortcomings of the contextualist methodology may be illustrated by considering the problems involved in using Gardiner's life to 'tell' his work. In his *The Victorians and the Stuart heritage*, the most extensive published study of Gardiner and his work of recent years,[2] Timothy Lang sees the work of Gardiner entirely through the prism of the historian's early Irvingism, later anglicanism and lifelong Liberalism. Lang tells his readers that Gardiner joined the Catholic Apostolic Church (the Irvingites) in 1851, was ordained a deacon in 1854 and married one of Irving's daughters in 1856. He then goes on to characterise the Irvingites as an amalgam that brought together a Laudian ritualism and a puritan millenarianism, and argues that in consequence Gardiner was able, and wished, to have sympathy for both sides in the great religious struggles of the seventeenth century. This theological *via media* was incorporated into Gardiner's life – both personal and professional – even after he left the Irvingites and became a communicant member of

1 Gardiner's *History* here means the combined ten-volume *History of England* (1883–4), the four-volume *History of the Great Civil War* (1893) and the four-volume *History of the Commonwealth and Protectorate* (1902): see editorial note above.

2 Lang, *Victorians*. The most relevant sections are chapter iv, 'Samuel Rawson Gardiner and the search for national consensus' (pp. 139–83) and part III of chapter v, 'Cromwell and the late Victorians' (pp. 198–212), although there are continuing references to Gardiner throughout the book.

the Church of England, Lang suggests, for thus Gardiner can be seen to have been both a dissenter and an anglican.[3]

Lang then discusses Gardiner's political leanings, specifically his Gladstonian Liberalism and dedication to the cause of Irish home rule. He suggests that Gardiner may have been turned into a follower of Gladstone at least in part by his experiences as an undergraduate at Christ Church, Oxford, at a time when Gladstone was MP for the university. Gladstone later became the politician who did most to abolish the religious tests that had, after Gardiner had joined the Irvingites, led to his expulsion from Christ Church. Whatever the reason for his political beliefs, 'Gardiner's decision to back Gladstone on Home Rule is perhaps the most telling indication of his political loyalties'.[4] As a result of his Gladstonian Liberalism, Lang believes, Gardiner put his books to the work of promoting good governance in Ireland and the movement for reform – to the promotion of a Gladstonian political settlement.

However, a close reading of the evidence that Lang presents weighs heavily against his own argument. According to him, '[b]y 1885 … Gardiner had become an advocate of Home Rule' and then '[l]ater that year, Gladstone announced his own conversion to Home Rule'. On Lang's own chronology, Gardiner was thus a supporter of Irish home rule before Gladstone. If Gardiner did not get his home rule beliefs from Gladstone, then the historian must look to other possible sources for his principles.

As late as October 1880 Gardiner was still clearly unconvinced by the arguments in favour of Irish home rule. In a review of the third and fourth volumes of Justin McCarthy's very successful account of contemporary and recent politics, *History of our own times*, Gardiner used some of McCarthy's own arguments regarding Africa to raise doubts with respect to the necessity and efficacy of the very home rule policy which McCarthy had used his book to promote. Gardiner pointed out how, in his discussion, McCarthy shows that the British people had opposed Bartle Frere's policies in southern Africa, sympathising with the Zulus in the process. For Gardiner, this event, and others, 'indirectly bear[s] testimony to the growth in English statesmen and in the English public of a capacity to enter into the feelings of those whose life and ways are other than their own'.[5] The reasons for this are clear to Gardiner, and he rejected McCarthy's limp analysis in favour of a more philosophical reading of recent changes in the British attitude to others, and from that a denial of the utility of granting Irish Home Rule: 'Mr. McCarthy may call this plain common-sense. It is rather the increased imaginative power which is able to comprehend what the rights of others are. No doubt this power is feeble as yet. But it exists, and its existence has made the Irish legislation of the last years possible.' Thus, the argument of the home

3 Ibid. 141–50. For Gardiner's religious life see chapter 3 below.

4 Ibid. 153.

5 'A *history of our own times*. By Justin McCarthy, M.P. Vols. III. and IV.' [review], *Academy* xviii (9 Oct. 1880), 251.

rulers that only the Irish can know what the Irish need is undermined by the imaginative powers of the British people and the 'United Parliament'. Moreover, the British are able to offer a better Irish policy than can the Irish themselves, because they have the benefit of an objective view from a distance: being of neither the Irish landed nor the Irish tenant class, they can balance the needs of each and better judge what benefits all.[6] Irish home rule was not yet a policy that Gardiner supported.

However, the terms which he employed in the anti-home rule arguments that he put forward in his review of McCarthy's book are instructive. In particular, his belief that the British were learning to 'enter into the feelings' of another society by applying their 'imaginative power' to events is striking. This is, arguably, what historians should always do; and it is what one contemporary school of thought in the philosophy of history argued that historians must do.

Despite what he had written in 1880, by 1885 Gardiner was a supporter of Irish home rule. Although there are no public statements of the basis on which he now supported the policy, he did enter into correspondence with his friend, the Liberal MP, historian and active advocate of home rule, James Bryce. In one of these letters, Gardiner puts forward an argument which suggests that he was not a liberal nationalist in the British political sense, as a result of listening to Gladstone, but a liberal nationalist in the philosophical sense, as a result of reading the German philosopher Johann Gottlieb Fichte: 'Much of the best part of the opposition to the present [Home Rule] Bill comes because men like Lord Hartington, Goschen, and Courtney & Co. haven't read, marked, and inwardly digested the meaning of Fichte's addresses for the modern world.'[7] Gardiner here is talking of the philosopher's *Addresses to the German nation* of 1807–8, in which, in reaction to the defeat of the Prussians by the French at Jena, Fichte set out his theory of the politics of the nation. In it, he had offered a conception of the nation as an aggregate 'Spirit'. This assured the self-determinism of the national polity, but also offered warnings about frustrating such great Spirits. Ireland was, for Gardiner, defined by a national spirit distinct from Britain, the satisfaction of which would avert a more revolutionary moment.

At the very least it is clear that Gardiner understood these events through a lens provided by Fichte's Idealist philosophy. Having recognised the British historian's engagements with, and use of, German philosophy in this respect, however, it is necessary to consider whether he also owed anything to German philosophy in the field with which he is most closely associated: historiography. Unfortunately, Gardiner left behind no explicit statements

6 In offering this analysis, Gardiner shows himself as either ignorant of, or willing to ignore, the large tracts of land that were owned by Britons, including British legislators. Hartington's family was an example.

7 S. R. Gardiner to James Bryce, 5 May 1886, Bodleian Library, Oxford, MS Bryce 68, fos 57–9.

of his historiographical theory, and the modern student must instead divine his theoretical preoccupations indirectly from his work. Such divination, however, requires some empirical evidence on which it is to be based.

As well as the letter to Bryce, Gardiner left behind much evidence of his engagement with German philosophy, historiography and literature. Of the last, for instance, uncredited lines taken from classics of German literature, sometimes misquoted or perhaps deliberately altered to suit the context, pepper his writings, in much the same way as lines from Greek and Latin literature, the Bible and other literature familiar to Gardiner and his readers might be expected. Such intertextual reference was strikingly prevalent in late nineteenth-century British historiography. It is different from direct quotation of sources, for the author is leaving the context and understanding to be read into the text by the reader, who is presumed to know the source and thus to be able to understand any relevant connotations carried by the word or phrase. The letter to Bryce contains an example from a common source in nineteenth-century literature: 'read, marked, and inwardly digested' would have been recognised by Bryce as being from the Book of Common Prayer, an integral part of any anglican's life. As well as informing about the author's religious affiliations, it suggests a role for Fichte's writings that is more than just informational – it is a text to be studied in a way similar to the way in which Scripture or the liturgy of the Church might be studied.

Two German writers of the late eighteenth and early nineteenth centuries feature often in Gardiner's work: Friedrich Schiller (1759–1805) and J. W. Goethe (1749–1832). The former was a dramatist, philosopher and historian, and a man whom Gardiner described as having 'a true historical instinct'.[8] His masterpiece, the *Wallenstein* cycle (1796–9), was used by Gardiner in his writing on Albrecht von Wallenstein, the Thirty Years War leader, to help to illustrate the character and life of the man. However, Gardiner also used Schiller's writings more widely, slipping phrases taken from a number of his plays into his own narratives. For example, in an article on the Scottish civil war general Montrose, Gardiner records his death with a slight misquotation from Schiller's *Die Räuber* (1781), 'So stirbt ein Held! – Anbetenswürdig!' ['A hero's death! – Meet for worship!'].[9] Schiller is an important literary referent in Gardiner's writings.

Goethe, however, appears more frequently. For example, while reviewing

8 '*Geschichte Wallensteins*. Von L. von Ranke' [unsigned review], *NBR* li (Jan. 1870), 552.

9 'The last campaign of Montrose. *The memoirs of James marquis of Montrose*, 1639–1650. By the Rev. George Wishart, D.D. Translated, with introduction, notes, appendices, and the original letters. (Part II. Now first published.) By the Rev. Alexander D. Murdoch and H. F. Morland Simpson' [unsigned review article], *ER* clxxix (Jan. 1894), 157. The lines from *Die Räuber* are to be found in act III, scene ii. For the English translation see F. Schiller, '*The robbers*' *and* '*Wallenstein*', ed. F. J. Lamport, Harmondsworth 1979, 98.

an edition of the thoughts of John Selden, Gardiner used a phrase from the German writer in what appears to be a gently critical sentence: 'There was so much in [Selden] of the Geist der stets verneint that the rare occasions on which he stood forth boldly for a great cause deserve to be emphasised.'[10] Here, Gardiner quite clearly means to draw attention to what he saw as Selden's failure to be a man of principle, rarely willing to fight for any 'great cause'. The phrase from Goethe ['the spirit that ever denies'] adds another layer of disapprobation, in a rather dismissive tone. But those of Gardiner's readers who would have recognised the phrase from *Faust* (1808/32), and would have thus known that it was Mephistopheles's description of himself, would have understood just how low an opinion of Selden the historian held – the association with Mephistopheles is, for Gardiner and his readers, damning indeed.

On a different occasion Gardiner used Goethe to express a positive judgement of another man. In a review of a biography of the seventeenth-century anglican bishop Joseph Hall, Gardiner described Hall's intellectual development in terms of 'ohne Hast, aber ohne Rast' ['without haste, but without rest'],[11] the motto copied into the front of the great German writer's notebooks. The phrase itself is a useful way to characterise a man who worked tirelessly, Gardiner suggested, always developing and growing intellectually, but who did so in a methodical and measured way. However, the use of Goethe's words also implies that Gardiner felt Hall to exhibit a Romantic model of intellectual striving which bore the imprint of an organic and imaginative intellect as distinct from the cool reason of rationalist models. Appreciating this contributes towards an understanding of Gardiner's vision of Hall, and recognising that for Gardiner this approach to one's intellectual life was something to commend, also contributes towards an understanding of the historian's own idea of what good thought might be – Romantic rather than Rationalist. Gardiner's regular use of German literature was not unique among British Victorian writers, although it is far from universal, and it is common only in the writings of such authors as Samuel Taylor Coleridge, Thomas Carlyle and others known to have engaged with German writers, both literary and philosophical – the 'Romantics' whose thought represents one British appropriation of Idealist concepts. Thus, Gardiner's use of such literature not only marks his reading of German literature, it suggests that there might have been Idealist and Romantic strains in his own thought.

Another route into English thought taken by German philosophy has long been considered to be the work of the German historians of the late nineteenth century and their impact upon British historical studies. Gardiner is no exception; where German strains in his work have been recognised, they

10 '*The table talk of John Selden*. Edited by S.H. Reynolds' [review], *EHR* viii (Jan. 1893), 161.

11 '*A life of Joseph Hall, D.D., bishop of Exeter and Norwich*. By the Rev. Geo. Lewis' [review], *Academy*, xxix (17 Apr. 1886), 267.

are usually described as 'Rankean',[12] although whether this term has been used as a shorthand for a German historiographical tradition or is meant to refer specifically to Ranke is often hard to ascertain. Leopold von Ranke was, and remains, the most celebrated representative of that late nineteenth-century German generation, a historian whose archival research and writings were rightly lauded for their volume and quality during his lifetime, but who has been subject to serious criticism since for his ideological convictions and his alleged methodological naivety. Whatever later historians have thought, it is clear that he was widely read and respected by late nineteenth-century British historians, and the relationship of his work and thought to that of the British writers is essential to any study of British historiography of the period. Tracing the influence of Ranke on Gardiner is difficult; whereas there is some evidence of Gardiner's correspondence with other German historians (for instance von Stern), there is none suggesting that Gardiner and Ranke wrote to one another. However, Gardiner did use, and comment upon, Ranke's work throughout his *History*, reviews and articles; moreover, it was Gardiner to whom the *Academy* turned for an appreciation of Ranke when the German historian died in 1886.

Gardiner opened his obituary of Ranke in the pages of the *Academy* with what appears to be fulsome praise: 'To speak of the great student whose long and fruitful life has at last been brought to a close as the greatest historian of his time, is to fail to appreciate his work at its due value.'[13] Elsewhere, Gardiner had made his positive assessment of Ranke clear: writing in 1875, Gardiner described him as 'the first historian of the day' whose knowledge of the documentary record of his chosen period was 'absolutely unrivalled',[14] and in 1884 as 'the father of modern historical research'.[15] Lang, however, chose in his study of Gardiner to emphasise the closing comments of the obituary in which, Lang claims, he 'criticised the German historian for not being sufficiently scientific'.[16] The words Lang quotes do indeed seem to support this notion: 'Is it not possible to do for history what Darwin has done for science? Ranke, at all events, did not do it. He knew of the influence upon individuals of great waves of feeling and opinion; but he does not seek for the law of human progress which underlies them.'[17] The implication, for Lang, is that Gardiner's ideal of history incorporated the search for (reduc-

[12] For example, P. Bahners, '"A place among the English classics": Ranke's *History of the popes* and its British readers', in B. Stuchtey and P. Wende (eds), *British and German historiography, 1750–1950: traditions, perceptions, and transfers*, Oxford 2000, 151–2; D. M. Kelley, *Fortunes of history: historical inquiry from Herder to Huizinga*, New Haven 2003, 245–6; and Kenyon, *The history men*, 286.

[13] 'Leopold von Ranke' [obituary], *Academy* xxix (29 May 1886), 381.

[14] '*A history of England, principally in the seventeenth century*. By Leopold von Ranke. In six volumes' [review], *Academy* vii (20 Mar. 1875), 285–6.

[15] *HoE* x, p. vii.

[16] Lang, *Victorians*, 165.

[17] 'von Ranke' [obit], 382.

tive) general laws, that is, the attempt to place history in the position of the physical or natural sciences.

The implications of Lang's argument are problematic. The mention of 'science' and 'law' offers the possibility that it was the theories of social science positivists such as Auguste de Comte or Herbert Spencer that Gardiner had in mind when he complained of Ranke's shortcomings. Spencer, in particular, was at the height of his fame and influence as Gardiner wrote these words. Could Gardiner be criticising Ranke for not attempting to seek the kind of positivist and 'scientific' general laws which Spencer and others like him advocated? There is a clue, however, in the word 'human' as applied in this extract. There may be some kind of laws operating in history, but the historian must study 'the men and women in whose lives these laws are to be discerned'. 'Either course [of studying laws, or these lives] is profitable', but the sole study of the laws of society leads to a mechanistic view that concentrates too heavily on external forces, failing to recognise that which comes from within – the human aspect.[18] This displays Gardiner's belief that the personal must always be kept in sight.[19] It is reminiscent of a Christian ethic of action, by which outward action is seen as caused by inward character, and its ideological opposite in historical studies is positivism. Of all of the labels that have been applied to Gardiner, 'positivist' is the least tenable. He reserved some of his strongest criticisms and his most biting sarcasm for the works of positivists and positivist-inspired historians such as Spencer and W. E. H. Lecky. For instance, in replying to a letter that had been sent to the *Academy* complaining about unfairness on the part of the original reviewer of Spencer's *Descriptive sociology*, Gardiner not only said that he felt impelled to agree with that review, but also suggested that Spencer might wish both to widen his reading of history, and begin to appreciate quite what historians do and how they go about it.[20] Gardiner was not a positivist, nor was he sympathetic to the positivist outlook, for it lacked what he understood as a historical understanding of the past.

The possibility that Gardiner was referring to positivist theories of the general laws of society arises due to Lang's very selective use of his source. By quoting only a short section from Gardiner's substantial obituary of Ranke, he does not let us see quite what was Gardiner's sense of 'science'. Thus the sentences that came before those quoted by Lang state that:

> The most devoted student cannot fail to perceive that there is something wanting which he would fain have there. Ranke, it is true, teaches him not to worship Luther and hate Louis XIV; but to discover the influences under which Luther and Louis XIV. grew to be what they were. Yet, when that is gained,

18 *HoE* x, pp. ix-x.
19 See chapter 5 below.
20 *Academy* v (24 Jan. 1874), 93–5. Gardiner was similarly dismissive of Lecky, in '*The political value of history*. By W. E. H. Lecky' [review], *EHR* viii (Apr. 1893), 394–5.

> is there not another step to be ascended? Ranke is cold and unenthusiastic; and, in judging individuals, it is well to be cold and unenthusiastic. But is there no room for warmth of feeling in recounting the efforts and struggle of the race? Is it not possible to do for history …

Ranke, Gardiner tells his readers, was a true historian in his conception of individuals and the past, successfully judging men in their times and not succumbing to party-spirit, but his writings suffer from a lack of warmth. It was this deficiency that prevented his history being on a level with Darwin's science. This 'warmth' comes from a close engagement, even sympathy, with man's struggles. Here the reader is reminded of the Romantic sense of humanity's struggles within and against the full majesty of nature. However, Gardiner was not talking merely of that which comes from a literary imagination, but of something different, a 'higher' imaginative faculty than that displayed by the hugely popular Romantic poets and historians, for

> it has been said, with truth, of Ranke that he interests students rather than the generality of readers. If this merely meant that he did not write as Macaulay wrote, it would mean that he was a better historian than Macaulay. Surely, however, it means more than this.

Gardiner appreciated the imaginative faculty in history-writing, and understood that it opened up history to an audience interested in more than just the dry collection of material and documentary evidence, but he also recognised that this imagination was not just of a dramatic or literary kind. It is that which makes for true history, for an understanding of the past that raises historiography to the level of a true science.

Gardiner's sense of scientific history is one in which the imagination plays an important part, and he saw the historian's task as much more than the recording of the facts of the past. Despite his strong commitment to *wie es eigentlich gewesen* (usually, if not altogether accurately, translated as 'how it really happened'),[21] for Gardiner such knowledge is never enough, and merely represents the first stage of historical method. The task of the historian in realising historiography, he believed, is two-fold: the historian does research, and then s/he writes it up. The former task is left relatively untheorised in Gardiner's work: his problematic of sources rests on their availability, and Gardiner's prefaces are often predominantly a series of 'thank yous' to the great and the good who have allowed him access to papers in their possession. He was clearly much more interested in what the historian does with the sources after having found them. In his review of a classic late nineteenth-century study of the practice of history, Langlois and Seignobos's introduction to the field published in 1898, Gardiner quickly skipped over the first part (about research techniques and the discovery of source-material) as being of little interest, before turning to a much more extensive

21 Many scholars prefer 'how it essentially happened'.

critique of the remainder of their text. This 'second part of the book', wrote Gardiner, 'naturally gives rise to more difference of opinion, as it concerns itself no longer with the examination of sources, but with the conditions and objects of historical writing'.[22] That this is the case is because documentary facts are not, Gardiner feels, inherently good nor interesting – nor indeed do they make up the knowledge of history,[23] for that is provided by the historian in the act of writing up research. The knowledge of history, for Gardiner, was in its writing.

This latter element is, Gardiner accepts, an imaginative act, but not in the sense that writing is inherently an imaginative act: the historian must imagine a causal sequence, as it is necessarily missing from the documentary evidence, and it is this which accounts for historical knowledge. Imagination, therefore, takes place prior to its representation in words on the page. Rather, '[t]he work of constructive imagination comes in where the work of investigation ends',[24] and before the putting of pen to paper. This act is most assuredly not the same as the historian putting forward accounts which seek to complete gaps in the documentary record – Gardiner had strong words for those whose preparations of documents he described as no more than '*lacunæ* filled up by conjecture'[25] – but the act of narrativisation, the construction of a story-like series of events with explicated causal relations from the unconnected events evidenced in the documentary record. Between the collation of information and the presentation of history in texts, Gardiner believed, an imaginative process of narration took place in the historian's mind.

In his obituary of Ranke, Gardiner used the word 'science' and appears to equate the biological sciences and the ideal historical sciences. However, it is indicative that the obituary appeared in the *Academy*. That journal was founded and initially edited by Charles Appleton, a disciple of the Idealists and a specialist in the Hegelian dialectical method.[26] Appleton had turned to Idealism during a short period studying in Germany, where he perfected his German, and amongst his publications is a translation of Ignaz von Döllinger's inaugural lecture as rector of Munich University, 'Universities past and present'. 'Science', in English Idealist thought, meant something quite different from its definition in the English empiricist tradition, particularly in its use as the translation of *Wissenschaft*, as used by the German Historicist school and central to German thinking after Leibniz's discussion of it as an understanding of intellectual enquiry that fully included the liberal arts. A central tenet of Leibniz's philosophy is the softening of

22 '*Introduction aux etudes historiques*. Par C. V. Langlois et C. Seignobos', 337–9.

23 'Mr. Green and Mr. Rowley' [correspondence], *Academy* viii (11 Dec. 1875), 604–5.

24 S. R. Gardiner and J. B. Mullinger *Introduction to the study of English history*, London 1881, p. xxii.

25 *The Fortescue papers* (Camden Society 2nd ser. i, 1871), 46.

26 See the *DNB* entry for Appleton, and J. H. Appleton and A. H. Sayce, *Dr. Appleton: his life and literary relics*, London 1881

the reason/unreason dichotomy, which can find an outlet in the softening of the science/humanities disciplinary boundary that the English language sets up. Fichte had taken Leibniz's understanding further by underlining the importance of the systematic nature necessary to make a science out of any philosophy. Such a systematic philosophy, or science (*Wissenschaftslehre*), must attend to the conditions of knowledge.[27] Empirical 'science' and 'objective history' are very different from each other for Gardiner. The comparison with 'science' that Gardiner is calling for is not one in which methodology is shared by History and Natural Science, nor one in which the senses they each use of 'laws' is the same. Gardiner's science was that of the *Wissenschaft*, probably of the Fichtean understanding of that 'science', better characterised as systematic intellectual inquiry than as 'science' in the Anglo-American analytic sense, and it is in this way that his historical project must be conceived.

A close reading of the rest of the obituary of Ranke suggests that Gardiner was indulging in a historicist analysis of the German historicists, a past generation: Ranke must be rejected as the consummate historian, for a true historical method does not allow for a 'finality in scientific [in the German sense] progress'.[28] No historian can imagine that they have obtained the endpoint of historical research, and this applies to Ranke's method as well as his documentary researches. Furthermore, Gardiner's refusal, despite his high regard for Ranke's work, to hero-worship the great German historian followed his own proscription of canonisations (and, indeed, gibbetings).[29] This approach is most clearly recognised in his refusal to follow either the Whig or Tory historiographical traditions in Britain, and it should not be a surprise that he followed his own precepts with German historiography, too. That approach is identical to that of Ranke's theory of *überparteilichkeit* ['standing above parties']. Gardiner's discussion of Ranke in the *Academy* obituary can be characterised as a typically Rankean historicist response to its subject. Gardiner appears to have used German historical methodology to shine a light upon one of its most famous exponents.

For Gardiner's method, both as it appears in his explicit statements and in his practice, is highly reminiscent of Ranke in particular, and the German historicist school(s) in general. Recognising this opens up the analysis of Gardiner to new and fruitful avenues of thought. The theological and political *via media* that Lang presents can, for example, be recognised as an example of the so-called 'Hegelian dialectic' in action. That phrase refers to the dialectical method whereby an idea, or thesis, is opposed to its antithesis, conceptually creating a pair of opposed ideas, from which a new synthesis

27 D. Breazeale, 'Circles and grounds in the Jena *Wissenschaftslehre*', in D. Breazeale and T. Rockmore (eds), *Fichte: historical contexts/contemporary controversies*, Atlantic Highlands, NJ 1994, 43.
28 'von Ranke' [obit], 382.
29 See chapter 5 below.

is formed as a subsequent move in the creation of knowledge. Although this method was clearly based on the work of Hegel, Hegel never actually used the terms: they are Fichte's.[30] Whereas Hegel's followers understood the dialectic as a forward-looking theory, using it to describe the movement of ideas, society and so on, as they progress, for Fichte the dialectic was intended as a way to look into, or through, an aspect of the real: it was the method for transcendental deduction. By analysing a historical concept thoroughly, it is inevitable that apparent contradictions will arise in the student's eye which will then need to be reconciled. This new synthesis represents an understanding which is not the thing itself; however, this synthesis itself will, on analysis, give way to a new set of contradictions, which will themselves require synthesis. For Fichte, this series of deductions will cease once the essential truth of universal reason has been reached in a concept not reducible to a set of contradictions.[31] Fichte's dialectic method is not a method for explaining the forward march of history, but rather a way of analysing what is and what has been in history.

The method has often been used in a relatively crude manner, and the late nineteenth-century usage of its terms often displays a simplistic understanding of the concepts covered by the method. Simplistic as those uses might be, however, they do appear to bear a resemblance to some of Gardiner's explanations. Thus can be read into Gardiner's work the thesis and antithesis of the puritan and the catholic producing a synthetic (and statist) anglican Church as a solution to the contradictions inherent in 1640s England; the thesis and antithesis of ultra-parliamentarianism and divine-right monarchy finding a synthetic solution in the modern English state; Oliver Cromwell's '[u]nion of apparently contradictory forces';[32] and, crucially for an understanding of Gardiner's historical philosophy, the thesis and antithesis of Whig and Tory historiography culminating in a synthetic truth in the unity of history. Gardiner's explanations can often be characterised in terms of the Fichtean dialectic.

That this Germanic theory should be evidenced in the theories and work of Gardiner should come as no surprise, for the influence of German theory on his generation and earlier has been widely noted. For example, Rosemary Ashton has traced the influences of German theory on Coleridge, Carlyle,

30 G. E. Mueller, 'The Hegel legend of "thesis-antithesis-synthesis"', *Journal of the History of Ideas* xix (June 1958), 411–14. For further discussion of the implications of this confusion see also G. A. Kelly, *Idealism, politics and history: sources of Hegelian thought*, Cambridge 1969, 208; D. Forbes, 'Introduction', to G. W. F. Hegel, *Lectures on the philosophy of world history: introduction: reason in history*, trans H. B. Nisbet, Cambridge 1975, p. x; and C. Sutton, *The German tradition in philosophy*, London 1974, 52.

31 Fichte's dialectic method is first presented in the 1794 *Wissenschaftslehre*, although it is the driving principle of all of his subsequent writings.

32 *CPH*, 114.

G. H. Lewes and George Eliot,[33] four writers whose work played an important part in the intellectual atmosphere of Britain during the 1850s and 1860s, the years during which Gardiner studied at university, began his researches and published the first volumes of his *History*. This influence is of particular interest, and relevance, amongst those writers with whom Gardiner shared intellectual (and political) affinities. Thus, the work of late eighteenth- and early nineteenth-century German philologists, and of German historians such as Reinhold Niebuhr, has been recognised as formative for the 'Liberal Anglican' historians of the mid-nineteenth century, as has its ideological inheritance in later liberal theology within the Church of England. Duncan Forbes has studied that group of historians – Thomas Arnold, Connop Thirlwall, J. C. Hare, A. P. Stanley and H. H. Milman – in detail. He has noted that Niebuhr was, for most of these historians, the immediate source for their engagement with German theory, and that liberal or Broad Church anglicanism shared roots with the Liberal Anglican historians in a German science of history; indeed, he suggests that the Broad Church approach was born of the Liberal Anglican's understanding of church history.[34] It is worth noting that Gardiner chose to support Archbishop Tait and the other drafters and promoters, generally characterised in older histories as Broad Church or liberal, of the erastian Public Worship Regulation Act of 1874 – which Gladstone deplored.[35] Where Lang sees a break from Gladstonian principles in Gardiner's political thought, a continuity in his historical and philosophical thought might be recognised. This led him to support Gladstone, on home rule, when the Liberal leader's thought and policies fitted Gardiner's reading of German Idealist philosophy, but also led him to oppose Gladstone when he believed that the politician's thought was not sufficiently Idealist in shape – as in the case of a measure intended by its essentially centrist proponents, under the influence of German theory, to promote tolerance, oppose the promotion of religious party-spirit and protect the spiritual life of the nation. Gardiner's historical work seems to have shared important principles with German historicism and, crucially, its followers in Britain.

This, however, can only be suggestive, for the traditions of German Idealist thinking are much more complex and multivalent than just the emphasis upon a thesis-antithesis-synthesis conception of the Hegelian dialectic can allow. For example, Gardiner's writing on nations and national sentiment often alludes to, or bears remarkable resemblance to, Fichte's theories of national spirit (*Geist*). It is these theories that Gardiner wished Hartington, Goschen and others had 'read, marked, and inwardly digested' during the

[33] R. Ashton, *The German idea: four English writers and the reception of German thought, 1800–1860*, Cambridge 1980

[34] D. Forbes, *The Liberal Anglican idea of history*, Cambridge 1952, 10–11, 95, 118.

[35] See his defence of Tait from Dean Hook's attacks: 'Hook's lives of Laud and Juxon. *Lives of the archbishops*. By W. F. Hook, D.D., Vol. XI.' [review], *Academy* viii (6 Nov. 1875), 467–8, and chapter 3 below.

Irish home rule debates. However, an appreciation of Fichte's understanding of national sentiment and the formation of political institutions is clear in Gardiner's historical writing as well as in his political activities. For example, he stated that '[t]he English Government of Scotland, as long as it lasted, was a good example of the government which fails, in spite of its excellent intentions and excellent practice, simply because it pays no heed to the spirit of nationality'.[36] Elsewhere, Gardiner commented on the contemporary South African situation in similar terms, in a passage in which he also wrote of studying the colonisation of New Zealand and its colonisers' relations with the 'natives' in his own century to help him understand the situation in seventeenth-century Ireland.[37] Gardiner's critical understanding of colonialism was very similar to Fichte's own rejection of colonialism,[38] in which the paired concerns of individual freedom and social justice necessitated a rejection of the 'universal Man' of both high Rationalist and Kantian thought.[39] It is interesting to note Gardiner's closing phrase –'the spirit of nationality' – on the relationship of England and Scotland, for it immediately conjures up Fichte. Fichtean thought was, in the late nineteenth century, acknowledged as the philosophical maturation of German national sentiment, grounded in Idealist notions of the state and the nation. For instance, in his 1881 study of Fichte – the first English-language study of the philosopher – Robert Adamson claimed that

> However widely the united German empire may differ in internal characteristics from that patriotic state to which Fichte, in his famous 'Addresses,' summoned his countrymen, no German who feels the full significance of his nation can fail to look with pride and gratitude to the eloquent thinker, who, with the thoroughness of a philosopher and the zeal of a patriot, drew in ideal form the outlines of that which has now been happily realised.[40]

For Fichte, the nation was *Geist*, or spirit, something not reducible to mere institutions or even to geographical expression. The obvious intellectual forerunner here is Johann Gottfried Herder, who viewed the nation as having organic unity, rather than a being united in territory, language or under a government.[41] As his letter to Bryce regarding Ireland, which explicitly referred to Fichte's *Addresses*, and his comments on Scotland and England show, the *Geist* was understood by Gardiner as a historical prin-

36 *CPH*, 63.

37 '*Calendar of the state papers relating to Ireland, 1608–1610*. Edited by the Rev. C.W. Russell, D.D., and J. P. Prendergast, Esq. Rolls Series' [review], *Academy* vii (26 June 1875), 654–5.

38 G. G. Iggers, *The German conception of history: the national tradition of historical thought from Herder to the present*, rev. edn, Middletown, CT 1983, 8–9.

39 A. J. La Vopa, *Fichte: the self and the calling of philosophy, 1762–1799*, Cambridge 2001, 316.

40 R. Adamson, *Fichte*, Edinburgh 1881, 5–6.

41 Iggers, *German conception*, 35.

ciple, not as a uniquely German political principle. Gardiner's reading of German Idealist and historicist philosophy, apparently engaged in as part of his historical studies, appears to have influenced both his historical writing and his political activities.

German historicism centred its attention on the nation and the state. The work of the nineteenth-century German historians that came after the earlier Idealist thinkers such as Fichte sought to understand the interplay between the Great Powers and the actions of the high political actors, and they did so by selecting for their sources diplomatic papers, communiqués and similar documents, and the personal testimonies written by those involved at the highest level in the events being described.[42] Certainly, Gardiner appears to share much with the Germans in this respect, with regard both to sources and the concentration of his gaze upon high politics. Thus, the large majority of source material that he made available in his books and through the Camden Society and other records societies consisted of the personal papers of central political actors, diplomatic papers, constitutional and other legal documents, and parliamentary reports,[43] and his prefaces to his main texts make constant reference to the papers of the great families of the realm and libraries of the stately homes of England.[44] There is an obvious parallel in this activity with Ranke's work with Venetian ambassadors' reports. Gardiner and the Germans both opened their historical researches in the documentary records left by high political actors.

Gardiner famously learned several languages in order to be able to read the papers of various ambassadors, the reports prepared for the relevant courts of Europe and the documents held in the national archives of certain countries whose history, certainly during the seventeenth century, was inextricably linked in Gardiner's eyes with that of England, for, '[w]ith the seven years which follow [i.e. 1617–23] all this [inward-looking English constitutionalism] is changed. Every English interest rapidly becomes a continental one'.[45] Here, in *Prince Charles and the Spanish marriage*, where Gardiner first paid particular attention to European concerns, his use of the archives at Simancas, Venice and Brussels was proudly advertised on the title-page. In those three archives, Gardiner had been able to research more fully than had previously been attempted the story of the knotty issue of Charles and the Infanta – and the diplomatic manoeuvrings that attended them. The story that the documents evidenced and that Gardiner told was very much the kind that the German historicists revelled in: a story of court intrigue, international jockeying for position, and the great struggle between national

42 Ibid. passim, but esp. pp. 4–12.

43 See appendix below.

44 See, for example, *HoE* i, p. vi; iv, pp. v–vi; v, p. v; ix, pp. vii–viii; *GCW* i, pp. vii–xi. Conversely, on one occasion Gardiner criticised Lord Fitzwilliam for not allowing access to papers in his collection: *HoE* ix, p. viii.

45 *Prince Charles and the Spanish marriage, 1617–1623*, London 1869, i, pp. vi–vii.

interests embodied in state institutions. Again, there appear to be striking similarities between the work of Gardiner and the work of the German historicists.

However, these apparent similarities with regard to high politics, national self-interest and state institutions in the approaches to history shown by Gardiner and the German historicists are just that – only apparent. Gardiner was much more a historian of ideas than a historian of high politics, and thus for him, in the final analysis, the struggles of which history is made up were those of ideas, of political and religious movements embodied not in institutions (or not just in institutions) but in social groups. Moreover, those social groups were not to be primarily understood as groups within the state, but rather as groups within the nation, as might be expected of a historian influenced by Fichtean national theory. This issue will be discussed in greater detail in chapters 3 and 4, and it is enough to note now that, on this point, Gardiner's position was not shared by the German historians of his own generation.

The German historicist conception of the state was based upon a borrowing of the sense of radical individualism held within Kantian Idealism, an individualism tempered by the events of 1789 to 1815 in France, such that individuation was seen by the later Idealists to take place in the state rather than the person.[46] These events were also the occasion of the rejection of sociology, tainted by association with the French revolutionaries whose application of abstract laws of society to the practical business of governance, the Germans believed, had led to those calamitous events. Again there are parallels with Gardiner's philosophy of history as evidenced in his treatment of British sociologists such as Spencer. Gardiner had a strong dislike for system-building in social theory and practice. He thought it the great failing of Francis Bacon and William Laud that they had tried to impose their theories, as systems, on to organic society.[47] It is also worth noting the Kantian understanding of the individuated state, a conception which gave birth to the concentration on states and their pursuit of their rational self-interest shown in later German historiography. It is important to recognise, therefore, that in rejecting the state-centred understanding of the historical process, Gardiner was not in disagreement with earlier philosophers such as Kant and those he inspired, but rather with a theory that had been developed through the nineteenth century by German historians. On the role of the state and state institutions, Gardiner was in disagreement with his German contemporaries rather than the earlier German Idealists.

One problem with a concentration on the states and their rational pursuit of self-interest is that it can lead to an anarchic conception of historical events, as the constant flux of politics lets history slip from its moorings.

46 Iggers, *German conception*, 39–43.
47 *HoE* iii. 240.

A stable anchor is required, and that anchor, that basis of an ultimate meaning, can be found in a divine plan which, according to Scripture, is invested by God in humans as individuals. This solution, it may be noted, was found by the historicists in returning to Kant's philosophy, although the problem that had arisen for the later historians had been occasioned by their development of the philosopher's theories away from what may be considered a purer Kantianism. In German historicism, then, there was a turn to the individual, not in a radical individualist sense, but in the sense that 'through them history gains meaning'.[48] This appreciation of the position of the individual within society or the state, and its role in historical inquiry, was not unique to Hegelian and post-Hegelian German historians. In Gardiner, too, can be found a version of this German historicist position – that the laws of society may be discerned in the lives of the men and women of history. For Gardiner, the object of analysis was not the state, as it was for the historicists, but rather the nation, as suggested by his apparent debt to Fichtean national theory. To be sure, the source of their difference may be explained by their different environments, rather than intellectual differences. The Briton had been born in a state made up of more than one nation, whereas the Germans had been born in a nation made up of more than one state. Therefore, if a German was to follow Kant's conception of the theoretically-individuated political unit, he might be more likely to see it in the states, individual components of their (divided) nation, whereas a Briton might be expected to look to the individual nations within the state as his political units. Nevertheless, whatever their differences with regard to what the political unit was, and no matter what the source of their difference might be, Gardiner and the German historicists could – and did – share a theoretical approach to the understanding of the world, for he and they both argued that it was only through study of its individuals that the theoretically-individuated object of analysis could be understood.

Having arrived at an answer to the question of what the 'true' or 'right' object of analysis might be (the state or the nation), and through which elements it must be approached (the individuals that comprised the membership of the state or the nation), both the German historicists and Gardiner were left with another question: what intellectual tools are available to, and should be used by, the historian in his or her attempts to understand the past? The historian, the Germans believed, needs to acquire and use the skills of 'rational observation' (*beobachtender Verstand*) and 'poetic imagination' (*dichtende Einbildungskraft*), for '[w]hat binds these fragments [of data], what puts the individual piece in its true light and gives form to the whole remains beyond the reach of direct observation'. What one must do is add 'the felt' (*empfunden*), 'the inferred' (*geschlossen*) and 'the divined'

48 Iggers, *German conception*, 58–9.

(*errathen*).[49] This is the intuition (*ahnung*) required for true understanding (*verstehen*), the consideration of which is found in the likes of Humboldt, Ranke and Dilthey[50] – the three great exponents of German historicism – which in Germany led directly to the 'professionalization of historical research and the development of canons of critical scholarship'.[51] These are the very elements of a discipline of History that Gardiner's disciple Firth spent his entire career campaigning to have applied at Oxford. It is thus understandable that a direct mirroring of this more complex German elaboration of the work of the historian can again be seen in Gardiner's (perhaps) simplified sense of the role of the imagination in narrativisation. Gardiner and his contemporaries in Germany seem to share a similar reliance on the imaginative faculty in understanding the past.

Tellingly, in the passage in which he most clearly discusses the role of the imagination in historiography, the preface to the tenth volume of the reprinted *History of England*, Gardiner again inserts some words from Goethe, without reference, this time from the ninth chapter of the seventh book of his *Wilhelm Meisters Lehrjahre* (1780): 'Nur ein Teil der Kunst kann gelehrt werden, der Künstler braucht sie ganz' ['It is but a part of art that can be taught; the artist needs it all'].[52] For Gardiner, as for Goethe, reason alone cannot produce the complete work; historians must use their intuition. In particular, the knowledge of facts – the very foundation of an empiricist conception of historical study – is never enough for understanding the past. Indeed, as Gardiner himself appreciated the principle, it is the understanding of the past rather than the facts of the past that is the true principle of historical study. In a debate via the review columns and letters pages of the *Academy* on the historiographical value of J. R. Green's work, Gardiner clearly declared his commitment to historicist *verstehen* against empiricist facts:

> There is an accuracy in detail which may exist quite independently of any perception of the larger truths of history. One is sickened by hearing how history is sometimes taught by men who, no doubt, are doing their best, but who have no idea that history cannot be got up like the rules of Latin grammar. 'Give me facts,' one sometimes hears of such teachers saying; 'I want to know in what year John of Gaunt was born, and what was the name of the youngest daughter of Edward I?' Such teachers have no sense of historical perspective. They do not rise up into the idea that facts are only of importance as they help us to understand the changes of thought, of feeling, or of knowledge which mark the growth of that complex social unity which we call a nation. A boy who does not know which side won at Blore Heath,

49 Humboldt, cited and translated ibid. 59.

50 Ibid. 10–11.

51 Ibid. 11.

52 *HoE* x, pp. vii–viii. Gardiner did not provide a translation; the English version given here is Carlyle's.

> or who has been taught that Henry VIII. had a wife called Margaret, may possibly know much more of history than many a man who has got all these facts at his fingers' ends.[53]

For Gardiner, then, the knowledge of history is to be found in the understanding, rather than in the empirical facts of which we have direct evidence.

It is useful to divide historians into those whom Wilhelm Dilthey would call 'empiricists' and those whom he would call 'historicists'. For Dilthey, the distinction is to be found in their respective commitments to the fundamentally different 'correspondence' and 'coherence' theories of truth. For those operating with correspondence theory, that which is true is that which actually happened – in other words, that for which we have direct evidence. However, historicists instead see a truthful statement to be one which coheres with other statements that are known to be true. This demands something beyond the accumulation of facts, for it requires the historian to go beyond the merely evidential and to use imagination and intuition in creating a coherent version of the past which accords with the evidence, to be sure, but which also offers a far larger picture, a panorama in which the full complexity and diversity of the past is represented. Gardiner's commitment to the principles of historical understanding and knowledge implied by coherence theory clearly places him in this historicist school.

Crucially, the use of Goethe's words, and Gardiner's apparent commitment to the principles they encapsulate, point to the origin of the theory of the imaginative conception to which Gardiner and the later German historians adhered. That theory was not formulated by the later historians, but early in the century by the philologist Wilhelm von Humboldt, whose statement of the theory is a recapitulation and, it may be admitted, sophisticated reorientation of the ideas put forward by the eighteenth-century theorist Herder, the contemporary and associate of Kant, Fichte, Goethe and Schiller. Although the appreciation of the need for the imagination in conceptualising the past can be, and has been, described as an historicist position, it is, rather, Idealist in origin, for the historicists had themselves taken the idea from the earlier theorists.

The need for an imaginative approach which went beyond the empirical facts was, for the German Idealists, much more than a merely theoretical point. Kant had argued that 'philosophy' – by which he meant the disciplines other than medicine, law and theology – had, as their final object, reason itself.[54] This, indeed, was the intended endpoint of Fichte's dialectic method which the successive analysis of apparent contradictions would eventually reveal. It is incumbent upon the philosopher (which includes the historian) to reach beyond the merely empirical, that is, the content upon

[53] 'Mr. Green and Mr. Rowley' [corresp.], 604.

[54] I. Kant, *The conflict of the faculties*, trans. M. J. Gregor, London 1992. See also the editor's introduction to *Kant: political writings*, ed. H. Reiss, Cambridge 1970, 35–8, 176.

which the disciplines rested,[55] to discover the laws of human society and its progress through history which account for natural reason. When Nicholas Tyacke convinces himself that the 'laws of human progress' that Gardiner talked of in his obituary of Ranke can only mean a Darwinian evolutionary theory applied to society,[56] he fails to recognise that that phrase has distinct Idealist connotations. Given Gardiner's clearly Idealist understanding of how one should reach beyond the empirical facts, it is not too much to at least consider, as a working assumption, that he also had an Idealist understanding of why one should reach beyond the empirical facts – and of what was to be sought there.

It thus becomes clear that Gardiner's criticism of Ranke is based on the belief that the German historian is not sufficiently Idealist in his historical writing. Such a position has important implications for any attempt to understand Gardiner. It challenges accepted opinion regarding the intellectual influences on Gardiner, suggesting that his thought needs to be appreciated as strongly German in origin, but not specifically Rankean. It is necessary, therefore, to discuss in greater detail whether it is the case that the British historian did differ significantly in practice from the German historian in his conception of the past and its study. Furthermore, if that does indeed prove to be the case, it becomes essential to attempt to draw out more precisely the origins of Gardiner's Germanic thought.

In his obituary of Gardiner, C. H. Firth wrote of his friend and master that

> In estimating Gardiner's place amongst historians, the comparison with Ranke, suggested in foreign appreciations of his work, inevitably arises in the mind. Gardiner possessed neither the qualities nor the defects of Macaulay or Froude, whilst in more than one respect he resembled the great German scholar. Like Ranke, he endeavoured to see things exactly as they were, and to let the facts speak for themselves; he was like Ranke too in his breadth of view, in his constant sense of the connexion between national and European life, and in the independence and equity of his judgements. As an investigator Gardiner was at least the equal of Ranke.[57]

What is remarkable here is not just the way it so succinctly puts forward both the positive and the negative aspects of the image of Gardiner that Firth advanced, but also that it so clearly articulates the image of Ranke held in much of the English-speaking world. Much of it, indeed, may be considered a fair representation. Gardiner's attempts at treading a path between Whiggism

55 Medicine, theology and law each had authoritative contents, thus denying them the status of philosophy.

56 N. Tyacke, *Aspects of English Protestantism,* c. *1530–1700*, Manchester 2001, 6–7. Tyacke refers also to Conrad Russell's assertion that Darwinian evolutionary theory explains the structure of Gardiner's narratives: Russell, 'Introduction', 4–5.

57 C. H. Firth, 'Samuel Rawson Gardiner' [obituary], *Proceedings of the British Academy 1903–4*, 300.

and Toryism in British historiography and Ranke's editorship of a journal initially dedicated to finding a way to truth between the liberal left and the reactionary right in German politics can both indeed be characterised as an 'independence and equity' of judgement. Both historians were dedicated to allowing the past, or rather the voices of the past, to speak without interference on the part of the historian, and both were great internationalists in their vision of how the political life of their objects of analysis should be mapped out. These shared theoretical and practical principles must be recognised for Gardiner had 'read, marked, and inwardly digested' German Idealist theory, the source for the methodologies of German historicists such as Ranke. Indeed, it would appear that, in philosophical terms, Gardiner may be considered an Idealist.

However, this possibility does come up against the objection that Gardiner was, after all, that which he has long been considered: a dry empiricist. This image has had a long history, probably due to the advocacy of Gardiner's friend, student and intellectual inheritor, Firth. Indeed, the usefulness of such an image of the historian for his admirers is hinted at in Firth's words: 'Gardiner possessed neither the qualities nor the defects of Macaulay or Froude'. Ranke and Gardiner were used to construct an image in opposition to the narrative history that a scientific historiography must reject as it aspires to disciplinary status – Firth's great project for historical studies which he never failed to promote throughout his career. To some extent, the new critical school of historians have been made victims of their self-representation. According to Firth, Gardiner did have the qualities of Ranke the empiricist, Ranke the impartial judge, Ranke the great promoter of a 'true' source-criticism in modern history, but he did not have the qualities of the literary historians Macaulay and Froude. There is a clear problem here: as his disciples constructed an idea of Gardiner which served their own purposes, they did a disservice to their master. In one recent survey of Victorian nonfiction, the single paragraph given over to Gardiner sounds mantra-like in its disdain for Gardiner the writer: his 'austere work' which is 'without any trace of excitement', its author warns, 'some readers may find … dull, due to its conscientious refusal to exploit the dramatic element … Understanding the past, rather than bringing it to life, was Gardiner's main object'.[58] As a result, it has not been the concern of any commentators on Gardiner to attempt to appreciate his work as a writer. In recent years, however, with the advent of new approaches to the analysis of nonfictional literature, broadly termed postmodernist, it can be recognised that all writing involves literary and linguistic choices and that, therefore, any writing that may appear nonliterary should be recognised for what it is: literature in which authorial choices have been made which work to occlude the literary nature of the text. Both Ranke and Gardiner were writers with the rhetor's powers, and

[58] P. Turner, *English literature, 1832–1890, excluding the novel*, Oxford 1989, 318–19.

no denial of the rhetorical nature of 'scientific' historiography can hide this. It may be that the intellectual sources for the work of Ranke and Gardiner played a role in their literary constructions: Anthony La Vopa has written that Fichte 'aspired to give the presentation of philosophy a certain rhetorical efficiency, even as he spurned the rhetor's arts of manipulation'.[59] The same can be said of the literary styles of Ranke and Gardiner. The image of the two historians as scientists, set up by well-meaning followers, belies a complexity of thought in both men with regard to the historical process, and a deep engagement with the creative force of history-writing.[60]

Christopher Parker has made another suggestion with regard to the representation of historicism generally, and Ranke specifically, in historiography which may help us to understand Gardiner.[61] In particular it sharpens the 'dull empiricist' vision of Gardiner that has come to dominate debate. Parker argues that Idealism has been left out of the equation when English historiography has been discussed. All of the schools of twentieth-century historiography have tended to posit an all-encompassing 'empiricism' to describe the methodological 'Other'. As a result, Idealist and Idealist-inspired historiography have been carefully subsumed into an empiricism that barely gives due credit to the intricacies of German theory and its impact on English historical thought. This has happened even with Ranke, although this may have been in part due to his rejection of much of Hegel's thought. The failure to appreciate Ranke's thought in all its complexity, and historiographical thought in all its diversity, has meant that the Idealist strains in his thought have been hidden from view. Parker's thesis is that an Idealist strain, separate from and even often opposed to empiricism, continued throughout the nineteenth century and has been conspicuously ignored, in part offering us the image of 'Ranke the empiricist' rather than the more fitting 'Ranke the Idealist'. This is perhaps best seen in the widespread reduction of historicism to the 'critical appreciation of documents, associated with Ranke' in its representation in historiographical analyses, as observed by Georg Iggers.[62] This stress on the documentary evidence is mirrored in reductive images of Gardiner's methodology. For example, Lang argues that when Gardiner spoke of 'science', 'he simply meant the thorough and objective analysis of facts, based on a first-hand use of documents culled from as many archives as possible'.[63] However, Gardiner's approach to history is so much more than this – and, indeed, where it can be seen to be so, it would appear that it is due at least in part to the influence of Idealist philosophy. The complexity of Gardiner's philosophy of history has been much neglected.

59 La Vopa, *Fichte*, 10.

60 See chapter 5 below.

61 C. Parker, *The English idea of history from Coleridge to Collingwood*, Aldershot 2000, 224–5. See also his *The English historical tradition since 1850*, Edinburgh 1990.

62 Iggers, *German conception*, 3.

63 Lang, *Victorians*, 166.

The problem for Parker is not just that a German historicist strain has been partially hidden from scholars, but that a more direct Idealist strain has been almost entirely ignored not just in historiography, but, remarkably, also in philosophy. He sees this happening in respect of the English Idealist thinkers in the tradition of T. H. Green who were centred on Oxford in the last third of the nineteenth century. For Parker, later modernists and post-modernists, through their failure to understand nineteenth-century thought and their reduction of it to 'empiricism', have lost sight of Idealism. But, if this account is a fitting rendition of the occlusion of Idealist philosophy amongst philosophers, then that is even more the case for Idealist philosophy's role in other fields, that is disciplines in which Idealism has had an impact but the practitioners of which are less inclined to study the history of philosophy. This is certainly the case with historical studies. According to Parker, history is one of the most Idealist-influenced disciplines, if only indirectly through the work of German historians, and yet this German philosophical tradition remains barely discussed in the historiography.

The influence of German historicism – meaning a specifically late nineteenth-century manifestation of German philosophy – has of course been recognised, and its situation as an inheritor of Idealism has been included in such accounts. No study of disciplinisation or professionalisation can possibly leave out the impact of the German university model, brought to Britain by students of German theory such as Acton and Firth.[64] However, although there has been plenty of research on the impact of German thought on the institutional expression of History, there has been less recognition of its direct impact upon historical practice. Moreover, German historicism is associated with Idealism, but it is not Idealism itself: it is a particular manifestation, or mediation, of the Idealist heritage. It is worth noting Iggers's point that the features recognised as being those of German historicism, such as the stress on documentary source analysis, are manifestations of, not identical to, German methodology.[65] It is for this reason that appreciating that Gardiner, and others, read the earlier Idealist thinkers without the mediation of the later German historicist school – historians such as Ranke, Droysen, von Sybel and Mommsen – can lead to new avenues of thought with regard to their work.

The development of pedagogical theory in Britain, particularly regarding higher education, is a case in point. It was Humboldt's reorganisation of the German educational system of 1809–10, inspired by Fichte's teachings, that appealed to British educational reformers. Here is another route to questioning the standard accounts of Gardiner. Gardiner's dedication to education outside the old universities has been widely noted, but it has generally

64 For Firth see *A plea for the historical teaching of history*, Oxford 1904, and *Modern history at Oxford, 1841–1918*, Oxford 1920; for Acton, see his *A lecture on the study of history*, London 1895.

65 Iggers, *German conception*, 3.

been presented as a pragmatic choice on his part, as a way of obtaining a salary as a historian after his expulsion, on religious grounds, from Oxford. The circumstances of Gardiner's life were such that he had to teach, and he had to teach outside Oxford and Cambridge. At most, these accounts suggest, Gardiner and the Idealists only shared an interest in education; unlike the German educationalists, however, Gardiner's interest was not a theoretical one. On this basis, Gardiner might fit into the standard accounts of the impact of the German model in British education through the impact of disciplinisation (which, in the British universities meant for History little more than source criticism) upon him. However, such an understanding of Gardiner's educational activities fails to deal with one simple question: if Gardiner taught because he needed to, in order to obtain a sufficient income, why, once he was in receipt of a civil-list pension, and academic preferment (and a salary) from Oxford, did he continue to teach? Gardiner did not teach because he had to; he taught because he wanted to.

Quite why he was committed to teaching may be suggested by his choice of where to teach. As well as his lecturing at King's College, London, Gardiner was a regular lecturer at the early women's colleges, such as Bedford College, and on behalf of the University Extension Movement and at Toynbee Hall. These movements, these colleges and these lectures were inspired, founded and staffed by the leading lights of English Idealism, and there were institutional and personal links between these Idealist educational reformers and Gardiner. Peter Gordon and John White have demonstrated that Idealism was a crucial intellectual source for educational reformers in Oxford and elsewhere. These reformers were not historicists and were not inspired by late nineteenth-century German thought, but had turned directly to earlier Idealists, in particular to Fichte and Hegel. Those involved came under the influence of the Oxford coterie around T. H. Green, such as the members of the 'Old Mortality Society' of the 1850s – A. V. Dicey, John Nichol (whose study of Carlyle stressed the importance of the sage of Chelsea to the reception of German philosophy),[66] Algernon Swinburne and James Bryce, Gardiner's correspondent on matters Fichtean. Another important influence was Green's tutor, Benjamin Jowett, whose disciples included F. H. Bradley and William Wallace, Gardiner's contemporaries as Fellows of Merton College. Amongst the associations and colleges these men founded or helped to found, were the Association for the Higher Education of Women in Oxford and the Oxford University Extension Movement (both topics close to Gardiner's concerns), the Working Men's College in London (where Gardiner lectured) and Toynbee Hall. The first director of the latter was Samuel Barnett, a Jowett pupil alongside Green and Toynbee, who used his contacts at Oxford to secure a number of members of that university to

[66] J. Nichol, *Carlyle* ('English Men of Letters' series), London 1892.

come to London to teach.[67] One of those lecturers – indeed one of the best, Barnett believed – was Gardiner. Gardiner was thus institutionally, personally and intellectually linked to leading British Idealists. Moreover, he shared their commitment to the teaching of women and the working classes, a commitment born of a theoretical engagement with early German Idealism.

The role of Idealism in late nineteenth-century British philosophy has often been minimised in historiography. Many accounts of educational history, for instance, have stressed disciplinisation (and therefore what was going on in the traditional universities and the new universities modelled on them) and failed to recognise the important issue of what was going on outside the traditional, elite-centred educational structures. This has also happened in studies other than those in the history of education. The conflation of historicism and Idealism in late nineteenth-century thought has become common as the historicist mediation of the earlier philosophers has been allowed to govern modern conceptions of Idealism. However, it has been shown that a more direct engagement with the early Idealists was practised by the educational reformers seeking to make changes in higher education outside of the traditional universities. It has been thus with Gardiner, too. His position as part of the new professional and disciplined order, Fellow of All Souls and of Merton, adhering to the principles of source criticism, has been the endpoint of much of the work on Gardiner the empiricist historian. However, throughout those later years of his career, he continued in his other educational activities. For the source of these, the historian must look to the theories of early Idealist thinkers. So, too, must the historian turn to these thinkers to explicate Gardiner's political principles and, indeed, to understand his philosophy of history. The late nineteenth-century historian's philosophy of history was not that shared by his German contemporaries, but rather that of the Idealists of the late eighteenth and early nineteenth centuries. Some of the implications of such a reading of Gardiner's intellectual formation for studies of his life activities (such as his educational work) or his practice (for example, his understanding of historical genre) must be left to future work (in the case of the former) or later chapters of this book (in the case of the latter). What can be concluded now is that, as the role of Idealism in late-Victorian thought has been neglected, so too has the Idealist Gardiner.

67 Gordon and White, *Philosophers*, 105.

2

Practice

German theories of history clearly played a significant role in the work of Gardiner. However Gardiner was interested not just in German theories of history, but also in German history, both as a part of the story that he told of seventeenth-century England, and in its own right. In the 1870s, perhaps as a result of the Franco-Prussian War, the subject of the internecine European struggles of the seventeenth century loomed large for Gardiner's conception of the political and religious crises in England in that century. As a result, the Thirty Years War plays an important part in the *History of England* and is dealt with in great detail, supplied at least in part by the British historian's use of the work of German historians. Furthermore, although Gardiner's interest in that war waned in later years,[1] in 1874 he published a book in Longmans' *Epochs of Modern History* series of introductory texts, entitled *The Thirty Years' War, 1618–1648*. A brief summary of the role of German historiography in Gardiner's main work, and a more detailed analysis of his own study of German history is therefore in order as a complement to his theoretical preoccupations and to provide a more nuanced account of his work.

Gardiner's *History of England* contains footnote references to at least thirty-six separate German-language works of history. Although these include books concerning European countries other than Germany, such as von Ranke's work on French history,[2] Julius Opel's *Der Niedersächsisch-Dänische Krieg* (1872–94)[3] and Adolf Buff's *Die Politik Karls des Ersten in den ersten Wochen nach seiner Flucht von London und Lord Clarendons Darstellung dieser Zeit* (1868),[4] the majority are concerned with German history. For example, Gardiner's study of the period before the Bohemian revolution of 1618 was carried out with the help of Moriz Ritter's *Geschichte der Deutschen Union von den Vorbereitungen des Bundes bis zum Tode Kaiser Rudolphs II (1598–1612)* (1867–73)[5] and Anton Gindely's *Rudolf II und seine Zeit, 1600–1612* (1863–8).[6] However, the majority of the works consulted were studies of the period of the Thirty Years War, such as August von Goschenbach's *Der General Hans Ludwig von Erlach von Castelen: ein Lebens- und Charakterbild*

1 Gardiner to W. Anson (?1884), MS Anson, All Souls College, Oxford.
2 *Französische Geschichte, vornehmlich im sechzehnten und siebzehnten Jahrhundert* (1852–6), referenced at *HoE* ii. 395.
3 *HoE* v. 293.
4 *HoE* ix. 136.
5 *HoE* ii. 91.
6 *HoE* ii. 92; iii. 263, 266.

aus den Zeiten des dreissigjährigen Kriegs (1880–2),[7] Rudolf Reuss's *Graf Ernst von Mansfield im Böhmischen Kriege, 1618–1621: ein Beitrag zur Geschichte des dreissigjährigen Krieges* (1865)[8] and Johann von Söltl's *Der Religionskrieg in Deutschland* (1840–2).[9] Some were German translations of texts previously published in other languages, such as Niels Slange's *Geschichte Christian des Vierten, Königs in Dännemark*, published in German in 1757–71 but translated from the 1749 Danish edition,[10] and Antoine Villermont's *Tilly, oder der dreissigjährige Krieg von 1618 bis 1632*, published in German in 1860, the same year as the original French edition.[11] As well as German books, Gardiner also read German-language journals, as evidenced in his reference to 'Gindely's paper in *the Proceedings of the Historical and Philosophical Class of the Vienna Academy for* 1859'.[12] Gardiner's use of German-language historiography in his *History of England* was extensive and displays his facility in that language.[13]

Moreover, Gardiner certainly read more German historiography than the list of directly referenced works suggests. For example, over three issues of the *Academy*, he reviewed separate volumes of Anton Gindely's *Geschichte des Dreissigjährigen Krieges* (1869–80).[14] For the *North British Review* he provided a lengthy discussion of von Ranke's classic biography of one of the leading generals of the war, *Geschichte Wallensteins* (1869),[15] his history of the war, *Zur Geschichte vom Religionsfrieden bis zum dreissigjährigen Krieg* (?1869) and Gustav Droysen's biography of *Gustav Adolf* (1869). His further reading for the history of the Thirty Years War is also displayed in his reviews of non-German studies of the war, such as J. L. Motley's *Life and death of John of Barneveld, Advocate of Holland: with a view of the primary causes and movements of the Thirty Years' War* (1874),[16] and Julius Fridericia's *Danmarks y dre politiske Historie, 1635–45* (1881).[17] He also footnoted non-German works that dealt with the characters and events of the Thirty Years War, such as

7 *HoE* ix. 64.

8 *HoE* iii. 292.

9 *HoE* iv. 178, 199, 222.

10 *HoE* iv. 180.

11 *HoE* iv. 302.

12 *HoE* iii. 267. Original not traced.

13 In the preface to *The Thirty Years' War*, Gardiner implied his awareness of the work of 'Ranke, Gindely, Ritter, Opel, Hurter, Droysen, Gfrörer, Klopp, Förster, Villermont, Uetterodt, Koch, and others', thus adding three German writers (Gförer, Förster and Koch) to the list of historians whose work was known to him, but who were neither reviewed by him nor directly referenced in any of his writings.

14 For vol. ii ('*Zweiter Band*') see *Academy* xiii (23 Feb. 1878), 162–3; for vol. iii ('*Dritter Band*') *Academy* xiv (14 Sept. 1878), 257; and for vol. iv ('*Vierter Band*') *Academy* xx (6 Aug. 1881), 101.

15 *NBR* li (Jan. 1870), 551–3.

16 'First Notice', *Academy* v (14 Feb. 1874), 161–3; 'Second notice', *Academy* v (21 Feb 1874), 192–4.

17 *Academy* xx (9 July 1881), 25.

Villermont's *Ernest de Mansfeldt* (1865).[18] Gardiner thus read widely in his attempts to understand events on the continent of Europe that were linked to, or played an essential part in, early Stuart England.

Gardiner's own contribution to the historiography of the greatest conflict in Europe of his chosen period has been recognised as one of 'the most satisfactory in English'.[19] *The Thirty Years' War, 1618–1648* (1874) is a densely-written narrative. However, although planned as an introductory text, it was not, according to Gardiner, designed for younger pupils, as he explained in his preface:

> If the present work should appear to be written for more advanced students than those for whom most if not all the other books of the series are designed, the nature of the subject must be pleaded in excuse. The mere fact that it relates exclusively to Continental history makes it unlikely that junior pupils would approach it in any shape, and it is probably impossible to make the very complicated relations between the German states and other European nations interesting to those who are for the first time … attempting to acquire historical knowledge.[20]

Gardiner knew the series to which his book was an addition well, having written an earlier contribution on British history,[21] and his wife Bertha was to contribute another volume of continental interest a few years later.[22] He understood, therefore, that his book need not be a work of original research, according to the principles that lay behind the series:

> But though, as I have said, the present work is not intended for young children, neither is it intended for those who require the results of original research … There must surely, however, be many, as well in the upper classes of schools as in more advanced life, who would be glad to know at second hand what is the result of recent inquiry in Germany into the causes of the failure of the last attempt, before our own day, to constitute a united German nation.[23]

Although his book was not, Gardiner felt, an addition to the historiography of Germany, it was based on the very latest original scholarship.

Such 'second hand' historiography however, has its pitfalls, and the writer of such a work must be aware that his 'impressions are less sharp, and are exposed to greater risk of error than those of one who goes direct to the

18 *HoE* i. 108; iv. 218; v. 276, 277, 285, 287, 290.

19 'Introduction', to T. K. Rabb (ed.), *The Thirty Years' War: problems of motive, extent, and effect*, Boston, MA 1964, p. xii. The other studies that Rabb recommends are C. V. Wedgwood, *The Thirty Years War*, London 1938, and the Czech historian Anton Gindely's *History of the Thirty Years' War*, in the 1884 English translation (originally published in German, 1869–80).

20 *The Thirty Years' War, 1618–1648*, London 1874, p. v.

21 *The first two Stuarts and the Puritan revolution, 1603–1660*, London 1874.

22 B. M. Gardiner, *The French revolution, 1789–1795*, London 1882.

23 *Thirty Years' War*, p. vi.

fountain head' of the documentary sources. Later in his preface, however, Gardiner asserted that 'in forming my own opinions I have had the advantage not merely of writing from original documents, but of having studied at least some of the letters and State papers of the time' and that he was thus in a position to question the conclusions of certain German historians whose work had been based on time spent in the archives.[24] Indeed, he claimed that some of the work that he had been able to carry out had given him a greater understanding than that of some specialist historians:

> More valuable than the little additional knowledge thus obtained [from documentary researches] is the insight into the feelings and thoughts of the Catholic princes gained by a very slight acquaintance with their own correspondence. To start by trying to understand what a man appears to himself, and only when that has been done, to try him by the standard of the judgment of others, is in my opinion the first canon of historical portraiture; and it is one which till very recent times has been more neglected by writers on the Thirty Years' War than by students of any other portion of history.[25]

As well as prefiguring critiques of the nineteenth-century historiography of the war later advanced by twentieth-century historians – such as in the failure by protestant liberals to understand the catholic participants in the war – these words remind the reader of the theoretical position taken by Gardiner with regard to the writing of history. Clearly, the documentary sources are necessary as a basis of work, but then there is the need for 'insight' and 'understanding' as part of what Gardiner, using an artistic metaphor, calls 'historical portraiture'. The practised reader of Gardiner's work can recognise here the principles of Idealist-inspired historiography. Moreover, Gardiner also asserts in this passage the need to judge a man through the eyes of contemporaries and the standards of his own time. Again, 'the first canon of historical portraiture' clearly retains the basic principles of historicist practice (in the wider sense of the term). The reader can be assured that Gardiner had maintained his usual critical standards in the writing of *The Thirty Years' War*.

Moreover, despite having earlier told his readers that in this instance he was 'the retailer rather than the manufacturer of history',[26] Gardiner actually went on to claim that to at least some small extent his account of the war was of his own conception. It is an original contribution to the historiography of the Thirty Years War. If that contribution is to be understood, however, it is necessary to turn to an analysis of the field, particularly the work of Gardiner's contemporaries in Germany and elsewhere. The Thirty Years War has remained a controversial and much-studied topic in German

24 Ibid. pp. vi–vii.
25 Ibid. p. vii.
26 Ibid. p. vi.

history, and many historians have sought to understand the development of its historiography, and in particular the role of the nineteenth-century writers in the development of later understandings of that war. A due consideration is required if Gardiner's work in German history is to be properly appreciated.

Theodore Rabb has both identified a 'traditional school' of thought on the war, and outlined the critique offered by subsequent 'revisionists'.[27] Rabb summarises the earlier view: the Thirty Years War was an isolatable and distinctly German war that took place between 1618 and 1648; the principal cause of hostilities, and motives of the participants, were religious; and it was a political, social, economic and cultural disaster for Germany. According to Sigfried Steinberg, a leading and particularly forthright revisionist writing in the 1960s, this 'war- and post-war propaganda' was first advanced under the patronage of the Swedish and Brandenburg governments,[28] by Bogislav von Chemnitz writing as Hippolithus à Lapide, in his *Dissertatio de ratione status in Imperio nostro Romano-Germanico* (?1640/1). Chemnitz, in later years the official historiographer to the Swedish court, wrote of the essential weakness of the imperial position and extolled the virtues of Frederick William, the elector of Brandenburg, in standing up to the tactics of the Holy Roman Emperor, Ferdinand.[29] In 1667 the cudgels were taken up by the Swede, Samuel von Pufendorf (also pseudonymously, in the guise of an Italian nobleman called Severinus de Monzambano) in a pamphlet entitled *De statu Imperii Germanici*, which was speedily translated into English, German, French and Dutch, and sold throughout Europe. Here, according to Steinberg, are the main elements of the traditional picture, such as the immediate start of the war being the rebellion in Bohemia in 1618 and the end being the Peace of Westphalia in 1648. Pufendorf then published three fuller accounts of the war, elaborating his version of events.[30] The 'traditional' account was thus a near-contemporary, propagandistic construction.

The traditional view only gained in currency in subsequent years. The Brandenburg line, wishing to advance its role as the chief defenders of German protestants, promoted this construction of the war through the eighteenth century, most notably in Frederick the Great's *Mémoires pour servir à l'histoire de la maison de Brandebourg* (1751), before it found its clearest version for a mass audience in the late eighteenth-century and early nineteenth-century

27 'Introduction', to Rabb, *Thirty Years' War*, pp. vii-xii.

28 S. H. Steinberg, *The 'Thirty Years War' and the conflict for European hegemony, 1600–1660*, London 1966, 92.

29 Chemnitz's work is discussed in some detail in Wedgwood, *Thirty Years' War*, 440.

30 Steinberg, *Thirty Years War*, 92–3.

accounts of Friedrich Schiller[31] and Gustav Freytag.[32] What Steinberg called their 'romantic', 'creative', 'poetic' and 'dramatic' accounts held sway due to their wide readership and, particularly in Schiller's case, their position as major books of study in German schools and universities. By the middle of the nineteenth century, a major historiographical tradition regarding the Thirty Years War had been instituted. Eventually, at the end of the century, a more critical generation of historians, particularly (but not exclusively) economic historians, began to question, one by one, the main elements of the traditional account. They did so from within the latest theoretical paradigms, basing their work on their researches in the archives. This generation was Gardiner's own, and it includes such men as Ranke, Gindely and Droysen, and many more historians whose work he referenced and reviewed. As he had stated in the preface to his study of the war, Gardiner was fully aware of 'recent inquiry' in Germany – the work, that is, of the historians engaged in the revision of the traditional account.

It might be expected, therefore, that Gardiner's conception of the Thirty Years War would share much with that of these early revisionists and that his study would form part of the new wave of thinking about the war.

The first element in the traditional construction is that the war was essentially a struggle for dominance in Germany between the Holy Roman Emperor and (some of) the princes of the states that made up the Empire. The war began with a rebellion against imperial control in Bohemia, continued to be played out on German soil despite the increasing involvement of non-German peoples and rulers, and ended with a peace treaty in which the heads of the various German states gained the right of virtual sovereignty within their territories and the powers of the Holy Roman Emperor to rule over Germany were drastically reduced. This germanocentric view is closely linked to the dating of the war at 1618–48. Those that have questioned this 'German' view have thus tended also to question this set of dates. For example, Nicola Sutherland, who sees the Thirty Years War as actually a small part of a larger conflict of the Habsburgs and the Valois against the Bourbons, dates the conflict of which it was a part as having begun in the 1490s (or perhaps even in 1477) and ending in 1715.[33] Steinberg also sees the fight in Germany as part of a battle for European hegemony between Habsburg Austria and Bourbon France, although he limits that larger battle to the years between 1609 and 1659.[34] George Pagès's understanding of

31 Ibid. 94. Schiller wrote two histories on aspects of the war, translated into English as *History of the secession of the Netherlands* (1788) and *History of the Thirty Years War* (1791), and a dramatic cycle centred on one of the great military leaders of the war, *Wallenstein* (1799).

32 Principally in his *Pictures from the German past* (1859–62); for a discussion of Freytag's work see Steinberg, *Thirty Years War*, 94–5.

33 N. M. Sutherland, 'The origins of the Thirty Years War and the structure of European politics', *EHR* cvii (July 1992), 589–90.

34 Steinberg, *Thirty Years War*, 1–2.

events in Germany is not limited to a set of identifiable dates, because for him the Thirty Years War was part of a more amorphous struggle, being 'one of the last manifestations of a much larger crisis: the passage from medieval to modern times in all western and central Europe'.[35] Dutch historians are wont to see events in Germany as part of, or merely linked to, their 'Eighty Years War' of 1568–1648; Spanish historians are more likely to interest themselves in the Hispano-French War of 1635–59, relegating events elsewhere to background or feeder conflicts for the more important struggle between the Spanish branch of the Habsburgs and the growing menace of Richelieu's France.[36] For writers such as Sutherland and Steinberg, however, historians should talk not in terms of certain states but rather of a European war, a point made also by Peter Limm, who stated quite categorically that 'the historian has to interpret [the Thirty Years War] as a major phenomenon in European history'.[37] These historians have tended not to concern themselves with the question of why a germanocentric construction had come about, although other critics, such as Pagès and Josef Polišenský, took a position on this historiographical issue. The latter blamed the failure of earlier generations to see the conflict as a European war as being due to their having been 'diverted by the distorting lens of nationalistic historiography'[38] although, as Graham Darby has pointed out, the Czech Polišenský's emphasis on Bohemia in his work suggests his own nationalistic bias.[39] Darby has made this point also about Pagès, whose stress on French policy as the harbinger of all things new in seventeenth-century Europe appears to give undue weight to his home nation. However, it is clear that the germanocentric conception of the war, tied to a dating schema of 1618–48, did indeed hold a dominant position in the historiography of the Thirty Years War until the twentieth century.

It would appear from a first cursory glance at his work on the war that Gardiner was very much within this mould. His book was, after all, called *The Thirty Years' War, 1618–1648*, in which, after opening with a frontispiece map of 'Germany at the commencement of the Thirty Years' War, 1618' and a discussion of 'Political institutions of Germany' and 'Protestantism in Germany' as historical background, he narrates a story from 'The Bohemian revolution' (the title of chapter ii) to 'The Treaty of Westphalia' (section two of the last chapter). However, what Gardiner writes about the periods both before and after those events is telling: the whole of chapter i is dedicated to the period 1440–1612, and the final section of the last chapter

35 Cited in Rabb, *Thirty Years' War*, 20. This passage, taken from Pagés's *La Guerre de Trente Ans, 1618–1648* (2nd edn, Paris 1949) has been translated by Rabb.

36 Rabb, *Thirty Years' War*, p. vii.

37 P. Limm, *The Thirty Years War*, Harlow 1984, 94.

38 J. V. Polišenský, *The Thirty Years' War* (1970), trans. R. Evans, London 1974, 9–10. See also his 'The Thirty Years War and the crises and revolutions in seventeenth-century Europe', *Past and Present* xxxix (1968), 34–43.

39 G. Darby, *The Thirty Years' War*, London 2001, 4.

is entitled 'Continuance of the war between France and Spain (1648–1660)'. This brings into question the issue of both the dating and the geographical limits of the war: Gardiner's interest is clearly in a struggle over a longer duration than the 1618–48 schema suggests, which went well beyond Germany's borders and indeed appears to have been a wider European conflict. This accords with Gardiner's conception of events in England, where he saw the 'Puritan revolution' not only as just part of a British conflict, but as part of a widespread European struggle. Gardiner thus saw the Thirty Years War not in isolation, in temporal or geographical terms, but as an element of a much bigger picture, one which incorporated much of the rest of Europe and which was not limited to even the seventeenth century, let alone 1618–48.

It is noteworthy that the germanocentric element of the traditional view was not questioned by the early revisionists of the nineteenth century. To some extent, this may be explained by the strength of nationalist theories in late nineteenth-century Europe. In particular, German intellectuals in this period – during which Germany was unified under the leadership of Prussia, home to many of the German historians whom Gardiner read – were in the main committed to a nationalist conception of Germany. Gardiner's position is a more complex one, in which Germany is appreciated as an entity, and yet is not treated as an island within Europe. This was a view of Germany held by many of the early Idealists of the late eighteenth and early nineteenth centuries, albeit a view which lost favour as the nineteenth century progressed. Fichte can be characterised as simultaneously both a German nationalist and a 'cosmonationalist', a position to which Gardiner's view of England in the seventeenth century appears analogous.

Gardiner's understanding of the issue of the German nature of the Thirty Years War is closely related to his Idealist conceptions of the nation, in contrast to those of the German historians of his and earlier generations. The issue of time and place is closely linked to differing perspectives on the motives behind the war. In the traditional account, the war was one of religion, although the details of that conception are often very different. For instance, it has been argued that the struggle between the (north) German princes and the Holy Roman Emperor was a struggle between protestants and catholics; or that the rebellion against imperial power was intended to assert the right of the protestant princes to decide on the religious allegiances of their state and peoples; or that, in a reversal of the model of power that this last argument suggests, this claim in Germany was part of a larger battle between powerful protestant princes and resurgent (roman) catholicism, that is, a battle between Reformation and Counter-Reformation. Some of these arguments with regard to the war necessarily suggest a non-confessional understanding: for instance, those historians that have argued that the war was part of a larger battle for hegemony in Europe between (catholic) Habsburgs and (catholic) Bourbons not only play down the role of protestantism but also clearly rest their analyses on matters of state, rather than theological, concerns. However, the issue of state or dynastic ambition is incorporated into the traditional view, for that perspective includes the recognition that, while the war started as a confessional war, it became a war of dynastic or state power as other nations, such as France, England and Spain, became involved. Thus traditional historians hold that the war was neither entirely confessional nor entirely non-confessional in nature, although religion remains a leading factor in their analyses.

This characterisation of the traditional view is unquestioned in twentieth-century studies of the historiography of the Thirty Years War. Both Theodore Rabb and Sigfried Steinberg use it as the basis of their critiques of the work of earlier historians, such as Anton Gindely, 'perhaps the most thoroughly researched and scholarly account to argue that religion was the principal issue at stake, with political concerns only a close second',[40] whose work Gardiner read and referenced in the *History of England*. According to Steinberg, the Thirty Years War 'was, so we have been taught, initially a war of religion between the German Protestants and Catholics, which the foreign powers of Spain, France, Denmark and Sweden exploited, each for political reasons of its own'.[41] Rabb tells his readers exactly what those political reasons were:

> It has ... been customary to call the Thirty Years' War the last of the religious wars and to stress that its basic cause was the conflict sparked by the Reformation and the Counter-Reformation. Although it is admitted that other interests were at stake ... the fundamental issue is held to be religion ... Only later, when foreigners entered the fray to plunder helpless Germany, did material aims triumph over spiritual.[42]

The term 'material aims' points the reader to the source of the counter-confessional argument, the Marxist economic historians. According to the revisionists, many of whom based their work on or referred to this Marxist historiography, material aims were all. The first writer to put forward this perspective in explicitly Marxist terms was Franz Mehring, in his short book *Gustav Adolf* (1894). The author of studies of Marx and historical materialism,[43] Mehring argued that economic forces were at work which account for the motives of all the states and leaders that became involved in Germany.[44] The strongest avowal of the position available in English has been that offered by Polišenský, a Czech historian working behind the 'Iron Curtain' during the 1960s and 1970s. He made his historiographical

40 Rabb, *Thirty Years' War*, p. viii.

41 Steinberg, *Thirty Years War*, 1.

42 Rabb, *Thirty Years' War*, pp. vii–viii.

43 Franz Mehring, *Karl Marx, Geschichte seines Lebens*, Leipzig 1918; *Aus dem literarischen Nachlass von Karl Marx, Friedrich Engels, und Ferdinand Lassalle*, Stuttgart 1902; 'Einem Anhange über den historischen Materialismus', in *Die Lessing-Legende*, Stuttgart 1893.

44 This biography has not been translated into English, but is discussed in Rabb, *Thirty Years' War*, p. viii.

position clear in the preface to his history of the war, arguing that, whereas the Marxist Christopher Hill represents the 'standard' understanding of the seventeenth century, the conservative Hugh Trevor-Roper's work is 'distinctly polemical'.[45] However, non-confessional accounts are not exclusive to a Marxist perspective and for Rabb, Michael Roberts and other non-Marxist late twentieth-century historians the religious motive has little relevance to their analyses.[46] Historians throughout the twentieth century have denied the centrality of religion to the Thirty Years War.

According to Steinberg, however, the religious argument had been overturned well before Polišenský. Turning back to the late nineteenth century, Steinberg has argued that the economic historians of that period had 'destroyed the legend of the preponderantly religious character' of the war.[47] Much of this work was not Marxist, despite its later adoption and reformulation by Mehring and others, and it is important to recognise that twentieth-century revisionists such as Steinberg see the reaction to the confessional argument as having been firmly stated much earlier – by Gardiner's generation. The best example of this is to be seen in the work of Gustav Droysen, whose biography of Gustavus Adolphus, which most clearly sets out this 'material interests' theory in which economic impulses lay behind the involvement of individuals and states in the war, was used by Gardiner. Other historians of the period who proposed a non-confessional analysis (or at least an analysis which questioned the importance that traditional historians had accorded to religion) include Ranke. According to the revisionists' narrative of the development of Thirty Years War historiography, then, it was Gardiner's generation that began to reject the traditional view that religious motives played an important part in the war, and instead held that the war was one in which material interests held sway over the minds of the participants. Crucially, Gardiner had studied many of the works by his contemporaries in which the non-confessional nature of the war had been asserted.

The death of the 'religious motives' argument has interested a number of students of Thirty Years War historiography. As well as accounting for the rise of the 'material interests' argument, they have attempted to understand quite why religion was written out of the discussion of war motives by so many historians. Religious motives and material interests could have been accorded equal status in explanations, but appear not to have been. Despite his own rejection of the 'religious motives' argument, Polišenský criticised nineteenth-century historians for their prejudice against the religious sensibilities of the seventeenth century: 'The views of contemporaries

[45] Polišenský, *Thirty Years' War*, 273.

[46] See the discussion of the historiography provided by Rabb, and the 'bibliographic essay' provided in G. Parker, *The Thirty Years' War*, London 1984, 281–303. Michael Roberts's analysis can be found in two biographies of Gustavus Adolphus, most recently *Gustavus Adolphus*, 2nd edn, Harlow 1992.

[47] Steinberg, *Thirty Years War*, 95.

were not of course readily adaptable to the liberal and chauvinistic models of thinking current in the last century, which looked down with a feeling of superiority on the "passions of religion" and with incomprehension on all phenomena transcending the purely national.'[48] Even though he argued for the economic and material interests account of the war, and which he incorporates here as 'phenomena transcending the purely national', the Marxist Polišenský took the opportunity to attack his liberal Victorian forebears for their lack of understanding of the earlier generation. A less forthright critique of nineteenth-century historians who rejected the 'religious motives' argument might be expected, however, from someone who has questioned the revisionist account and sought to reassert the centrality of religion in the narrative of the Thirty Years War. According to the twentieth-century historian Carl Friedrich, unable to 'feel ... the religious passions' of a past age, nineteenth-century historians spurned the 'religious motives' explanation of the Thirty Years War.

However, many nineteenth-century historians of the seventeenth century did not deny the crucial role that religion played in the lives of the people of the age that they studied. Gardiner repeatedly and vigorously argued that the Thirty Years War was in great part a religious war. He may have read Droysen's counter-argument, but he had also read Gindely's eloquent account of a religious war later merely tempered by material considerations. In reviews of the work of these two historians, Gardiner contrasted Droysen's failure to comprehend the 'close connection' between religion and politics, and his subsequent reliance upon the political model of the war,[49] with Gindely's 'truth-loving spirit' and 'sobriety and impartiality'.[50] Elsewhere, denying Droysen's emphasis on less lofty motives than religion, Gardiner stated that he felt able to 'neglect [his] elaborate argument that Christian IV. took part in the war through jealousy of Gustavus Adolphus'.[51] Gardiner was a nineteenth-century liberal historian who was not only capable of appreciating the religious factor in seventeenth-century life, but was also a historian who appreciated historiography which stressed the role of religion in the past and attacked, as weak and deficient, the work of historians who sought to downplay such motives in favour of exclusively political, or rather secular, explanation.

Furthermore, Gardiner practised what he preached. His narrative of the Thirty Years War, for instance, traces the cause of the war back to the Treaty of Augsburg in 1555, which offered an unstable settlement on the ownership and control of church lands and the rights of sovereigns to declare the

48 Polišenský, *Thirty Years' War*, 10.

49 '*Gustav Adolf*. Von G. Droysen' [unsigned review], *NBR* li (Jan. 1870), 550.

50 '*Geschichte des Dreissigjährigen Krieges*. Von Anton Gindely. Zweiter Band', *Academy*, xiii (23 Feb. 1878), 162; '*Geschichte des Dreissigjährigen Krieges*. Von Anton Gindely. Dritter Band', *Academy* xiv (14 Sept. 1878), 257

51 *Thirty Years' War*, p. vii.

religious affiliations of their states and peoples, and its subsequent gradual erosion by catholics.[52] The 'three parties' in the increasing tensions in Europe were not dynasties or states, but 'Catholics,' 'Lutherans' and 'Calvinists'.[53] The struggle in Bohemia which sparked war may have been between the Estates and the House of Austria, but the root of the dissension was their respective religious affiliations.[54] And so on, through the entire history of the war, until it was settled in 1648, ostensibly with a parcelling up of territory, the importance of which for Gardiner, however, was much more than the merely material:

> The importance of the Peace of Westphalia in European history goes far beyond these territorial changes ... That which gives to the Peace of Westphalia its prominent place amongst treaties is that it drew a final demarcation between the two religions which divide Europe ... Thirty years of war ended by a compromise under which the religious position of each territory was fixed by the intervention of foreign powers, whilst the rights of the central government were entirely ignored.[55]

Thus, the issue of religious tolerance and the right of princes to choose their religion was the crucial issue, both in 1618 and in 1648. Indeed, for Gardiner, the 'unity' of conception that made the Thirty Years War a fit subject for a history was 'the growth of the principle of toleration as it is adopted or repelled by the institutions under which Germany and France, the two principal nations with which we are concerned, are living'.[56] 'Toleration' is a key word in Gardiner's *The Thirty Years' War*, and he usually associated it with protestantism. Thus, in the war up to 1635, 'Protestantism and Catholicism, tolerance and intolerance' were 'the immediate objects of strife'.[57] However, elsewhere Gardiner presented toleration as a living principle that can take root in all cultures, even though it can find fertile soil in some nations more easily than in others: 'In that great country [i.e. France], then as now, ideas of the most opposite character were striving for mastery. Old thoughts which had been abandoned in England in the sixteenth century were at issue with new thoughts which would hardly be adopted in England before the eighteenth.'[58] Tolerance and intolerance were not represented separately by different states; they were both present in all states. The 'national interest' argument could not take hold in the mind of a man who thought like this, that the issues that mattered were not national

52 Ibid. 10–13.
53 Ibid. 14.
54 Ibid. 23–8.
55 Ibid. 210–11.
56 Ibid. p. v.
57 Ibid. 187.
58 Ibid. 69.

issues. Gardiner's entire conception of the war was based upon religious and related intellectual concerns.

This account of Gardiner's understanding of the Thirty Years War contradicts the standard view held by students of historiography, that historians of the late nineteenth century had rejected the older tradition of viewing the Thirty Years War in terms of religion, in favour of a 'material interests' argument. Why then did Gardiner assert the religious dimension, and why has Thirty Years War historiography failed to account for the position of Gardiner, Gindely and other late nineteenth-century historians for whom religious matters were crucial? One critic of those historians who argue that religion was a leading motivating factor in the war has stated that he believed that earlier generations had been led astray by the rhetoric of seventeenth-century leaders who were, quite genuinely, religious men, but who used the language of religion to convey other concerns:

> As religion was still the pivot of men's political thoughts and social activities, and as even secular ideas found expression most commonly in biblical and ecclesiastical language, arguments of statecraft and political propaganda readily appeared in the guise of religious or theological controversy. There is no doubt, however, that all decisions of consequence were taken in the cool light of what at the time became known as *raison d'etat*.[59]

This 'guise' however, was not conscious disguise

> [f]or down to the middle of the seventeenth century members of every community considered life in all its aspects as one integrated whole. There was no division between their religious convictions, their political aspirations, their economic theory and practice: all of them flowed from the concept of human life as one undivided and indivisible universe.[60]

Carl Friedrich argued in similar terms, albeit suggesting that religious issues were not just part of the mentality of a seventeenth-century political actor, but the dominant concern, adding that it was for this reason that Gardiner's generation had failed to understand the 'religious passions' of the seventeenth century: 'Liberal historians found it difficult to perceive that for baroque man religion and politics were cut from the same cloth, indeed that the most intensely political issues were precisely the religious ones.'[61] For Steinberg, the failing of historians of Gardiner's generation, and of the years before and after Gardiner had been writing, lay in how they had sought to understand these religious, political and economic issues as divisible and, indeed, divided:

59 Steinberg, *Thirty Years War*, 2.
60 Ibid. 96.
61 Cited in Rabb, *Thirty Years' War*, 33.

> The label of a 'war of religion' between Roman Catholics and Protestants has been attached to the 'Thirty Years War' by German writers whose philosophy of history was determined successively by the rationalism of the eighteenth, the liberalism of the nineteenth and the agnosticism of the twentieth century. They wrote in an intellectual atmosphere in which religion, philosophy, politics, science, economics and other spheres of human thought and action had become separate entities, divided from one another in almost watertight compartments.[62]

Historians have compartmentalised human thought and have thus allowed themselves to see religion as an identifiable and isolatable facet of human existence, and thus of the historical process, in particular, of the Thirty Years War. It is as a result of this generalisation that Steinberg's model does not account for Gardiner. According to that particular nineteenth-century liberal, '[h]istorians coolly dissect a man's thoughts as they please, and label them like specimens in a naturalist's cabinet. Such a thing, they argue, was done for mere personal aggrandisement; such a thing for national objects; such a thing from high religious motives. In real life we may be sure it was not so.'[63] Steinberg's critique of nineteenth-century historians therefore does not hold for Gardiner, as the rejection of compartmentalisation was the very source of Gardiner's thesis, at least at the theoretical level. The reason for both Steinberg's and Friedrich's sense of superiority in the appreciation of the seventeenth-century mind is clear to any student of the nineteenth century: whereas Friedrich claimed, in the middle of the twentieth century, that in the seventeenth century, 'for the last time, life was seen as meaningful in religious, even theological terms',[64] presumably an apparently unproblematic claim for a historian of the seventeenth century to make, the student of the Victorian era knows that this is simply not true, at least in Britain. Gardiner was able to understand fully the role of religion in seventeenth-century minds, because his thought also was not compartmentalised into the religious, the political, the personal and so on – his thought and action were unified in conception, and it was made meaningful in religious terms.

This appreciation of the indivisibility of seventeenth-century thought is clear in Gardiner's understanding of one of the more controversial figures of the Thirty Years War, a man whose 'motives' have been much debated: Gustavus Adolphus, king of Sweden. It is possible to see in Gardiner's treatment of Gustavus that the rejection of compartmentalisation was not just a theoretical principle, but one that was acted on throughout his work. Much of the writing on Gustavus falls before the critiques of Steinberg and Friedrich, compartmentalising as they do the possible motives behind his intervention in the wars in Germany. Erik Ringmar has created a further

62 Steinberg, *Thirty Years War*, 96.

63 *Thirty Years' War*, 81.

64 Cited in Rabb, *Thirty Years' War*, 33.

set of divisions, namely the set of arguments that have been put forward by historians with regard to Gustavus' motives: a religious commitment to the fight against the Counter-Reformation; a pro-active defensive move against the threat of Austrian invasion; and the need to expand markets and trade.[65] This model of the sets of theories available is based on the more detailed account of the historiography given by Sverkar Oredsson[66] in which eleven basic explanations are delineated, and then collected into three sets of theories that he calls religious/ideational, military/political and economic/socio-economic. According to Ringmar, Oredsson has surveyed 166 writers in seven languages, including English, and assigned them to one or more of these groups of theories.[67] For example, eighty-six writers, such as Edmund Burke, Hegel and August Strindberg, are included in the first group. The latter two are included in the subset of those seeing Gustavus as 'acting as an "instrument of God or History"'; as Ringmar describes it, Hegel 'regarded him as a vehicle of the progress of the World Spirit'.[68] Included in the second group there are 122 writers, such as Droysen and Michael Roberts, the leading twentieth-century biographer in English of Gustavus Adolphus. The third group contains just fourteen writers, and it includes Mehring. A fourth group is also considered – those who sought not their own understanding of Gustavus Adolphus' motives, but rather took at face value the *Manifesto* that he published when he invaded Germany. They include his contemporaries Chemnitz and Pufendorf, as well as later writers such as Voltaire. Some writers are included in more than one group, such as the German historian and dramatist Friedrich Schiller, whose account of the Swedish king includes both an acceptance of his *Manifesto* and an argument for the religious motive. Through a careful reading of Oredsson's analysis, Ringmar has provided a narrative of the development of the historiography: during the seventeenth and eighteenth centuries the *Manifesto* was at the centre of explanations of Gustavus' conduct; at the end of the eighteenth century, an ideational account began to appear; from 1870 the military argument took over; and at around the turn of the twentieth century the economic argument made headway, eventually supplanting all other accounts. According to this analysis of the historiography, then, Gardiner and his generation were the originators and popularisers of the military/political explanation.

However, the work of Gardiner on the wider issue of the Thirty Years War does not sit easily with the accounts that have been presented of the historiography, and his understanding of Gustavus might also be expected to defy the generalisations of such analyses. Indeed, one might question

65 E. Ringmar, *Identity, interest and action: a cultural explanation of Sweden's intervention in the Thirty Years' War*, Cambridge 1996, 11.
66 See S. Oredsson, *Gustav Adolf, Sverige och trettioåriga kriget: historieskrivning och kult*, Lund 1992.
67 Ringmar, *Identity*, 20–4.
68 Ibid. 11.

the analysis itself. In the late nineteenth century, two principal images of Gustavus Adolphus existed in English-language literature. There was the great military leader and brilliant fighter on behalf of his nation's interests that Ringmar states as being the leading construction of the late nineteenth century, but the protestant saint-hero of an earlier age was still very much in evidence and often presented unproblematically. For instance, J. Johnson Leak's *King and hero* (1891), published by the Sunday School Union, treats Gustavus Adolphus only in a religious light, unsurprisingly given the interests of its publisher, as the defender of the protestant cause. C. R. L. Fletcher, in his volume in T. Fisher Unwin's *Heroes of the Nations* series, presented the Swedish king in similar terms, as the full, rather melodramatic, title of his book suggests: *Gustavus Adolphus and the struggle of Protestantism for existence* (1890). These nonfiction accounts were given support by fiction. In 1885 the bestselling author of tales for boys, G. A. Henty, had published *The lion of the north*, which Gardiner reviewed, remarking on his success in offering 'a very interesting tale, conveying a good deal of historical information', despite 'the difficulties inherent to his subject', that is, the complexities and banalities of the actual events.[69] In the previous year, Frederick Swinborne had published an epic poem in which he sought to present 'the recognised soldier-hero of the Reformation, the military Luther of Protestantism',[70] in unambiguous terms:

> Gustavus, King of Sweden, who his life
> Gave free for Freedom, in defensive strife,
> The Hero of Religion's war.
> *He* sought not selfish empire to extend,
> Nor dared *he* Sweden's blood and treasure spend
> For glory or for fleeting fame[71]

Swinborne's rejection of arguments concerning personal aggrandisement or imperial (and military) conquest is explicit, and flies in the face of the new image of Gustavus that Ringmar has noted. However, these four examples of the protestant-hero conception of the Swedish king are all from what might be called 'popular literature,' as opposed to the apparently more moderate 'academic' texts to which Ringmar (exclusively) refers. Such accounts, born as they are of a need to proselytise or to provide exciting heroic narratives, might be dismissed in favour of the work of university historians such as Droysen, but it is important to recognise that such accounts were an integral part of the discourse surrounding Gustavus Adolphus in late nineteenth-century Britain. Gardiner read Henty's book, and knew at least some of the volumes in the *Heroes of the Nations* series to which Fletcher's book

69 'Historical gift-books', *Academy* xxviii (28 Nov. 1885), 355.

70 F. P. Swinborne, *Gustavus Adolphus: an historical poem and romance of the Thirty Years' War*, London 1884, p. vi.

71 Ibid. 5.

belonged. This latter volume in particular, but others also, were intended for use in schools, and the school textbook was a genre very familiar, and very important, to Gardiner and to other historians. Indeed, Gardiner's own *Thirty Years' War* was a textbook for use in schools. Ringmar is interested only in the study of a small and limited genre of historical writing, the academic text, and his confident conclusions regarding the chronology of Gustavus Adolphus historiography must be treated with care.

Gardiner's conception of Gustavus Adolphus is spread across two works, his study of the Thirty Years War and his *History of England*. The historian's characterisation of the Swedish king must hence be understood with reference to both works. Each has its own concerns, born of the nature of its genre, and yet a composite picture can be drawn from them.

Gardiner's first mention of the Swedish king in the *History of England* describes him as 'the great Gustavus Adolphus'.[72] In his *Thirty Years' War* the first reference is much more detailed, and he provides an extended eulogy which is worth quoting at length for both the large picture that it draws and the detail he provides of that drawing:

> Gustavus Adolphus, King of Sweden, was a man of higher stamp [than Christian IV of Denmark]. His is one of the few names which relieve the continental Protestantism of the seventeenth century from the charge of barrenness. Possessed of a high and brilliant imagination, and of a temperament restless and indefatigable, to which inaction was the sorest of trials, he was never happier than when he was infusing his own glowing spirit into the comrades of some perilous enterprise … he had, too … the power of seeing facts in their infinite variety as they really were, and the self-restraint with which he curbed in his struggling spirit and his passionate longing for action whenever a calm survey of the conditions around showed him that action was inexpedient. In all the pages of history there is probably no man who leaves such an impression of that energy under restraint, which is the truest mark of greatness in human character as it is the source of all that is sublime or lovely in nature or in art.[73]

Here is not the reduced mortal of revisionist accounts, but the shining hero of Romantic accounts: 'brilliant imagination', 'glowing spirit', 'struggling spirit', 'passionate longing'. The eulogy also closes with a phrase familiar to Romantic criticism, talking of the sublime and the lovely in relation to nature and art. It also reminds the reader of the religious element in Gustavus, only making reference to the earthly man in providing his title, 'King of Sweden'. As Gardiner introduces his readers to Gustavus Adolphus, there is no sense of the problematising of his character or actions that appears in much of the contemporary historiography.

72 *HoE* ii. 136.

73 *Thirty Years' War*, 77–8.

In the *History of England*, Gardiner provides the words of one of Gustavus' contemporaries as part of his assessment of the king's character. Simonds D'Ewes (1602–50) was a member of the Long Parliament who planned to write a history of England, and who thus collected a number of papers of the Elizabethan and early Stuart periods and kept a diary of his own times for posterity. He was a presbyterian, but not a protestant ideologue, and was expelled from Parliament in Pride's Purge in 1648 as a royalist sympathiser. For Gardiner and other historians, D'Ewes's diaries opened a window on the political society of his times. D'Ewes never met Gustavus, but he did offer an assessment which Gardiner appreciated gave a voice to the Swedish king's reputation in England at this time. Gardiner quoted 'the plodding antiquary' on Gustavus' victory at Breitenfeld in 1631, and on the king's death the following year. D'Ewes's words on Gustavus display the characteristics that the historians of the historiography have recognised as being central to protestant propaganda. At Breitenfeld, 'the sole honour and glory of the victory, next under God – to whom the religious King of Sweden gave the only glory – redounded to the Swedes and the Scots and other nations in the Evangelical army'. This ensured that 'infinite comfort [is] afforded to the distressed and persecuted and oppressed Protestants in Germany, so all men hoped [Gustavus] in the issue would assert fully both the true religion and the ancient liberties of Germany'.[74] Here are the familiar strains of protestant hero-worship, accepting at face value the claims of Gustavus' manifesto that he was fighting for the glory of God, the defence of protestantism and to secure the liberties of the German princes. These attributes – and the king's reputation in England – are given added strength with D'Ewes's report of the death of the 'heroic king': 'Never did one person's death in Christendom bring so much succour to all true Protestant hearts.' Presented without criticism by Gardiner, D'Ewes's words help to construct the image of the protestant hero which resounds in the work of the popular writers of the late nineteenth century.

Although Gardiner's basic conception of the Thirty Years War relied on a religious analysis, the level of the stress that he placed on the confessional argument was not consistent. Indeed, his dedication to a religious explanation of the Thirty Years War was stronger earlier in his career than it was towards the end. In 1865, prior to the publication of Droysen's study and other key early revisionist works, Gardiner's analysis was more clearly one based on the religious issue. In a volume of papers published in that year dealing with Anglo-German diplomacy during the Thirty Years War, he described the 'struggle of the two religious parties in Germany which lit up the flames' of that war.[75] However, by the 1870s, as the revision of the

[74] D'Ewes, cited in *HoE* vii. 190.

[75] *Letters and other documents illustrating the relations between England and Germany at the commencement of the Thirty Years' War: from the outbreak of the revolution in Bohemia to the election of the Emperor Ferdinand II* (Camden 1st ser. xc, 1865), p. v.

traditional accounts began in earnest, the historian began to recognise the possible role of issues of strategic interest in the birth, conduct and end of the war. Thus, Gardiner's assessment of Gustavus published during the 1870s and reprinted after thorough revision in 1883–4, does not neglect to bring forward questions of the king's less idealistic motives, although they were, for the historian, clearly linked to religion:

> Gustavus Adolphus was bound by every conceivable tie to the Protestant cause. He had to fear a Catholic pretender to the Swedish crown in the person of his cousin Sigismund [of Poland]. If the Emperor extended his authority to the shores of the Baltic, the throne of Gustavus and the national independence of Sweden would be exposed to danger. The dominion over the Baltic was for him a question of life or death.[76]

Here, are the personal and national motives – the trade-related and strategic needs of the revisionist accounts – for control over the Baltic and thus over a principal trade-route for northern Europe, at the very centre of 'materialist interest' accounts of Gustavus' actions. Gardiner does not shy from references to Gustavus' need to defend his own crown, the territory of his nation, and the control of the Baltic trade routes. Along with his contemporaries in the historical profession, Gardiner recognised that Gustavus' interests were not just ideational, but material. It thus appears from the evidence of Gardiner's writings on Gustavus Adolphus that he was at least partly influenced by the prevailing historiographical trends of the end of the nineteenth century.

However, Gardiner's understanding of Gustavus' character was not presented in the compartmentalising way that this initial, brief analysis suggests. According to Gardiner, 'Protestantism and the national right of each separate country to go its own way untrammeled by [the Holy Roman Empire's doctrine of legal right] appeared in [Gustavus'] eyes, as in his days for the most part they really were, but two forms of the same spirit.'[77] Steinberg's appreciation that religious and secular motives were not to be compartmentalised, as in the seventeenth century they were not divisible, is here mirrored in Gardiner's understanding of Gustavus Adolphus. Indeed, according to Gardiner, in Gustavus 'the love of law and orderly government was *indissolubly blended* with the desire to propagate the faith on which [his] own spiritual life was based'.[78] Countering the analysis of Droysen, then, Gardiner argued that to Gustavus, 'the consummate warrior and statesman, the defence of Protestantism was no empty phrase … [it] filled him with the consciousness that he was sent forth upon a high and holy mission'.[79] Gustavus Adolphus was, for Gardiner, a protestant and national hero, a defender of both his faith and liberty, not separately, but indivisibly so. This

76 *Thirty Years' War*, 293–4.
77 Ibid. 79.
78 Ibid. 81 (emphasis added).
79 *HoE* v. 293.

appreciation, moreover, was not based solely on Gardiner's analysis of what these apparently separate motives meant for Gustavus, but on the historian's own sense of their indissolubility. That Gardiner argued in the same book that Gustavus' 'first duty, and he never forgot it, was to his own country', but also that the 'establishment of Protestantism in Europe as a power safe from attack by reason of its own strength was the cause for which he found it worth while to live, and for which, besides and beyond the greatness of his own Swedish nation, he was ready to die'[80] should not be read as a contradiction, then, but as a result of Gardiner's own refusal to countenance the division of the great king's interests into the secular and the spiritual, the material and the ideational. For Gardiner, the apparently competing claims of the Church and the nation were indivisible, in theory and in practice.

Gardiner's maintenance of the practical-spiritual image of Gustavus was in contrast to the prevailing orthodoxies of the historicist school of his own time. It may be the case that the British historian was influenced by the continental historians that he had read, but he was not as ready as they were to reject entirely the confessional explanation. Late nineteenth-century German historians were at the forefront of the revision of past orthodoxies with regard to the Thirty Years War. The work of many of them may, at first glance, appear to be products of their time. For example, to Droysen, a leading intellectual of Bismarckian ideology and a committed German nationalist, might be ascribed a political source for his emphasis on the 'national interests' argument. His book was published in 1870, at the height of tension between Germany and France, created at least in part by the push for a Prussian-centred German unification. In such a climate, and given his own political activities, Droysen would be likely both to cast doubt on the idealism of non-Germans (such as Gustavus Adolphus), and to downplay or even to exclude religion – which divided rather than united Germans – from the debate over the Thirty Years War. However, it is more valuable to look behind the merely political, to the philosophical underpinnings of such a nationalist and state-centred theory. German Idealist and, in particular, historicist philosophy was predicated upon a model of the nation as state, and as an individual agent in its own right. Droysen's political philosophy was intimately related to his philosophy of history. The German historicists, whose philosophy was based on an Idealist conception of the state as a freely-acting entity pursuing its own interests, understood the actions of seventeenth-century politicians in this light – as leaders expressing their nations' interests, not as ideologically-charged fighters on behalf of (non-national) religion.

Ranke, then as now the great exemplar of late nineteenth-century German historicism, viewed the Thirty Years War as a struggle between great powers fighting for their own interests. His conception of the war was very

80 *Thirty Years' War*, 78, 162.

different from that of Gardiner. Since Gardiner was not a follower of Ranke in terms of his approach to history, this should not be a surprise. However, it is not enough to say that Gardiner differed from Ranke; it is necessary also to attempt to discover the source of Gardiner's understanding of the Thirty Years War.

Although he had shown an interest in Gustavus Adolphus, the individual who appears to have most fascinated Ranke was Albrecht von Wallenstein. One of the great military leaders of the Thirty Years War, Wallenstein won a number of victories for the emperor, before first being sacked under pressure from powerful members of the imperial aristocracy, then reinstated, and then murdered. In 1869 Ranke published a biography of the general, albeit a 'biography which expands into history',[81] which Gardiner reviewed.[82] According to Theodore Rabb, that biography, after the earlier traditional 'one-sided portrayals' of 'the tragic, idealistic hero' exemplified by the work of Friedrich Schiller, represented the 'first serious attempt at an impartial assessment of the most controversial figure in seventeenth[-]century German history', a 'careful, modest scholarly evaluation' which 'remains … one of the most satisfactory accounts ever written'.[83] Gardiner agreed that Ranke's biography was a 'very full and impartial narrative', but expressed concern that it lacked something which only Schiller appeared to have appreciated. Gardiner quoted a line from Schiller's dramatic cycle *Wallenstein* in the original German, 'sein Lager nur erkläret sein Verbrechen' ['His camp must help us understand his crime'][84] and then, although he admitted that the assessment is in the main wrong, argued that Schiller, unlike Ranke, was right to 'bring the "Lager" [the 'camp'] into special prominence'.[85] By relying solely on the documentary record, and seeking to produce a dry, impartial narrative, Ranke had fallen short of Schiller's conception of the character of Wallenstein. According to Gardiner, the dramatist's better understanding of the military leader was the result of 'a true historical instinct', an instinct thus denied for the German historian. Ranke, the great example of the 'scientific' historian had not, in Gardiner's eyes, been able fully to appreciate Wallenstein, and certainly not to the level that the Idealist dramatist and poet – and historian – Schiller had.

Schiller's literary qualities, and the uses to which they could be put, may have appealed to Gardiner. Schiller himself claimed to offer, in his plays, a representation of the character of Wallenstein that would be better than had ever before been attained by historians:

81 Ranke, cited in Steinberg, *Thirty Years War*, 124.

82 '*Geschichte Wallensteins*' [unsigned review], 551–3.

83 Rabb, *Thirty Years' War*, pp. 64, x.

84 Translation taken from the Lamport edition. The words are from the prologue, line 118 at p. 168.

85 Indeed, the first part of the cycle is entitled 'Wallenstein's camp'.

Partisan hatreds and affections shroud
His character, as history portrays it;
But art shall bring him closer, as a man,
Both to your eyes, and to your feeling hearts.[86]

It is this 'art', aimed at the reader's 'feeling heart', which Gardiner believed carried the 'true historical instinct'. Schiller's play was, for Gardiner, the best representation of Wallenstein's character, and it was so as a result of what art had brought to it.

Gardiner used Schiller's *Wallenstein* in the *Thirty Years' War* in order to help him present to his readers not only the character of Wallenstein, but also other features of the Thirty Years War. For example, he used lines from the second part of the cycle, 'The Piccolomini', to describe the inherent problems of military government and to defend the principles of the old order:

> A new form of government, to be exercised by a soldier with the help of soldiers, could never be founded on justice
>
> For always formidable was the league
> And partnerships of free power and free will.
> The way of ancient ordinances, though it winds,
> Is yet no devious path. Straight forward goes
> The lightning's path, and straight the fearful path
> Of the cannon-ball. Direct it flies, and rapid.
> Shattering that it may reach, and shattering what it reaches.[87]

Similarly, Gardiner inserted a long section from a speech of an Irish captain to illustrate the character of Wallenstein's army, emphasising its multinational character and the personal obedience and loyalty owed to Wallenstein by his soldiers, introducing the lines thus: 'The great German poet has breathed the spirit of this heterogeneous force into one of its officers.'[88] Schiller offered Gardiner an understanding of certain aspects of the Thirty Years War which he did not find in the work of mere historians, and which he believed he could not put forward in words more fitting or beautiful than the poet's.

Ranke had presented a Wallenstein who was a supremely able military adventurer, inspired by religion, but essentially a man seeking aggrandisement and the satisfaction of his own, selfish ends. The success of his

[86] Schiller, *Wallenstein*, 'prologue', lines 102–5 at p. 168.

[87] *Thirty Years' War*, 123. The lines are from act I, scene iv and, with a few small changes of spelling and grammar, are taken from the translation of S. T. Coleridge: *Collected works of Samuel Taylor Coleridge*, ed. J. C. C. Mays, xvi (Poetical Works iii), lines 65–71. In the Lamport edition, the lines are at p. 235.

[88] *Thirty Years' War*, 151–2, quoting parts of Butler's speech in 'The Piccolomini', act I, scene ii (Lamport edn, 226–8).

'balanced' view was in his argument that Wallenstein should not be judged for this because he was but a man of his times – a decidedly historicist project. Schiller's Wallenstein was a wholly different creature. He was – as Gardiner had pointed out in his review of Ranke's work – a leader of men, allied to the camp and tied less to states or high politics than to his army. Furthermore, he was a soldier fighting not for the *status quo*, on behalf of a despotic and intolerant Emperor, but a soldier who wished, above all else, for a peace founded on religious liberty. Finally, he was no mere plunderer of Germany, as some have thought, but rather a man of honour and strong religious principles. Schiller's Wallenstein was the very model of the Romantic-Idealist hagiography dismissed by both the historians of Gardiner's day and the historians of the late twentieth century.

What is remarkable about Gardiner's Wallenstein, however, is that, despite his engagement with, and use of, the work of the German historicist school and their disciples in other countries, it quite clearly owes much more to Schiller's Wallenstein than to Ranke's. Thus, for example, just as Schiller (a protestant) lauds Wallenstein (a roman catholic) for his multinational and multidenominational army and his spirit of tolerance, Gardiner tells his readers that 'Wallenstein wished Catholic and Protestant, already united in his army, to be equally united in the Empire'.[89] The historian's closing eulogy on the soldier-hero, although suggesting that Gustavus Adolphus was a greater man, retains a warmth, and views his faults as being not of the lowness of his aims and objectives, but of the impractical nature of his dreams:

> In spite of all his faults, Germany turns ever to Wallenstein as she turns to no other amongst the leaders of the Thirty Years' War. From amidst the divisions and weaknesses of his own country, a great poet enshrined his memory in a succession of noble dramas. Such faithfulness is not without reason … Wallenstein's wildest schemes, impossible of execution as they were by military violence, were always built upon the foundation of German unity. In the way in which he walked that unity was doubtless unattainable … But during the long dreary years of confusion which were to follow, it was something to think of the last supremely able man whose life had been spent in battling against the great evils of the land, against the spirit of religious intolerance, and the spirit of division.[90]

Gardiner's Wallenstein was not a man of mere military prowess, interested in the place of his own family in the social order, or seeking his own aggrandisement; he was a man of principle, a man dedicated to liberty and tolerance. He was, in short, Schiller's Wallenstein.

Gardiner's conception of Wallenstein, and of the Thirty Years War, was not that held by the majority of the historians of his own day. He had read

89 *Thirty Years' War*, 96.
90 Ibid. 178.

the works of the likes of Ranke and Droysen, and indeed had used them and referenced them in his own work, but he had remained unconvinced of their analyses. Rather, Gardiner retained a commitment to the older, traditional account, exemplified by Schiller. That he did so at least in part due to Schiller's qualities as a man of literature in contrast to the later historians' empirical approach is of utmost importance to a deeper appreciation of Gardiner's theory and method.[91] However, analysis of Gardiner's writings on the Thirty Years War leads to another important conclusion. Schiller was a central figure in late eighteenth-century Idealist circles in Germany, whose work – as a historian, as a philosopher and as a dramatist – retains its status as a leading contribution to Idealist theory. Gardiner's theory of history drew on an earlier tradition, and Fichte was an important source for him. However, whereas Fichte's theories were taken on by Gardiner and helped him to reach an understanding of wider philosophical issues regarding the past, it was Schiller's historiography that Gardiner employed to help him to reach an understanding of a specific set of events and historical actors. Gardiner's practice of history, just like his theory of history, drew not so much from the German historians of his own generation, but from the German Idealists of an earlier one.

91 See chapter 5 below.

3

Religion

> With the stately periods of Hooker English prose entered on a new stage. For the first time it sought to charm and to invigorate, as well as to inform the world. In Spenser and Shakspere are to be discerned the same influences as those which made Hooker great. They, too, are filled with reverence for the reign of law. Spenser, in his *Faerie Queen*, set forth the greatness of man in following the laws which rule the moral world – the laws of purity and temperance and justice; whilst Shakspere, in the plays which he now began to pour forth, taught them to recognise the penalties which follow hard on him who disregards not only the moral but also the physical laws of the world in which he lives, and to appraise the worth of man by what he is and not by the dogmas which he accepts. That nothing might be wanting to point out the ways in which future generations were to walk, young Francis Bacon began to dream of a larger science than had hitherto been possible – a science based on a reverent enquiry into the laws of nature.[1]

In these words, taken from one of Gardiner's school textbooks, can be recognised a number of emblematic features of his philosophy, such as the desire to judge men as they were rather than through a religious or political lens, a moral code founded on the classical virtues of purity, temperance and justice, and the search for a higher science. They are also witness to Gardiner's deep respect for the culture of the periods in which he was interested as a historian. What is particularly noteworthy is Gardiner's close engagement with, and appreciation of, the thought of that period that had directly preceded his immediate object of inquiry. Given the prevailing image of Gardiner as a historian of high politics, it is perhaps surprising that he believed that the history of action could not be understood without first embarking upon a study of the ideas of the generations that had lived before, and whose thought reached forward into, the Stuart period. The vision of Gardiner as a historian of ideas carries significant implications.

In his brief survey, Gardiner named four writers – a canon for the Elizabethan period. Gardiner's engagement with the two prose writers in this list of the masters of late Elizabethan and early Stuart literature, Richard Hooker (*c.*1554–1600) and Francis Bacon (1561–1626), taken with his wider understanding of, and engagement with, both seventeenth-century and nineteenth-century religion and politics, demonstrate the impact of his ideas on his writing of history.

1 *A student's history of England*, London 1890–1, ii. 473–4.

Hooker was an ardent churchman, a parish priest whose depth of learning made him many friends in the hierarchy of the Church of England. Despite his general acceptance of much of Calvin's teachings, he engaged in the anglican-puritan debates of the late sixteenth century, and published in 1593 the first books of *The lawes of ecclesiasticall politie*. This work, intended as an anglican riposte to puritan teachings against, and within, his Church, has ever since been considered an important, if not essential, element of the core principles of the Church of England.

For Gardiner, a historian always looking further back in time for a more nuanced history of ideas, the early Stuart historicism of Hooker was prefigured in the late Elizabethan generation in which Bacon had been nurtured. Despite being, ostensibly, a historian of the Stuart epoch, Gardiner was considerably more attracted to the Elizabethans. For him – as indeed for many Victorians – their England was a lost Golden Age prior to the divisiveness of the seventeenth century. This Golden Age was experienced both in culture and in the state. In one of his school textbooks, Gardiner said that '[g]reat writers and great poets arose at the end of Elizabeth's reign' and he felt moved to finish his discussion of the period by quoting one of them, 'Shakspere, the greatest of them all'. However, the words he used (from *King John* V.vii.112–14) expressed not a literary message for Gardiner, but a political one that encapsulated the happy effects of the Elizabethan state settlement:

> This England never did – nor never shall –
> Lie at the proud foot of a conqueror,
> But when it first did help to wound itself.[2]

The man that represented that settlement, and whose work epitomised its literary culture, was Richard Hooker. For Gardiner, it was Hooker who personified the great intellectual statement of that *via media* within and between Church and State in the late sixteenth century which was the basis of late Tudor peace and prosperity.[3]

What made Hooker's thought so attractive to Gardiner was his 'strong historical sense',[4] a sense that context and experience can be a source of knowledge of equal value to the Word of God. According to the historian, the great Elizabethan churchman had been of that 'school of theological students' who 'based their convictions on historical study'.[5] Indeed, Hooker not only believed in truth in a history outside Scripture, but believed fervently in the historicity of Scripture itself.[6] This historical understanding Hooker contrasted to what he considered the 'Truth' of the puritans to be –

2 *Outline of English history, B.C.55–A.D.1895*, London 1896, 194.

3 *HoE* i. 40.

4 A. P. D'Entrèves, *The medieval contribution to political thought*, New York 1959, 119.

5 *CD*, pp. xxi–xxii.

6 N. Sykes, 'Richard Hooker', in F. J. C. Hearnshaw (ed.), *The social and political ideas*

a truth which was situated solely in Scripture, and which was anathema to him.[7] For Gardiner, this was Hooker's great contribution to English philosophy: 'In the *Ecclesiastical Polity* of the great Hooker these ideas were set forth with a largeness of mind and a breadth of charity which made his work memorable as a landmark in the history of thought. It was the starting-point of a change which was to substitute reasonableness for dogmatism.'[8] Human reason, learning and experience – as the outward expression of the Word – contained the ineffable mystery of God and the moral lessons imparted in Scripture: 'the will of God which we are to judge our actions by, no sound divine in the world ever denied to be in part made manifest even by light of nature, and not by Scripture alone'.[9] Unfortunately, the puritans had rejected this history, and in their teachings 'the name of the light of nature is made hateful with men; the "star of reason and learning," and all other such like helps, beginneth no otherwise to be thought of than if it were an unlucky comet'.[10] Gardiner's conception of Hooker as a historicist is largely shared by a number of later intellectual historians. For example, Peter Munz, writing in the 1950s, argued that Hooker's 'subtle sense for historical realities' was not just an advance on earlier thought, but was in advance of the irrational and relatively limited understanding of history which characterised the eighteenth century.[11] Robert Eccleshall, writing in 1978, even likened Hooker to the German historicists, placing some of Hegel's words[12] into the mind of Hooker:

> Hooker endeavoured to 'portray the state as something inherently rational … To comprehend what it is, this is the task of philosophy, because what is, is reason … To recognise reason as the rose in the cross of the present and thereby to enjoy the present, this is the rational insight which reconciles us to the actual.' The words, of course, are Hegel's, but they would not be out of place in the preface to Hooker's treatise. Hegel sought to portray the State as the objective manifestation of its members, an historically evolved, concrete scheme of life in which the individual's striving for freedom was made actual. Likewise, Hooker's intention was to reveal the rational structure of the Elizabethan State in order that its members might consciously identify with it and willingly comply with its legal requirements.[13]

of some great thinkers of the sixteenth and seventeenth centuries: a series of lectures delivered at King's College University of London during the session 1925–26, London 1926, 74.

7 *CD*, p. xxii.

8 Ibid.

9 R. Hooker, *The lawes of ecclesiasticall politie*, bk III, ch. iii.3.

10 Ibid. bk III, ch. viii.4.

11 P. Munz, *The place of Hooker in the history of thought*, London 1952, 197.

12 These are taken from G. W. F. Hegel, *The philosophy of right* (1821), at pp. 11–12 in T. M. Knox's Oxford 1952 edn.

13 R. Eccleshall, *Order and reason in politics: theories of absolute and limited monarchy in early modern England*, Oxford 1978, 126

Hooker's mind was essentially historicist, both in terms of an awareness of the role of history in the formation of knowledge and also in terms of his appreciation of the development of human institutions.

Gardiner's interest in Hooker was far from unusual in nineteenth-century Britain. W. E. Gladstone, Edward Irving (who bought his first Hooker volumes in Scotland, in an Edinburgh edition), both 'broad' and 'high church' anglicans, and the Liberal Anglican historians all claimed an intimate knowledge with, and intellectual descent from, the thought of Richard Hooker. An early marker in Gladstone's conversion to what has been characterised as high churchmanship, for instance, was his reading while at Oxford of Hooker.[14] Indeed, despite the Calvinism of Hooker, the great anglican theologian of late Elizabethan England was a central thinker for the kind of high churchmen who adhered to the concept of a national Church, whose brand of churchmanship was 'High,' and yet whose theological politics were of a moderate variety that rejected the Church of Rome as readily as it rejected nonconformist protestantism. Thus, Gladstone described Hooker's central principle as '[t]he great doctrine that the State is a person, having a conscience, cognisant of matter of religion, and bound by all constitutional and natural means to advance it'.[15] At the height of Tractarian activity in Oxford, John Keble produced an edition of Hooker's work, and expressed the hope that '[s]hould these volumes prove at all instrumental in awakening any of [the Church's] children to a sense of that danger [of a "fall … towards rationalism"], and in directing their attention to the primitive, apostolical Church, as the ark of refuge divinely provided for the faithful, such an effect will amply repay the Editor'.[16] The volumes had the opportunity to do that, passing through seven editions by 1888, at which point they was substantially revised by Dean Richard Church and Professor F. E. Paget, the Gladstone-appointed canon of Christ Church; the original preface was retained. Although Keble's clear interest was in opposing the spread within the Church of England of the low church principles he associated with the nonconformist Churches, just as it had been for Hooker, his preferred answer lay in a national Church, and Keble, unlike some of his Tractarian associates, remained loyal to the Church of England throughout his life. For anglicans, particularly anglican intellectuals and advocates of orthodox 'high church'[17] principles, Hooker was an important historical benchmark in the

14 After reading Izaak Walton's *Life of Hooker* in December 1828, Gladstone turned to the *Ecclesiastical polity* on 12 July 1829, reading it almost daily from then until 6 September; on 29 September, he began writing an 'analysis' of the book, a task which took up much of his time for the next ten days.

15 W. E. Gladstone, *The State in its relations with the Church*, London 1841, i. 14.

16 Editor's preface to *The works of that learned and judicious divine*, Mr. *Richard Hooker*, ed. J. Keble, London 1836, pp. cxv–cxvi.

17 The phrase 'orthodox High Church' here bears comparison with Peter Nockles's discussion in *The Oxford movement in context: Anglican High Churchmanship, 1760–1857*, Cambridge 1994

development of the theology of their Church and of continuing interest and relevance in the nineteenth century.

The Elizabethan church settlement was even more central to the thought of those anglicans who distanced themselves from faction within the Church of England. The *via media* model of the English Church was very much a contemporary concern for those liberal churchmen who, later in the nineteenth century, sought out the space between ritualism and evangelicalism, between Rome and Geneva. One such was Archibald Campbell Tait, whose solid orthodox anglicanism gained him the support of the queen as candidate for the bishopric of London in 1856 and archbishopric of Canterbury twelve years later – the latter despite the opposition of the prime minister, Disraeli.[18] The nature of his church politics can also be seen in the moderate position he took over the Athanasian Creed controversy, agreeing with such broad church luminaries as Benjamin Jowett and Connop Thirlwall, but against the resurgent catholic party (led by Edward Pusey, a canon of Christ Church at the time of Gardiner's expulsion for his Irvingite associations), that its compulsory use in anglican ceremony should be ended, but adding the proviso that it should be retained through insertion into the Thirty-Nine Articles – the basis of anglican theology. Tait was one of the tutors who had denounced Tract XC in 1841, doing so against the advice of friends who thought that circumspection was required in such times of strife; even a voice calling out against division might fall prey to the prejudices of less enlightened Fellows, they counselled.[19] He also corresponded with the historian and cleric Arthur Penrhyn Stanley over their shared opposition to the writers of the *Essays and Reviews*, a group of churchmen of quite a different colour from the Puseyites, but causers of another fractious debate within the Church. Tait opposed faction, but he also urged tolerance towards those guilty of fermenting divisiveness, even those, such as Bishop Colenso, whom he believed were in the wrong.[20] The future archbishop was also renowned as an energetic and effective evangelist for the Church of England during his time as bishop of London, with pastoral care for a city which, although the centre of national life, was a source of grave concern for those who foresaw testing times ahead for the Church's historic mission in the country.[21] Tait established a programme intended to draw new or lapsed members into the fold of the Church, sending out men and women to preach in the open air and to minister to the people of London. It was during these years that Gardiner, then living within Tait's diocese, became a member of the Church of England.

18 P. T. Marsh, *The Victorian Church in decline: Archbishop Tait and the Church of England, 1868–1882*, London 1969, 15–17.

19 R. T. Davidson and W. Benham, *Life of Archibald Campbell Tait, archbishop of Canterbury*, London 1891, i. 87.

20 Ibid. i. 360–3.

21 Marsh, *Victorian Church*, 6–7.

The controversy with which Tait's name is most closely associated, that which raged over the Public Worship Regulation Act of 1874, was also the occasion of perhaps Gardiner's only public comments on contemporary political or religious matters. At the time, and subsequently, Tait's name was inextricably linked with both the provisions of that act and the debates that it engendered in society, parliament, the Church and the pages of *The Times*. The measure was intended as one which would reinvigorate the Church of England as an active Church relevant to modern society and also ensure that ritualist and evangelical practices which its promoters viewed as unorthodox were brought to an effective end, returning the Church to the core of its teaching and acting against the factional battles that had the potential to destroy it from within. In order to begin to understand Gardiner's position within the Church and the nature of his theological politics – which arguably is essential to an adequate appreciation of the historian's writings on those earlier centuries in which catholic-protestant intellectual battles were at the very forefront of English politics – it is worth giving space to an analysis of the 1874 act and his intervention in the large-scale and sometimes venomous debates it occasioned.[22] Gardiner's response to the Public Worship Regulation Act controversy provides an important window into his mind.

The original bill, first drawn up in January 1874, was to all intents and purposes Tait's. Its principal clauses asserted the need for, and attempted to institute, greater coercive power for the bishops to ensure 'correct' anglican practice, although it also defined what that 'correct' practice was where it was currently at issue. Most notably it provided for the banning of the eastward positioning of the celebrant, a matter of great concern to many catholic adherents, particularly those of Tractarian or ritualist sympathies, and indeed to their opponents. Catholics had asserted at the very least their right to maintain this practice, if not the theological necessity of its adoption by all anglican priests for all ceremonies and services. These provisions governing correct practice proved most controversial, as it was felt by many adherents that decisions on such matters should be left to the Church's internal governing structures, and they were removed before the bill finished its journey through parliament. Thus, the final act was considerably reduced from the intentions of its authors, although it still provided greater coercive power for the episcopate.

The controversy burst upon the political life of the country in response to a report on the provisions of the original bill printed in *The Times* on 10 March. Essentially the work of Tait, the report stressed the need to rein in

[22] For a more detailed account of the act and the surrounding debates see especially J. Bentley, *Ritualism and politics in Victorian Britain: the attempt to legislate for belief*, Oxford 1978, and N. Yates, *Anglican ritualism in Victorian Britain, 1830–1910*, Oxford 1999.

the ritualists and paid scant attention to evangelical practices that many in the orthodox centre or on the catholic wing of the Church might question. As a result, the initial opposition came from ritualists and Puseyites, led by Pusey himself, who felt that the catholic traditions of the Church were under threat from what they saw as the growing erastianism within the country and the church hierarchy. However, evangelical opposition built quickly as well, on the basis of their general resistance to strong episcopal authority as well as their concerns over a presumed want of anti-ritualist fervour on the part of the bishops. On the other hand, as well as receiving the expected assent of centrist protestants, Tait and the bill also received the tentative support of moderate high churchmen, who were not unfriendly to the strengthening of episcopal authority and were as concerned at the fractious words and actions of the high ritualists as they were at the spread of evangelical practices. Parliament, less attuned to the intricacies of theological debate than it perhaps had been in previous generations, and essentially erastian in flavour, was less dangerous territory for Tait, although debate still raged there. The bill was first presented to the House of Lords in a speech of the archbishop's which served to intensify the controversy: as in the earlier article in *The Times*, Tait emphasised the need to bring ritualism under control and brought enormous disapprobation down upon his head from certain catholic elements within the Church. Potentially worse, however, was the opposition that the bill received from the most renowned and theologically knowledgeable of MPs, Gladstone, on its presentation to the House of Commons on 9 July. However, the author of the insistently anti-erastian *The State and its relations with the Church* was forced to withdraw his opposition upon finding that he was almost entirely isolated both within his party as a whole and on the Liberal front benches, from where close associates such as William Harcourt, Viscount Goschen and W. E. Forster (the son-in-law of Thomas Arnold) launched strong defences of the bill and its promoter. Receiving a great deal of support within parliament in its reduced state, the bill duly passed into law, and the last great theological controversy to excite all of parliament came to an uneasy end. Tait had secured a notable victory, and received the public commendations of many 'liberal' churchmen, such as Thirlwall and Jowett.

For Timothy Lang, who discusses Gardiner's position in the debate at some length, it is interesting as the only example that he can find of the historian diverging on a political matter from the man Lang portrays as his political master – Gladstone. However, given the isolation of the erstwhile prime minister within the Liberal party over this matter, the Public Worship Regulation Act controversy tells much less about Gardiner's Liberalism than might be hoped – and than Lang presumes. It does, however, add to knowledge of the historian's religious beliefs, his understanding of the much more acute religious controversies of the seventeenth century, and the roots of his overarching philosophy. Gardiner's comments came in a review of the eleventh volume of Walter Farquhar Hook's *The lives of the archbishops of*

Canterbury for the *Academy* in 1875.[23] In the article in that volume on Laud, Hook – the high church dean of Chichester and one of Hurrell Froude's 'Z's[24] – had launched a stinging attack on Tait for his despotism, using the comparison as part of his defence of the seventeenth-century churchman to whom the description 'despot' had been most readily ascribed by historians. In the introduction to his book, Hook offered a sideswipe at those 'latitudinarians and political primates'[25] who had attempted at various times in the history of the Church of England to alter its liturgy and practices according to their own interests and without the assent of the Church as a whole: 'The appointment of the whole order pertaineth not to private men, therefore no man ought to take in hand nor presume to appoint or alter any private or common order in Christ's church, except he be lawfully called and authorised thereunto.'[26] If the target of this attack was not clear to all Hook's readers, they could not have failed to notice the subject of the more personal attack offered in the main body of his text. Although rather lengthy, it is worth quoting in full in order to appreciate its nature and to help contextualise Gardiner's defence of Tait:

> That Laud was despotic no one will deny, but he exerted his powers not to exceed but to enforce the law upon those who had sworn to its observance. We can imagine a primate equally a despot in disposition, who, in waging war with a party against whom he had formed a prejudice, instead of being contented with the law as it stands, seeking by a new act of parliament to increase his own temporal power, and thus to betray the independency of the Church. We can imagine a primate – who, born and bred a presbyterian, has been led by circumstances to conform to the Church, to be oblivious of his solemn ordination vow, 'with all faithful diligence to banish and drive away all erroneous and strange doctrine.' We can suppose him to co-operate with the propagators of those same erroneous and strange doctrines, which every bishop is pledged both privately and openly to oppose. Laud, on the contrary, boasted that he was born and bred in the Church, and the cause of the Church he died to sustain. He did not nullify the Creed by regarding as 'the Holy Catholic Church' a gathering together of discordant sects, to express a belief in the existence of which is a mere un-meaning truism; but he believed that Christ, his Master, had established that one Church mentioned in the Creed, a kingdom upon earth, of which there are many colonies, some of them in much need of reformation.[27]

Gardiner, a Scot born and bred within what amounted to a breakaway presbyterian sect, but now a member of the Church of England, and a wholehearted believer in the great institutions of the British state, must

23 'Hook's Lives of Laud and Juxoni' [review], 467–8.

24 Nockles, *Oxford movement*, 20.

25 W. F. Hook, *Lives of the archbishops of Canterbury*, London 1860–75, xii, p. xi.

26 Ibid. p. xiii.

27 Ibid. 389–90.

have personally felt the sting of this rebuke to Tait; certainly, he pulled few punches in the archbishop's defence.

Around the time that this volume was published, its author died. Gardiner's obituary of Hook for the *Academy*, published at the end of October 1875,[28] prefigures in a general sense the more pointed and particular criticisms of the review of Hook's volumes which he provided in the following week's issue. Although on the surface a rather gentle criticism, which suggests the need for non-scholars in the study of history, and the usefulness of men involved in contemporary debates and with knowledge of the real and the practical writing historiography which attends to present concerns, a practised reader of Gardiner's pronouncements on historiography might recognise the depth of his concerns regarding the limitations of Hook's approach. 'He did not take up a subject and examine it on all sides with a purely scientific interest', the professional practitioner opined, but 'flung upon it straight out of the living present'.[29] This 'holder of definite opinions for which he had done battle in the world', 'a man so involved in the questions of his day' could not, and did not, care for his subjects as a true historian should. '*The Lives of the Archbishops* … was evidently undertaken', wrote Gardiner, 'not from any pre-eminent interest in the occupants of the see of Canterbury, but because they enabled him to group round their biographies the main facts of the opposition to the influences which he disliked.'[30] Hook, according to Gardiner, wrote his historical works for the benefit of his present concerns.

As Gardiner correctly noticed, this was never more the case than in the volume on Laud. In reply, he made explicit reference to the controversy of the previous year, first suggesting, against Hook, that the behaviour of the earlier and current archbishops was closer than the dean had cared to recognise:

> Is there any parallel to be drawn between [Laud's] mode of dealing with Church questions and that which was accepted by the House of Commons in the session of 1874? No candid person can fail to trace a resemblance reaching very deeply between Laud and the authors of recent legislation, especially those who were lawyers by profession. In both was a profound respect for the authority of the law; in both was a contemptuous dislike of the irregular manifestations of religious sentiment; in both was a desire to establish uniformity of ritual with a corresponding want of zeal for unity of doctrine.[31]

However, at this point Tait and Laud diverge, for, unlike Hook, Gardiner saw the wrong not in the current archbishop's behaviour, but in his predecessor's:

28 'The late Dean Hook' [obituary], *Academy* viii (30 Oct. 1875), 453–4.

29 Ibid. 453.

30 Ibid. 453–4.

31 *Academy* viii (6 Nov. 1875), 467.

> But it is seldom that comparisons run on all fours, and the main difference consists in this; that Laud became unpopular by appealing against use and wont to the unrepealed law, while his modern successors, having the legislative power in their hands, were able to produce a new law, the operation of which was intended to favour the popular use and wont. Nor must the great distinction between the seventeenth and nineteenth centuries be left out of sight because Dean Hook deliberately closes his eyes to its existence. When Laud forbade the clergy to conduct the worship of their congregations according to a certain form of ritual, he forbade them to officiate anywhere within the King's dominions. At present the enforcement of the law leaves them perfectly free to continue any practices they please outside of the Established Church.[32]

Here, Gardiner presents a classic historicist argument: Laud's attempts to renew the Church were carried out against the times themselves, and therefore failed, whereas Tait's were of their times, and thus, at least in part, successful. This historiographical point is lost on the amateur historian. Modern liberty of conscience represents an entirely different context for ecclesiastical law, something not recognised by Hook: it makes Laud's actions despotic, but Tait's essentially not despotic. According to Marsh, the Public Worship Regulation Act of 1874 shows that the idea of religious toleration was no longer at the core of moderate anglican belief,[33] but for Gardiner the general nature of Victorian religious life was one of liberty within which the act could, and did, operate in a liberal manner. The 1874 act was, in Gardiner's eyes, legislation fully compatible with a liberal and tolerant approach to modern religious practice.

That Gardiner understood the religious debates within the Church which took place during his own lifetime in historicist terms is a point worth labouring, for it reminds the reader of the close intellectual connections between the principal actors in this drama. After Oxford, Tait had succeeded Thomas Arnold as headmaster of Rugby School. Arnold, the hero of Conybeare's 'broad Church' party[34] and a key member of the group of 'Liberal Anglican Historians' identified by Duncan Forbes as the great popularisers of German historical method in Britain,[35] had left Rugby to become Regius Professor of History at Oxford in 1840. Although he died soon after, his lectures continued to have an influence in the university long after his death, still having an audience during Gardiner's time at Christ Church, continuing through to and beyond Stanley's appointment as canon there in 1858. Tait was initially pressed to go forward as a potential successor to Arnold by Stanley, Arnold's disciple, who wrote to him in recognition of his

32 Ibid.

33 Marsh, *Victorian Church*, 176.

34 A. Burns, 'Introduction' to W. J. Conybeare, 'Church parties', in S. Taylor (ed.), *From Cranmer to Davidson: a Church of England miscellany*, Woodbridge 1999, 226.

35 Forbes, *Liberal Anglican idea*, passim.

'reverence for your great predecessor'.[36] Stanley was similarly pleased to see Tait elevated to Canterbury, arguing that '[i]t is the very best thing for the Church, for the country, and for him'.[37] Stanley's appreciation of Tait was not just intellectual; they had shared a close friendship ever since Tait had been the young man's tutor and they had travelled together in Europe in 1840–1.[38] The future archbishop was closely allied with those Oxford men whose philosophies were based on an intimate knowledge of the past and close attention to the possibilities of historical knowledge.

The opening vignette of the standard Victorian biography of Tait tells a story in which Stanley is a leading character:

> On Thursday, February 11th, 1869, Archbishop Tait was presiding in the Jerusalem Chamber at Westminster over a meeting of the Ritual Commission. Dean Stanley was sitting by his side. In the course of certain works in the adjacent Abbey a search had for some time been in progress to discover, if possible, the unknown burial-place of King James I. Just as the meeting closed, a messenger entered into the Jerusalem Chamber, and whispered to Dean Stanley that the coffin had been discovered in one of the vaults under Henry VII's chapel. The excited Dean sprang up, and, inviting the other commissioners to accompany him, hastened to the spot. As they all drew near, the Dean motioned them back. 'It is fitting,' he said, 'that our first Scottish Archbishop should lead the way into the tomb of our first Scottish King.'[39]

As well as displaying the anglican attention to history and particularly the history of that period in which the Church had, it was claimed, been at its happiest and most content, this story was told by the authors of the biography in order to stress what they saw as the singular aspect of Tait that marked him out: his Scottishness. It was something that Stanley could hardly not be aware of; Tait had, many years earlier, given him a 'Scotch plaid shawl' as a memento.[40] It was of more than trivial interest to his contemporaries, as evidenced in Hook's criticism, and raises some interesting points. As a Scot with a presbyterian family background, trying to make his way in England and as a member of the Church of England, Tait shared much with such men as Gladstone and Gardiner, men whose commitment in adult life to anglicanism opened up to them brilliant careers in their chosen fields. However, the connections are closer than this simple description of background suggests, for Gardiner shared much intellectually with Tait and Gladstone.

36 Davidson and Benham, *Life of Tait*, i. 113.

37 This is cited in A. V. Baillie and H. Bolitho (eds), *A Victorian dean: a memoir of Arthur Stanley, dean of Westminster*, London 1930, 245.

38 R. E. Prothero, *The life and correspondence of Arthur Penrhyn Stanley, D.D., late dean of Westminster*, London 1893, i. 256.

39 Davidson and Benham *Life of Tait*, i, 1.

40 Baillie and Bolitho, *Victorian dean*, 27.

Nowhere is this companionship clearer than in their shared reverence for Hooker. For men such as Tait, Gladstone and Gardiner, Hooker's work was the highest intellectual achievement of his age and of English theology. For orthodox Churchmen, Hooker was the father of the modern non-Roman, non-puritan Church of England; for Gladstone, Hooker was the greatest theologian of his age, an intellectual giant whose work proved the catholic claims of the English Church; and for Gardiner, Hooker was the exceptional prose writer and thinker of the high point of England, the late Elizabethan era. Although it is impossible to situate Gardiner's theology within the tradition and parties of the Church of England with any great accuracy, it can be said, with a high degree of probability, that he was not a 'low' protestant, as some readers have suggested on the basis of what they see as his sympathies with the independents and presbyterians of the parliamentarian party, but rather a solidly protestant orthodox and liberal anglican of high church leanings.[41]

Another Scot of presbyterian background who found fame in London, and for whom Hooker was an important intellectual figure, was Edward Irving. He was, if not the formal founder of the Catholic Apostolic Church, its source and inspiration. This Church was a strange creature, even in heterodox London, for it trod neither solely a catholic nor solely a protestant path. Its followers were committed to ceremony and the physical manifestation of faith, and yet the Church was millennarian and its congregations took part in such 'low' expressions of spirituality as speaking in tongues. The sect enjoyed a brief maturation in the 1840s and 1850s, but then shrank to a rump which, to this day, takes communion within the Church of England. This is quite a journey from Irving's days as a presbyterian in Annan, a journey represented metaphorically and literally by the Victorian cleric and writer on the religious life of the capital C. M. Davies as one from 'the dim conventicle in Newman Street into the cathedral-like edifice in Gordon Square'.[42] For Irving at least, this journey had been partly inspired by Hooker, his 'idol for style' according to one regular attendee of his sermons.[43] In her biography of Irving, Mrs Oliphant writes:

> There is a story told, which I have not been able to trace to any authentic source, of [Irving's] having found in a farm-house, in the neighbourhood of

[41] In the light of recent work regarding parties in the Victorian Church of England, the term 'orthodox' has been preferred here for describing non-factional centrist thought within the anglican spectrum, while recognising the descriptive validity of 'Low', 'Broad' and 'High' where they refer to a characterisation which would be understood during the late nineteenth century. The use of the term 'orthodox' is intended to unite an appreciation of Gardiner with both Newman's characterisation of his opponents as orthodox or evangelical and Laud's use of the term to mean a non-Puritan churchman.

[42] C. M. Davies, *Unorthodox London: or, phases of religious life in the metropolis*, 2nd edn, London 1876, 87.

[43] W. Jones, *Biographical sketch of the reverend Edward Irving*, London 1835, 28.

> Annan, a copy of Hooker's *Ecclesiastical Polity*, which is said to have powerfully attracted him, and given an impulse to his thoughts. He is also said to have expended almost the whole sum which he had received for the expenses of a journey in the purchase of Hooker's works; 'together with some odd folios of the Fathers, Homer, and Newton,' and to have trudged forward afoot with the additional load upon his stalwart shoulders, in great delight with his acquisition. There can be no doubt, at least, of his own reference to 'the venerable companion of my early days – Richard Hooker.'[44]

In Gladstone's own copy of Oliphant, he left his mark in the margins next to this passage, or rather next to the mention of the *Lawes*, writing 'NB' against that and the quotation from Irving. In his diary, he recorded 'Read & finished Life of Irving: a noble creature shipwrecked in judgment not in soul.'[45] With a shared reverence for Hooker and the Elizabethan settlement, and a shared interest in the road between Rome and Geneva in their own times, it comes as no surprise to discover that Gladstone, despite reservations, was sympathetic towards Irving, as was Tait towards Irvingism:

> I have read the greater part of the second volume of Irving's life. He was plainly mad, and so for the time were all the people who prophesised to him, though one of them – Baxter, the solicitor – is a shrewd man of business, whom I often see in London. I was struck, however, this morning, in reading the 2nd Lesson from the Acts, with the thought how completely they lived as St. Paul and his company, looking for distinct guidance at every turn. The Apostle had good grounds, and they had not; but the frame of mind in both was much the same – a waiting upon God for guidance at every step.[46]

Tolerant in their attitudes towards other Christian traditions, Tait and Gladstone shared an interest in, and yet critical distance from, the Irvingites.

Gardiner was brought up an Irvingite, expelled from Christ Church before he took his MA for having become a deacon at Gordon Square Central Church in London. He was, along with the rest of his family, very much at the centre of the Church; his first wife was the daughter of Irving, and one of his brothers became an 'Angel' of the church in Southampton. By the 1860s, however – while Tait was ministering to Londoners as their bishop – he had literally crossed over (Gordon Square) to the anglicans, to whom he remained loyal for the rest of his life.[47] Nevertheless, it was while he was an Irvingite that Gardiner began his historical researches, and indeed

[44] M. O. Oliphant, *The life of Edward Irving, minister of the national Scotch Church, London: illustrated by his journals and correspondence*, London 1862, i. 30–1. A. L. Drummond has the place as Armadale: *Edward Irving and his circle*, London ?1934, 20.

[45] W. E. Gladstone, *Diaries*, ed. M. R. D. Foot and H. C. G. Matthew, Oxford 1968–94, vi, entry for 22 June 1862.

[46] Davidson and Benham *Life of Tait*, i. 531

[47] A. R. Gordon (vicar of All Saints', Gordon Square) to the council of King's College, London, 21 Nov. 1871, Kings College, London, KA/IC/G48.

published his first book, a translation of Heinrich Wilhelm Josias Thiersch's fifth book, *Über Christliches Familienleben* (?Munich 1854), as *Christian family life* (London 1856; 2nd edn, London 1880). Thiersch had been the founder of philological study in Bavaria, associated with the school of von Humboldt, and Professor of Theology at Marburg until he resigned in 1850 in order to work on behalf of the Catholic Apostolic Church. He had been converted through Irving's close associate Thomas Carlyle and was probably one of its most brilliant converts – certainly its most brilliant convert in Germany. A renowned theologian in his home country and correspondent of Döllinger and other Old Catholics, it was only right that his works should be translated into English for the edification of the Irvingite community. The Church organised the work and put it in the hands of trusted members: Carlyle himself translated one volume. That Gardiner acted as a translator of one of Thiersch's books suggests that he was very much at the centre of the intellectual activity of the Catholic Apostolic Church in England during the 1850s.

Gardiner's edition repays attention. The 'translator's preface' contains a number of ideas characteristic of him. He introduces 'this little work of Dr. Thiersch' and warns his reader that

> Written in a country where the condition of society is in many respects so different from that of our own country, there are necessarily some parts which will be found, in some respects, inapplicable to our circumstances. But such passages are of rare occurrence, and even these will often be found of practical use to ourselves. For it often happens that we may in other countries watch the results of schemes and principles which have there been reduced to practice, but which are still under discussion amongst ourselves. The author's remarks upon education, for example, will be found to bear upon many questions which are agitated on this side of the channel, although there is considerable difference between the existing German and English systems.[48]

Here is visible, very early on in Gardiner's career, his respect for German models of education. Thiersch's own father had been the protestant reformer of catholic Bavaria's education system, creating the set of basic principles which still govern Bavarian and, through their absorption into the unified nation's policies on teaching at school and university level, Germany's educational system today. For many of Gardiner's generation – most explicitly C. H. Firth – the Germans offered the finest example of how universities in particular should be arranged and their syllabuses organised and taught. Of Thiersch's many treatises, each dedicated to a particular theme, *Christian family life* is the one in which he concentrated on the issue of education, and it is telling that it is this one which Gardiner translated. Several years before

[48] H. W. J. Thiersch, *Christian family life*, trans. J. R. Gardiner [S. R Gardiner], London 1856, pp. iii–iv.

he was to become a teacher of history, Gardiner was reading and thinking about educational theory, and doing so using German sources.[49]

As might be expected of a German writer on educational theory, Thiersch's principal references were to German philosophers. Although a number of the authorities he drew upon were contemporaries, most commonly theologians (including Döllinger), he relied in the main on figures associated with the Idealist school of the late eighteenth and early nineteenth centuries, such as Goethe and Schleiermacher. In particular, he discussed Fichte's theories in great detail. Although he took issue with many of Fichte's ideas as expressed in the *Orations to the German nation*, such as his proposals for a system of educational 'conscription' – similar to the compulsory system later devised for English schools and implemented by Gladstone's government in 1870 – Thiersch accepted that his principles were of a higher stamp and a necessary starting-point for any adequate theory of man and his intellectual and ethical life; he was, the theologian opined, a 'man of such uncommon moral worth and activity, that his doctrines of ethics is certainly to be reckoned amongst the best which has ever been written'.[50] Although Gardiner may have encountered Fichte at an earlier stage – certainly his abilities in the German language must already have been impressive, given the task that he was here carrying out, and thus his reading of German literature surely would have been far advanced by this time – it is well worth noting that in *Christian family life*, a theologian for whom the future historian presumably had high regard recommended the very same book, Fichte's published lectures on the theory of the nation, that Gardiner was later to recommend to his fellow Britons as a guide to politics.[51] The twenty-six-year-old student of the German language read in the writings of an important thinker of his own Church an evaluation of Fichte that was as positive as that he was later to offer as a fifty-six-year-old historian to his friend, the politician James Bryce.

This chapter has so far concentrated upon seeking to understand Gardiner's own religion, and his engagement with the religious life of the nineteenth century. However, to carry this into the study of Gardiner's appreciation of seventeenth-century religion is an inadequate historiographical method, for it inscribes the context into the text. Perhaps all that can be taken from the discussion are deconstructions of the traditional view of his church party affiliations, and his connections to orthodox churchmen inspired by history and Hooker. Rather, it is necessary to deal more directly with the historian's own writing on his chosen period, in this case his study of the religious strife and parties of those times. In the study of historiography, the work must be understood first; then it is possible to bring the conclusions drawn to the biographical account of the historian, and attempt to understand the man

49 See chapter 1 above for a detailed analysis of the German intellectual atmosphere within which Gardiner's educational beliefs were formed.

50 Thiersch, *Christian family life*, 108.

51 See chapter 1 above.

and his work within this textualist account. It may well be that Gardiner's religious life is interesting; certainly it must play a part in an intellectual biography of the historian. But it is less clear that it should be so central to an intellectual history of his historiography. What is important is not Gardiner as a religious man, but Gardiner as a historian of religion.

The issue of religion is one in which all accounts to date of Gardiner and his work have most clearly gone awry. It has become an unquestioned assumption of the literature that the (ex-)Irvingite Gardiner sympathised with the puritans in the theological and politico-religious battles of the early Stuart period. Thus, writers as diverse as Kevin Sharpe, Roger Howell, James Holstun, David Norbrook and David Kelley have in recent years chosen to stress the 'nonconformist' (to use the most popular label) Gardiner, and attempted to explain his work, methods or sympathies in those terms.[52] Most later accounts make explicit reference to the standard work on the nineteenth-century historiography of the Civil War, Lang's *The Victorians and the Stuart heritage* and all appear to bear its imprint, principally indirectly through Richardson's *Debate on the English Revolution*, which relies heavily on Lang. Richardson makes much of Gardiner's 'Nonconformist background' in his explanation of the historian's account of the English Revolution, mentioning only in passing his conversion to anglicanism.[53] Using Lang, recent studies of Gardiner's work assume that his Irvingism led him to look favourably upon seventeenth-century dissenters.

However, even the most cursory reading of Gardiner's writings on the 'puritans' (the catch-all term he uses for dissenters of all kinds)[54] shows him to have been highly critical of puritanism as a movement. He did, in the main, look with favour on puritan persons, and wrote of the beneficial impact of puritanism on the characters of individuals.[55] Although he was highly critical of some of puritanism's more extreme exponents, such as the controversialist Marginal Prynne, in the main his accounts of puritans reveal deep respect. For example, on his first appearance in the *History*, the politician John Pym is the subject of a laudatory account of his intellect and abilities,[56] which is repeated in greater detail and in even more lavish terms in Gardiner's discussion of his character after describing his death.[57] However, puritanism as a movement and as an idea were clearly anathema

52 Sharpe, *Personal rule*, 880; Howell, 'Who needs another Cromwell?', 28; J. Holstun, *Ehud's dagger: class struggle in the English revolution*, London 2000, 24; D. Norbrook, *Poetry and politics in the English renaissance*, rev. edn, Cambridge 2002, 301; D. M. Kelley, *Fortunes of history: historical inquiry from Herder to Huizinga*, New Haven, CT 2003, 245–6.

53 R. C. Richardson, *The debate on the English revolution*, 3rd edn, Manchester 1998, 95, 91.

54 Gardiner advocates the term 'Puritans, as the Nonconformists and the Presbyterians began to be alike called in derision [during Elizabeth's reign]': *HoE* i. 29.

55 *GCW* i. 9–10.

56 *HoE* iv. 242–5.

57 *GCW* i. 256–9.

to him. Thus, Gardiner attacked what he perceived as puritan intransigence and narrow-mindedness. In his textbooks he used simple terms such as 'dogmatism' and 'stern doctrine' to characterise puritanism,[58] but in his *History* he discussed in much greater detail the ways in which puritanism can be seen to be not 'animated by a conciliatory spirit',[59] which he perceived as the principal reason for the failures of the puritans at the Hampton Court conference ('their inferiority in breadth of view is conspicuous'[60]), and the ways in which 'it refuses to take account of a large part of human nature'.[61] Reading Gardiner's history suggests that modern historians should take a more circumspect view of the Victorian historian's sympathies with regard to seventeenth-century nonconformity.

Lang's analysis of Gardiner's sympathies is, indeed, considerably more sophisticated than those studies purportedly based on his work would suggest, and he recognises that Gardiner had what appears to be a less Manichaean appreciation of the leading political parties of his chosen period. According to Lang, 'it would be misleading to regard Gardiner as a nonconformist whose religious dissent led him to write a history of the Civil War from a distinctly Puritan point of view'.[62] In part this is due to the unusual nature of Irvingism, an amalgam of ritualism and millenarianism, but it is also in part due to Gardiner's conversion to anglicanism. According to Lang, this is perhaps best illustrated in 'Gardiner's ability to appreciate the Laudian movement in the Stuart Church, which he termed an appeal to the senses, [which] may have derived in part from his own exposure to ritual'.[63] This is an important observation, for Laud can be treated as an important case study in the study of Gardiner's conception of seventeenth-century religion.

William Laud rose to the position of archbishop of Canterbury under Charles I. Prior to that he had held various appointments around England, most notably as chancellor of the University of Oxford and bishop of London. Laud's own theological beliefs were very much towards the catholic pole within the national Church, and he had caused offence during his earlier career for wearing a surplice, insisting upon the eastward position of the communion table, promotion of bowing to the east upon entering a church, and his outspoken criticism of Calvinist tenets coupled with his assertion of episcopacy as the only correct system of government for the Church. His promotion to Canterbury gave him the opportunity to enact nationally those policies that he had been assiduous in promoting within the more limited domains of Oxford and London. Suspected of crypto-romanism, he became the *bête noire* of the puritans who, in 1645, secured his execution

58 *Puritan revolution*, 75; *Student's history of England*, 511.
59 *HoE* i. 149.
60 *HoE* i. 155.
61 *HoE* i. 39.
62 Lang, *Victorians*, 149.
63 Ibid. 150.

for treason. However, it was not just that Laud the person was the enemy of puritans, but that his system was opposed to puritanism in all its manifestations. If Gardiner was a historian influenced by his own nonconformist background into having sympathy with the puritans, one should expect him to have held as low an opinion of Laud as appears to have been the case amongst seventeenth-century puritans and which had become, by his time, a commonplace amongst (protestant) historians.

Gardiner's view of Laud and Laudianism was, as Lang rightly judges, not as antipathetic as might have been expected. Indeed, this had been recognised by J. R. Green, the great populariser of a more obviously protestant account of England's past, when he wrote in a letter to E. A. Freeman that 'I suppose you have got Gardiner's new vols anent the Duke of Buckingham.... I see he is going to make Charles and Laud the champions of "free inquiry" against the Puritan House of Commons'.[64] Such an account of Laud was naturally shocking to Green, not only a sympathiser with both liberalism and puritanism, but one who believed – alongside such Whig luminaries as Macaulay – that the two movements were inextricably linked, the puritans of the seventeenth century having created the possibility of liberty within nineteenth-century parliamentary democracy. According to Green, whose conception of the religious struggles of the seventeenth century posited the existence of two antipathetic parties, Gardiner sympathised with one party only – the party of Laud.

Green's understanding of Gardiner's sympathies is, however, as inaccurate as those modern studies which place his contemporary's sympathies firmly with the opposite party, that of the puritans. This inaccuracy in both nineteenth-century and modern accounts is based on the same analytical error: by assuming an either/or approach to seventeenth-century religion, Gardiner must be placed with one party or the other – either a puritan or a Laudian in his sympathies. Even more sophisticated accounts such as Lang's suffer from this same error. For instance, recognising that Gardiner cannot simply be placed in one party or the other, Lang places Gardiner in both parties, assuming in the same way as other studies that such an apparently complex position can be considered the result of the historian's personal religious life: having been both a nonconformist and an anglican in his own life, Gardiner was sympathetic (perhaps in different ways) to both the puritans and the anglicans of the seventeenth century. The crucial error, however, is the seeking of positions either for or against each of the two parties. Such an account fails entirely to appreciate the complexity of Gardiner's critiques of both the puritans and the Laudians.

Gardiner's account of Laud is a sophisticated combination of criticism and applause. This, indeed, is to be expected of a writer who called for

64 J. R. Green to E. A. Freeman, 13 Feb. 1875, in *Letters of John Richard Green*, ed. L. Stephen, London 1901.

neither canonisations nor gibbetings. However, the example of Laud gives fresh insight into Gardiner's method of finding the good and the bad in everything and everybody. Throughout the *History* and his *DNB* article on the archbishop, Gardiner is very critical of Laud's character, his 'hard and unsympathising temper'.[65] On the other hand, his comments on Laud's ideas – and thus on any 'Laudianism' we may wish to posit – are often laudatory, in particular noting what he regarded as their advanced nature. Laud and his party were 'intellectually the Liberal Churchmen of their age', Gardiner argued,[66] who had received criticism from those unable to see beyond mere surface to the ideas beneath, for '[i]t was natural that the outward ceremonialism of the men should attract more notice than that principle of intellectual liberalism which, though yet in its germ in their minds, brings them into connection with modern thought'.[67] Although in this passage Gardiner is apparently referring to Laud's contemporaries, it is a criticism which may be deemed to have fallen upon those historians who have continued in the tradition of heaping opprobrium on the archbishop's name. Gardiner also made clear that he felt that the historical sources of the thought of the Laudian party were the major contributory factors in their 'rightness':

> It was by looking back to the earlier days of the English Reformation, when Calvinism was but stealing in, that they found what they needed. The theology of Cranmer, fixing itself upon the principle that all practices were to be maintained, all doctrines held, which could not be proved false by the authority of Scripture and the custom of the early Church, suited them exactly ... It gave employment to minds to which the history, especially the ecclesiastical history, of the past was an attractive study. It appealed to the poetic and artistic instinct which was almost smothered under the superincumbent weight of dogmatic theology ... Their life was more sympathetic, more receptive of a higher culture than that of others.[68]

The historical interests of the Anglican hierarchy, and their cultured minds – the result, surely, of their historicist minds – had led them to a far greater ideal than their adversaries. One past thinker in particular, Gardiner believed, was implicated in the new anglican theology, for Laud and his colleagues were amongst those to be considered to have been those 'followers of Hooker [who] were at first the few who, in spite of their appeal to antiquity, were in their central convictions in advance of their age'.[69] According to Gardiner, Laud – despite his character flaws – was part of a great tradition in English political and ecclesiastical thought which reached back through

65 *HoE* viii. 117.
66 *HoE* v. 357.
67 *HoE* v. 359.
68 *HoE* v. 358–9.
69 *CD*, p. xxii.

Hooker to the English Reformation, and reached forward to the liberalism of the nineteenth century.

That Laud's theories reached forward to Gardiner's own day, however, was for the historian not only a matter of modern liberalism, but also of modern anglicanism. Thus, he agreed with those who have 'said that Laud's system, and not that of his opponents, prevailed in the Church of England, and that the religion of that church showed itself at the end of the seventeenth century to be less dogmatic than that of the puritans, while its ceremonies were almost precisely those which had been defended by Laud'.[70] The Church had only settled into a Laudian intellectual mould once the character who had advocated it in the seventeenth century had left the stage: 'The result … was only finally obtained by a total abandonment of Laud's methods.' The religious party whose members were to be applauded for their characters was the puritan party. Although these distinct views of the commendable aspects of Laud and his opponents suffuse Gardiner's work, he appears to have only once directly compared them:

> It is evident that each of these systems supplied something which was not to be found in the other. At the same time, it was evident that a considerable time must elapse before they would agree to tolerate one another. For some time to come, a violent controversy was to be expected … but if the Government would be content to maintain order between the contending parties, no great harm would be done. The great body of the laity would refuse to listen to the violence of noisy partisans. Something would be learned from the more moderate on either side. Puritanism, with its healthy faith and manly vigour, would long have continued to supply the muscle and sinew of English religion, but its narrow severity would have given way before the broader and gentler teaching of the disciples of Hooker and of Andrewes.

At first glance, these words appear to support Lang's contention that Gardiner's religion lay, as it were, in between puritanism and anglicanism, taking the good of either side. However, it is clear that, although he openly stated what was to be commended on either side, he believed that only the good of the anglicans survived: the synthesis given is only hypothetical, and would only have been attained 'if the Government would be content to maintain order between the contending parties'. Charles's government had done no such thing, and neither had the Independent and Presbyterian parliament. The result was 'the stagnation of the eighteenth century',[71] which had, we may presume, only found an end with the Church of the nineteenth century, now a thoroughly (moderate) Laudian Church. The religious synthesis that Lang thinks that he sees in Gardiner is merely hypothetical.

Nevertheless, Gardiner did understand seventeenth-century religion in dialectical terms. Lang, Richardson and others are quite right in that regard

70 *DNB* xi. 635.

71 *HoE* ii. 126.

– what has been wrong in the writing on Gardiner has been the characterisation of his dialectic. Gardiner's posited set of religious parties looked very different from that put forward by those who have sought to understand his account of seventeenth-century English religion. However, in order to discover how he understood the theological dialectic of the period that he was studying, it is necessary to step back and approach the issue of Gardiner's perspective through an analysis of the perspective within which he has been understood in recent years. Recognising both Gardiner's sympathies with the Laudian party and the continuing belief among students of Stuart historiography that Gardiner sympathised with the Laudian party's opponents, an obvious question arises: how has this confusion come about? The answers to this problem can be found in two distinct, but related issues concerning the continuing tradition of misunderstanding Gardiner and his work: the nature of his project, and the nature of the theoretical approaches that he used to explicate the past.

The first issue, that of the nature of Gardiner's project, has already been introduced in discussion of his view of Laud. The archbishop, Gardiner believed, was fundamentally flawed in his character, and as a result behaved in a way which was to be criticised. Nevertheless, what he had been trying to do was both good and right. The contrast, of course, is with the puritans: good men led astray by projects unworthy of support. Puritans were to be commended for their character, whereas anglicans were to be commended for their thought. Historians of 'high politics', such as Gardiner's revisionist critics, are interested in the behaviour, and therefore the characters, of leading political actors. Gardiner has himself most often been characterised as a political historian, and, if this characterisation is recognised, then he appears to be sympathetic to the puritans. If it is character and behaviour he is interested in, and it is the puritans whose character and behaviour he applauds, then Gardiner must be on the side of the puritans. Such a logic merely finds even greater support from historians who are themselves political historians, for they will tend to seek out – and find – Gardiner's comments on character as a priority. Thus, they understand the historian within the prism that they are themselves using to understand the seventeenth century. View Gardiner as a historian of ideas, however, and a wholly different picture of his sympathies emerges. His main interest was in thought, and it was Laudian (or anglican) thought which he applauded. As a result, he was, in the final analysis, with the Laudian party rather than against it.

The second issue, that of Gardiner's methods for understanding the past, not only helps to answer the question of the inaccuracy of traditional historiographical views of his religious sympathies, but it also answers the question of why it was that he commended anglican, or Laudian, thought. Gardiner was committed to the dialectical method, as has been recognised by some of his critics, such as Conrad Russell. In the introductory comments to one of his later books, Russell sought to define 'revisionism', a historiographical tradition with which he aligned himself. Revisionism, he wrote,

> had many practitioners, whose positions were never identical, yet it may be claimed that all versions of revisionism ... enjoyed certain broad similarities. Perhaps the most important of these was the rejection of a dialectical framework for history, a disinclination to see change as always happening by means of a clash of opposites. To those aware of the strength of Hegel's influence on the philosophy of the nineteenth and early twentieth centuries, it should come as no surprise to realize that the dialectical framework was never confined to the followers of Marx. It influenced Gardiner as much as Tawney, and Notestein as much as Hill, and revisionism has always been directed against the historiographical assumptions Whigs and Marxists held in common. So far, it has been the Whigs who have given us a run for our money.[72]

This was a claim that Russell had made in an earlier book, and which throughout his work formed the basis of his critique of Gardiner: that the late Victorian historian, along with his contemporaries, structured the past with the assumption that 'there were two sides to every division'.[73] This two-part understanding of the dialectical method is present in modern writing on Gardiner even where the German Idealist roots of his thought have not been recognised or explicitly referred to – such as Richardson's and Lang's consideration of the nonconformist and anglican 'sides' of the historian and his sympathies. If a bipartite understanding of religious parties is sought in Gardiner's *History*, then 'puritans' and 'anglicans', are to be found for they are the two parties that he almost exclusively discussed. With these two parties available to the reader of Gardiner, the next step is merely to discover which of them he sympathised with, or with seeking to place him somewhere between them – both in his own life, and in his historiography. The understanding of the dialectic as a dyad limits the understanding of Gardiner's application of the method.

For the dialectic is always already a triad, not a dyad. It requires not just a thesis and an antithesis (anglicanism and nonconformity, orthodoxy and heterodoxy, puritanism and Laudianism) but also a synthesis. It is this synthesis, of course, which Lang and Richardson find, in Gardiner, between nonconformity and anglicanism in his own time and thus also between puritans and anglicans in his appreciation of an earlier time. Unfortunately, Lang's and Richardson's syntheses have been worked out by them – not by Gardiner – and have been worked out on the basis of the analysis of the two parties considered most often by the earlier historian. Recognising that the dialectic is a triad, however, allows the reader to seek three parties in Gardiner's work – a thesis, an antithesis and a synthesis. Rather than posit a synthesis, it is far better to find that which Gardiner himself posited as synthesis.

72 C. Russell, *Unrevolutionary England, 1603–1642*, London 1990, p. ix.

73 Idem, *Parliaments and English politics, 1621–1629*, London 1979, 5.

Gardiner posited a tripartite set of religious parties in seventeenth-century English theology: Roman Catholicism, puritanism and anglicanism.[74] His almost exclusive discussion of just two of these, puritanism and anglicanism, is due to their almost exclusive presence in English religious life; in English religious thought, however, all three are clearly present. Indeed, Roman Catholicism appears in England as a ghostly presence, in particular as a historical presence, closely related to politics. For example, Gardiner argued that 'Laud's view of the constitution [as set out in the 19 June 1625 sermon at the opening of parliament] was no new theory evolved out of the recesses of his own mind. It was in the main the doctrine of the Tudor sovereigns, the doctrine under which England had won its national independency from Rome.'[75] Here, the role of the past in Laud's thought is again stressed by Gardiner, placing him in a tradition of English Reformation theologians. On another occasion Gardiner put forward another argument regarding the historical sources of Laud's thought; however, the 'opponent' of Laudianism in this case was not Roman Catholicism:

> The difference between Laud and the House of Commons was one which had been inherent in the church of England since the days of Henry VIII. Laud was the intellectual successor of the men of the new learning, who had attempted, with the king at their back, to reform the church under the influence of constituted authorities and learned inquiry. The commons were the intellectual successors of the men who, under the influence of continental teachers, first of Zwingli and afterwards of Calvin, attempted to extract a definite system of doctrine from the scriptures.[76]

The puritans are the enemies of Laud's party, the latter characterised as the inheritors of the men of Henry's time – such as Cranmer – but also, by extension, those of Elizabeth's time: Hooker had offered his theological treatise against those puritans who sought the truth only in Scripture. In the final analysis, therefore, Laudian Anglicanism held the middle course between, on the one hand Roman Catholicism, and on the other hand puritanism – and did so in national, political terms as much as it did so in universal, theological terms. Thus, '[t]he unwritten tradition of Anglicanism, that it was the duty of kings to support a learned and large-minded clergy against the dogmatism of Rome on the one side and of Geneva on the other, found a hearty supporter in Laud'.[77] For Gardiner, Laud – and seventeenth-century anglicanism – represented the synthetic position between the thesis and antithesis of Roman Catholicism and Puritanism.

74 Gardiner preferred to use upper case letters (for example Anglicanism rather than anglicanism), which stresses a 'party' interpretation rather than one based on a tendency of thought.

75 *HoE* vi. 205.

76 *DNB* xi. 627.

77 *DNB* xi. 628.

Just as it is now possible to suggest that a conceptual problem has led to an inaccurate impression of Gardiner's view of seventeenth-century religion being put forward, so it might also be said that a similar problem existed for Laud, in the eyes of his contemporaries. Certainly, Gardiner thought so:

> Such a system [as Laud's] might be regarded as holding a middle place between Rome and Calvinism; but it might also be regarded as a more feeble copy of Rome. Those who valued the independent reasoning and the freedom of inquiry upon which it was based would take the more favourable view. Those to whom freedom of inquiry was an object of terror would have nothing to say to it. They would desert it for the infallibility of Rome, or they would attack it in the name of Calvinism. Between the negation of individual religion and the assertion of individual religion, a compound of free thought and ceremonial observance was likely to have a hard time before it could establish itself in the world.[78]

Laud's contemporaries, too, saw the theological world in terms of two parties, a problem which dogged him throughout his life. As early in his career as his time as a student at Oxford, he faced criticism for his attempts to hold a middle course in religion. 'In 1614', Gardiner tells us, 'he was violently attacked by Dr. Robert Abbot from the university pulpit for having declared in a sermon that presbyterians were as bad as papists, and was scornfully asked whether he was himself a papist or a protestant.'[79] And yet, twenty-five years later, his *Conference with Fisher* (1639) was 'received with jeers by Catholic and Puritan'.[80] Just as Gardiner's critics have found only two parties in his characterisation of seventeenth-century religion, so too did Laud's critics understand theological controversy in terms of 'two sides in every division'.

Laud, however, clearly understood there to be three principal theological parties. This may, Gardiner suggests, have been due to his intellectual formation at Oxford under the tutelage of John Buckeridge, a man who had himself come to this position under the Tudors:

> Buckeridge was one of those who, during the closing years of Elizabeth's reign, headed at the two universities a reaction against the dominant Calvinism, and who, standing between Roman Catholicism on the one hand and puritanism on the other, laid stress on sacramental grace and on the episcopal organisation of the church of England.[81]

Laud's tutor, then, had been part of the Hookerian response to continental religious influences. This quotation also includes the names of the three

78 *HoE* v. 360.
79 *DNB* xi. 626.
80 *HoE* viii. 390.
81 *DNB* xi. 626.

parties as Laud understood them – but also as Gardiner understood them. In a passage describing Laud's attempts to promote his and Buckingham's policy of 'Thorough' – on pages with the running header 'The religious opposition. Puritans and Catholics' – Gardiner wrote that '[u]nder no circumstances was this system of repression likely to take permanent root in England. To have given it even a temporary chance of success it must have been applied fairly on the right hand as well as on the left. The Catholic must suffer as well as the Puritan'.[82] The 'stumbling-block [which] stood in Laud's way', ensuring the failure of 'Thorough', was the king, whose 'support was not to be relied on for any persistent course of policy'. That persistent course could only be the thoroughgoing restatement of protestantism in the face of the religious opposition, allied with a serious assault upon the religious liberties of the Puritans and Catholics, the enemies of the Church of England. Laud and Gardiner saw, from their respective anglican positions, two other parties contending for theological supremacy in early Stuart England.

Gardiner's use of the term 'protestant' is particularly telling. He did not use it to describe those allied with Geneva, for they are always called 'puritans'. Rather, the 'protestants' were those who have thus far been called anglicans, or the Laudian party. In terms of ideas, of theology and philosophy, this is certainly the case. Thus, Gardiner says of Laud, 'as far as the intellect was concerned, he was more truly Protestant than any Puritan in England'.[83] This, perhaps, is an additional source of confusion for writers on Gardiner: his sympathies are clearly with protestantism, which may be confused with dissent. In the *History*, there is no such confusion. For Gardiner, protestantism is the synthesis which resolves the problems of the thesis and antithesis of Roman Catholicism and puritanism; and this protestantism is anglicanism, for it is Canterbury which is situated between Rome and Geneva. Laud, the archbishop of Canterbury, represents the truth, for he represents also synthesis in history.

Moreover, Laud does not just represent a monolithic point of synthesis between Rome and Geneva, for he holds a position much more finely-tuned than even that characterisation would suggest. According to Gardiner, the arguments which Laud put forward in his debate with the Jesuit Fisher, which was intended as a battle for the allegiances, and soul, of the countess of Buckingham, 'mark his ecclesiastical position in the line between Hooker and Chillingworth'.[84] Gardiner had a high regard for Hooker as a representative of intelligent, moderate anglicanism; that he would place Laud between him and a man whose book, *The religion of protestants* (1637), written at the insistence of the archbishop, made him worthy of the description 'the great latitudinarian,'[85] shows the exceptionally high (theological) regard in which

82 *HoE* viii. 235.

83 *HoE* iii. 224.

84 *DNB* xi. 627.

85 *Puritan Revolution*, 135. Chillingworth's book is discussed in detail at *HoE* viii. 260ff.

Gardiner held the archbishop. Laud was a synthesis of two positions which were themselves syntheses.

This finding of a synthesis within a synthesis is familiar to students of Fichte's dialectical method. The Hegelian dialectic, although apparently identical to Fichte's, particularly in their shared used of the thesis-antithesis-synthesis triangulation, proceeds in a significantly different manner. In particular, the movement from the thesis-antithesis contradiction on to synthesis is understood by Hegel as a movement forward in the progress of the world. In Fichte's method, however, it is a further movement toward the final goal of reason in the rational analysis of the world. When the final synthesis is reached – when there is no longer contradiction – then truth has been attained. Here, perhaps, might Laud be found – and the Church of England, as Gardiner did.

A close reading of Gardiner's writings on seventeenth-century religious disputes, demonstrates that the standard works dealing with his account of the past have failed properly to appreciate the full complexity of his understanding of the history of the Church in England. In particular it may be noted that it is impossible to generalise with regard to his historiographical methods on the basis of his own religious life, beyond the recognition of a relatively undifferentiated concern with the past shared with certain churchmen. Rather, it is better to see the relatively close relationship between his religious affiliations and his sympathies with religious groups in the past in terms of the close intellectual relationship between their theological premisses and the ideas of their leading proponents. Certainly, in Gardiner's account of the religious upheavals of the early Stuart period they were understood by him in a classic Idealist, dialectical manner.

4

Politics

Richard Hooker and Francis Bacon were crucial elements in Gardiner's understanding of the early seventeenth century. Bacon was a very different kind of public figure from Hooker, a politician and lawyer whose slow rise through the ranks of the servants of the state led him, eventually, to the post of lord chancellor to James I in 1618. In 1621, however, he was accused and convicted of bribery and thus fell from his lofty position. He died five years later having spent the intervening time continuing the literary and philosophical studies that he had begun in the 1580s. These works – most notably the *Advancement of learning* (1605) and the *Novum organum* (1620) – constitute some of the most important British philosophy of the early modern period. On the surface very different men, Bacon and Hooker may be considered two of the most powerful and influential thinkers of their age, while also two of the most important figures in the development of the early modern state. Thus, just as Hooker was treated by Gardiner as a central figure in his work, subject to both the historian's respect and his close literary, philosophical and historical scrutiny, so too was Bacon worthy of admiration and careful analysis. A study of his writings on Hooker provides an appreciation of Gardiner's unique understanding of religion; similarly a discussion of his account of Bacon will go some way towards uncovering his understanding of politics.

Gardiner's fascination with Bacon may well have been explained, inadvertently, by the Marxist critic James Crowther. Although Crowther is on very dubious grounds when he asserts that '[i]n his primary conception, Bacon does not belong to the capitalist period, but to the socialist society of the future', he follows this by reminding his readers that 'S. R. Gardiner pointed out that "Neither of the great English parties which were so soon to spring into existence could claim [Bacon] as their own; and as long as the influence of those parties continued to lay its spell upon history, his memory was left without a champion."'[1] Gardiner, for whom the breaking of that spell was the great aim, had good reason to be so interested in a man who could never be reduced to understanding in either Tory or Whig terms. Indeed, Gardiner became Bacon's missing champion.

Gardiner clearly believed that Bacon had been unfairly represented in the ideological atmosphere of the eighteenth and nineteenth centuries, arguing that

[1] J. G. Crowther, *Francis Bacon: the first statesman of science*, London 1960, 5.

> It was hardly possible for any generation earlier than the present one to take other than a prejudiced view of the career of a statesman whose more prominent political views lay athwart the political current of the two centuries which followed his life, and in which historical writing was more political and less scientific than it is at present.[2]

Gardiner performed a double manoeuvre here; not only did he align modern historical practice with science and set it up in opposition to political prejudice, but he also expressly aligned himself with the politics of Bacon. He had rejected the politics of the last two centuries, represented by what he saw as the polarisation of the Whig–Tory system, and in declaring Bacon to be the opposite of such petty rumblings, Gardiner announced his political affinity with Bacon.

Bacon had been an object of interest for much of the nineteenth century, and already had a number of admirers within English literary circles such as Percy Bysshe Shelley and Samuel Taylor Coleridge. Similarly, he had had his detractors, most famously Macaulay, whose stinging attack for the *Edinburgh Review* was anathema to Gardiner. In the late nineteenth century, however, the debate over Bacon and his legacy shifted ground. During the 1880s, partly as a result of a renewed interest prompted by the publication of James Spedding's huge edition of the works of Bacon and his conjoined seven-volume *Life and letters* (1857–74), a number of scholars were involved in a controversy in the pages of leading journals and in their respective studies or editions of his writings regarding the reputation of the great philosopher and statesman. According to the literary historians Percy and Elizabeth Matheson, looking back over forty years, the articles and books that were central to the debate were E. A. Abbott's *Bacon and Essex* (1877) and *Francis Bacon* (1885), Thomas Fowler's *Bacon* (1881), R. W. Church's *Bacon* for Macmillan's *English Men of Letters* series (1884) and Gardiner's article in the *Dictionary of national biography* (1884).[3] Abbott, an anglican educationalist, grammarian and biographer, wrote in the introduction to his second intervention in the debate that opinion regarding Bacon was split into two camps, one sympathising with Bacon, and in the main exonerating him from all historical and contemporary charges against his conduct and character, and one – Abbott's own – which held the statesman in very low esteem, criticising both his thought and his practice. The exception was one writer who had struck out on an original and perhaps lonely path:

> Professor Fowler ... closely follows Mr. Spedding in his views of his character. Dean Church has been led to conclusions very similar to those which I endeavoured – very roughly and imperfectly – to express in my edition of the

[2] '*The letters and life of Francis Bacon*. By James Spedding. Vol. VII.' [review], *Academy* vii (10 Oct. 1874), 393–4

[3] *Francis Bacon: selections: with essays by Macaulay & S. R. Gardiner*, ed. P. E. Matheson and F. Matheson, London 1926, p. vii.

> essays (1878), and to which I still, in the main, adhere. Professor Gardiner has viewed Bacon in a new light.[4]

That new light was one that saw Bacon, not through a political lens – which inevitably led to a rejection of the apparently corrupt royal courtier – nor through the lens of a later science – which inevitably led to the rejection of the flawed scientist, unable or unwilling, despite his theoretical work, to engage in practical scientific endeavour – but through an analysis of Bacon as a statesman, a historical actor. According to Abbott, the political historian Gardiner studied the statesman Bacon in terms of his involvement with the politics of his day, rather than in terms of either his character or his ideas.

Much evidence can be drawn from Gardiner's work to support Abbott's contention. For example, although Macaulay appeared to be dealing with Bacon as an actor, Gardiner considered that Macaulay and other detractors had viewed Bacon politically, rather than as a politician.

> In our own days, the most brilliant of historians … took the case against Bacon under his patronage, and in language which will be read as long as the English tongue endures, painted the great statesman and the great philosopher in colours as odious as they are untrue to nature, because his thoughts and principles did not square with the system of a Whig politician of the nineteenth century.

Rather than take this approach, the later historian, alluding to Pope's infamous epigram in *An essay on man* (1734) describing Bacon as the 'wisest, brightest, meanest of mankind', said that '[i]t is time that Bacon should be known as he really was. He was not the faultless monster which it has pleased some of his too enthusiastic supporters to represent him. But far less was he that strange congeries of discordant qualities which were never found united in any human being'.[5] Bacon, thought Gardiner, must be studied within, and according to the perspective of, his own time, with the sufficiently balanced judgement that the modern, scientific historian could offer.

In his 1885 biography of Bacon, Abbott criticised Gardiner's views regarding the statesman. Indeed, it is suggested in the introduction that it is against Gardiner that Abbott is arguing in the main work, despite his rebuttal of a number of other writers on Bacon too. In particular, he expresses much dissatisfaction with what he sees as the historian's failure to discuss Bacon as a thinker, for he believed that the statesman-philosopher was too complex to be 'adequately explained … by Professor Gardiner's suggestion that the greater part of Bacon's life was spent in shaping political history'.[6] Abbott does recognise that Gardiner had not succumbed to the recent fashion of denying that Bacon had been guilty of 'perversion of justice' during his

4 E. A. Abbott, *Francis Bacon: an account of his life and works*, London 1885, p. xiii.
5 *HoE* iv. 104.
6 Abbott, *Francis Bacon*, p. xv.

time as lord chancellor, although the defence that Gardiner had included in his *DNB* article against the conclusions regarding this matter offered by Bacon's more intemperate critics – such as Abbott – received short shrift.[7] Furthermore, although Abbott tells his readers in his introduction that it is 'seldom that Professor Gardiner makes a mistake',[8] the main body of the work contains many corrections of, and objections to, Gardiner's factual accuracy, conclusions and methods.[9] Abbott criticised Gardiner for many failures he perceived in his study of Bacon.

To these criticisms Gardiner, at least in part, replied in a review written for the *Academy*.[10] He first side-stepped the blow by stating that '[o]f Dr. Abbott's criticisms of my own work, all that I can say here is that they will receive respectful consideration, if ever I am in a position to avail myself of them'. Then Gardiner went onto the attack himself. He briefly granted that Abbott's understanding of Bacon was based on 'diligent study of all that Bacon wrote', but argued that such study was insufficient for the historical biographer:

> Unfortunately, though his apparatus would have been complete if the subject of his biography had lived in the nineteenth century, and therefore in an atmosphere with which both the author and the subject are familiar, it is not enough where the subject of the biography has been dead for more than two hundred years. The author who would succeed under such conditions must be not merely thoroughly, but instinctively familiar with the problems of the age in which the personage he described lived, and with the aims and ideas which were natural to it, however strange they may seem to us. It is in this necessary knowledge that Dr. Abbott most distinctly fails.

Abbott, Gardiner makes clear, lacked a proper historical or historicist understanding with which he could situate Bacon; and this was so because he lacked the deep cultural knowledge, the empathy, the instinctual imagination, that was necessary for the historian.

The renewed interest in Bacon at the end of the nineteenth century may be traced to the work of James Spedding, Bacon's greatest nineteenth-century editor, who was concerned, like Gardiner, to break the Macaulayan view of the corrupt courtier. In his *Evenings with a reviewer* (originally privately printed in 1848 as *Evenings with a reviewer; or a free and particular examination of* Mr. *Macaulay's article on Lord Bacon, in a series of dialogues*, but better known to a later generation in its 1881 edition as *Evenings with a reviewer; or Macaulay and Bacon*), Spedding took Macaulay to task, and it is interesting to note that Gardiner was initially full of praise for Spedding's

7 Ibid. pp. xviii–xix.

8 Ibid. p. xxi.

9 See, for example, 32n, 37, 58–9n, 61, 80–1, 112, 116, 226, 231, 237.

10 '*Francis Bacon: an account of his life and works*. By Edwin A. Abbott' [review], *Academy* xxvii (13 June 1885), 411–12.

work. He felt that, with his edition of the works of Bacon and multi-volume *Life and letters* of the great statesman, Spedding had done a great service to scholarship, and had produced a valuable resource. With it, Gardiner was able to mount a vigorous defence of Bacon against the accusations regularly brought up by his contemporaries, claiming that '[i]n meeting the first charge [regarding Bacon's alleged interference in the marriage of Coke], all that was necessary to do was to give the story completely, and to add, as is now done for the first time, a collection of all the documents bearing upon it, arranged in proper chronological order'.[11] Here is not only Gardiner's much-vaunted and commented-upon reverence for the chronological method and his dedication to the documentary record, but also his clear appreciation of the practical use of Spedding's edition of the works of Bacon.

As Spedding's project turned to a biographical treatment, Gardiner was again initially supportive, for example writing that Spedding's 'book is more than a history, more than a biography. It is a moral school, teaching historical writers to combat the sin which most easily besets them, the tendency to put their own interpretation upon doubtful facts, and their own thoughts into the minds of men of other ages'.[12] The lesson was in Spedding, but the message was in the contrast with past tellings which viewed Bacon, not from the perspective of his own age, but from the perspective of their own times. Thus, Macaulay and Abbott had criticised the scientist for not following through his theoretical musings with the kind of practical science expected in the nineteenth century, and criticised the politician for not displaying the norms of action and probity expected of men of government in their own times. Spedding, in contrast, viewed Bacon as a seventeenth-century man would – at least, as a seventeenth-century man as understood by Gardiner would – and had thus produced a work to be admired as an example of how to write good historical biography. Gardiner reviewed Spedding's work positively as an example of historicist practice to be followed by others.

Gardiner had his reservations, however. Spedding, he wrote, 'has hardly been able to throw much new light upon the subject', and thus had failed as a biographer. Eight years later, Gardiner extended this criticism, arguing that Spedding ultimately failed also as a historian. He deals with an aspect of Bacon's life, Gardiner tells us, but then 'it is flung aside, and whatever is next in order is approached.… At the end of the seven volumes, when the reader expects to get a picture of Bacon as a man, drawn by the hand which was most competent to portray his lineaments, he is sent away disappointed'.[13] The book is no longer 'more than a history, more than a biography', it is a failure on both counts and, although Spedding 'throws over the judgment

[11] '*The letters and life of Francis Bacon*. By James Spedding. Vol. VI', [unsigned review] *Athenæum* 2337 (10 Aug. 1872), 173–4.

[12] *Academy* vi (10 Oct. 1874), 393–4.

[13] '*Evenings with a reviewer;* or, Macaulay and Bacon. By James Spedding. With a prefatory notice by G. S. Venables' [review], *Academy* xxi (18 Mar. 1882), 187.

of feeling and of prejudice ... he has no scientific conception of history to fall back on'. He might have learned that one should not judge ahistorically from the perspective of one's age, but he had not actually taken on the historicist philosophical precepts which Gardiner saw as the source of that understanding and which he considered necessary for an adequate, scientific, practice of history. The reader is left with a 'craving after unity of conception' which Spedding fails to satisfy. Here, Gardiner's fully developed philosophy of history is displayed: as well as utilising it as a method of criticism, he seeks it out in the work of others. Spedding failed as a historian, according to Gardiner, for failing to adopt an historicist position.

And yet, as Gardiner narrated a story of the British state, full of actors, and based on this philosophy, he rarely dealt directly with the philosophy of Bacon. He made it clear that he was well immersed in Bacon's work and willingly admitted Bacon's intellectual influence, but necessarily discussed him principally as a statesman. For Gardiner, there were strong empirical reasons why Bacon should be treated in this way. In his review of Church's contribution to the controversy, Gardiner wrote that 'it is evident that [the author] does not take any great interest in political history, and yet it was in an attempt to shape political history that the greater part of Bacon's life was spent'.[14] This was the perspective which Abbott criticised so heavily. As Gardiner sought to criticise other writers for not engaging sufficiently with the life of the statesman in politics, it is tempting to believe not merely that he engaged with Bacon predominantly as an actor in the political events of James I's reign, but that he understood Bacon only in those terms.

However, a closer analysis of Gardiner's writings on Bacon teases out a different view. Gardiner's view of Bacon the statesman is not consistently a supportive and sympathetic one, but it was an attempt to provide a balanced account that did, in the final analysis, fall into a putative pro-Bacon school. Rather than following the fashionable position of attacking him at every turn, a fashion made all the more popular by Macaulay's full-frontal assault, Gardiner lauded Bacon's 'transcendent abilities', 'noble objects' and 'genius'.[15] According to the historian, 'the great political thinker of his age'[16] – indeed, 'the deepest thinker … of the age',[17] political or otherwise – was to prove to be a quite brilliant chancellor once he had finally received the promotions his talents deserved. His genius, however, was not reliant merely on his high intellectualism, for that could separate the man from the real world, but was an intelligence that always held the immediate and possible in view, with close attention to that which would be of assistance in the world: 'The distinguishing characteristic of Bacon's intellect was its practical tendency. In speculative as well as in political thought, the object which he set before

14 '*Bacon*. By Dean Church' [review], *Academy* xxv (3 May 1884), 305.

15 *HoE* i. 164.

16 *HoE* i. 146.

17 *HoE* ii. 211.

him was the benefit of mankind.'[18] This could be witnessed in his writings, such as in his 'Tract on the Plantation of Ulster' which 'teem[s] with lessons of practical wisdom',[19] and also in his work within the state: the 'prudence' of the 1604 parliament, by which it was able to achieve much, was solely due to 'Bacon's guidance'.[20] Gardiner considered Bacon to be the greatest statesman of his age, a result of his intelligence and his ability to apply it to practical matters.

Gardiner's intellectual understanding of Bacon has been neglected in all previous accounts of his views on the politician. The Mathesons used the work of two writers as introductory essays for their edition of *Selections* (1922) from Bacon – that of Macaulay and Gardiner. For them, these two not only held opposing views, but appeared to have opposing interests. Macaulay was used to illustrate Bacon as a philosopher and writer, whereas Gardiner was used to offer a political narrative. Yet much of Macaulay's essay had been taken up with politics; it was this aspect that Gardiner complained of when he attacked Macaulay's position, in so doing decrying those who 'have taken the utter darkness of Macaulay's essay for light'.[21] For students of Bacon, the two historians held mutually compatible attractions. Macaulay told a laudatory story of Bacon's philosophy, whereas Gardiner was renowned for writing a sympathetic variation of Bacon's political life. However, by linking Macaulay with a literary-philosophical analysis and Gardiner with a political analysis, the Mathesons reinforced the artificial division between the great literary historian in the English tradition and the archetypal dry political historian. This dichotomy was in many ways a false one: both Macaulay and Gardiner considered Bacon to have been a great philosopher and writer.[22] Their real split was in their differing conceptions of Bacon as a political actor, or rather their differing philosophies of history and methodological approaches. Method, not object, was their point of departure, Macaulay displaying his eighteenth-century, rationalist, mind[23] and Gardiner his nineteenth-century, Idealist, mind. Thus, whereas Macaulay the biographer judged Bacon ahistorically in terms of, and according to, the ethics of his own times, Gardiner recognised Bacon as a great statesman of his time.

The radical difference between Gardiner's and Macaulay's views regarding Bacon's status as a statesman is thrown into relief by their apparently shared approval of him as a philosopher. Indeed the Mathesons had used Macaulay's

18 *HoE* ii. 193.

19 *HoE* i. 435.

20 *HoE* i. 168–9.

21 *Academy* vi (10 Oct. 1874), 393–4.

22 According to Gardiner, 'Bacon . . . was a wise man and a great philosopher': *The Stuart period* (Longman's 'Ship' Historical Readers), London 1894, 16.

23 The reaction of the early nineteenth-century Romantics to eighteenth-century literary style – a reaction exemplified by Macaulay – tends to occlude the fact that their claims to an objective truth arrived at through reason is virtually indistinguishable from, and clearly owes a lot to, the rationalism of the preceding century.

essay to offer a gently critical account of Bacon's philosophy. In the passages from the *Edinburgh Review* essay the Mathesons printed in their volume, Macaulay praised Bacon for the all-encompassing nature of his attempted philosophical system. According to the early Victorian essayist, the 'knowledge in which Bacon excelled all men was knowledge of the mutual relations of all departments of knowledge'.[24] This knowledge was attained through his 'power of perceiving analogies between things which appear to have nothing in common, [in which] he never had an equal'.[25] However, although this appreciation of analogies was judged to be the basis of his brilliance, Macaulay argued that 'he sometimes appeared deficient in the power of distinguishing rational from fanciful analogies'.[26] According to Macaulay, then, Bacon's philosophical writings were ultimately flawed, for he stretched his system beyond the boundaries which later empiricists, such as his eighteenth-century followers, would allow – the purely rational. Indeed, it was in George Berkeley's writings that Macaulay found the beginnings of this critique of Bacon.[27] For Macaulay, Bacon was not systematic enough, and thus prone to metaphysical speculations unsupportable according to the precepts of the later science to which the Victorian had had the privilege of access. Gardiner, however, held Bacon's philosophy in much higher regard – there are no statements mitigating the applause that he offered in the words quoted above – portraying him as the greatest thinker of his time. For the historicist Gardiner, this was the highest possible praise; Macaulay could not, in the final analysis, so unproblematically praise Bacon, as he could not consider the seventeenth-century writer to have been adequate for the nineteenth century. Thus, Macaulay's criticism of Bacon as a thinker was based on the same, ahistoricist, method by which he accounted also for Bacon's life as a statesman; in contrast, Gardiner's understanding of Bacon as both a philosopher and a political actor relied upon a historicist reading.

Gardiner entertained a profound respect for Bacon's ideas. Realising this raises an important question: to what extent were Gardiner's ideas influenced directly or indirectly by Bacon's philosophy? Paulo Rossi, a friendly twentieth-century critic of the seventeenth-century philosopher, has written that his subject's

> later attitude to traditional philosophy … stems from what Bacon called in the *Advancement of Learning* the 'liberating function' of historical awareness … In the *Temporis partus masculus* the Greek philosophers were summoned to defend their guilt; in the *Cogitata et Visa* and the *Redargutio* their guilt emerges as the result of an historical background evoked by Bacon. Direct violent attack is now abandoned for a cautious enquiry that might be described as

24 Matheson and Matheson, *Bacon: selections*, 3.

25 Ibid. 4.

26 Ibid. 6.

27 Ibid.

'sociological' or 'historicist' (not that I have any intention of tracing the origins of historicism back to Bacon).[28]

Although it may be the case that the sense of 'historicist' being used here is Karl Popper's rather bastardised variant, it may indeed be possible to trace a lineage from Bacon to historicism. For example, it is worth noting that Edward Caird, the late nineteenth-century British student of Idealist thought, argued that Kant united the *a posteriori* of Bacon and Locke and the *a priori* of Leibniz.[29] Kant's approval of Bacon's philosophy led him to use a quotation from *The advancement of learning* as a motto in the second edition of his *Critique of pure reason* (1787); potentially of more interest to the subject at hand is Fichte's use of those same words (perhaps taken directly from Kant) as the motto of his *Wissenschaftslehre*.[30] The Baconian tradition is implicated in the development of early nineteenth-century German thought.

The Idealist and historicist accounts of Bacon, and of the school of English empiricism to which his name is usually attached, did not lack a critical reading. Hegel believed that British philosophy was a limited discourse, and had historically been so, but that the best of British philosophy, such as it was, appeared in the work of Bacon. He was, said Hegel, the apotheosis of 'what is in England called Philosophy'.[31] Bacon's empirical method was essential to a true knowledge:

> What Cicero says of Socrates may be said of Bacon, that he brought Philosophy down to the world, to the homes and every-day lives of men ... To a certain extent knowledge from the absolute Notion may assume an air of superiority over this knowledge; but it is essential, as far as the Idea is concerned, that the particularity of the content should be developed.[32]

'Empiricism', Hegel tells us, 'begets what pertains to the region of the Idea.'[33] It was an important stepping-stone in the development of a modern historiographical style, for 'an important point is that Bacon has turned against teleological investigation of nature, against the investigation into final causes'.[34] For Hegel, however, the empirical method could only be one part of a full method or philosophy of history, as it did not itself contain the recourse to an imaginative, empathetic and truly historical understanding. In the

28 P. Rossi, *Francis Bacon: from magic to science* (1957), trans. S. Rabinovitch, London 1968, 46.

29 Caird, in his *Philosophy of Kant*, 119–20, cited in H. Jones and J. H. Muirhead, *The life and philosophy of Edward Caird*, Glasgow 1921, 274.

30 J. G. Fichte, *Introductions to the Wissenschaftslehre and other writings (1797–1800)*, ed. and trans D. Breazeale, Indianapolis, IN 1994, 2–3.

31 G. W. F. Hegel, *Lectures on the history of philosophy*, trans E. S. Haldane and F. H. Simson, London 1896, iii. 172.

32 Ibid. iii. 175.

33 Ibid. iii. 176.

34 Ibid. iii. 183–4.

writing, so also in the life. The British literary critic Henry Morley (a fellow lecturer of Gardiner's at Toynbee Hall), in his edition of the *Essays* released at the height of the debate over Bacon, argued that

> Life is directed best by those who allow due influence to each of its elements in man – the will, the intellect and the emotions; and Bacon's failures both as an actor in life and as interpreter of action may depend chiefly, as Dr. Kuno Fischer has suggested, upon undue predominance of the intellectual over the emotional part of man's nature.[35]

There was, in Bacon's thought, too much emphasis upon system for it to operate well where humans are involved. This was a principal point of a critical reading for Morley, and it is one that he shared with Gardiner. However, Morley and Gardiner were, on balance, sympathetic towards Bacon and recognised his role in the history of modern thought. He was, perhaps, a proto-historicist, a writer of genuine historical understanding, whose example and teaching had become part of the prevailing intellectual atmosphere in Germany and England.

In his own edition of Bacon's *Essays*, the philosopher Richard Whately,[36] in complaining of those writers that have lately 'accustomed their disciples to admire as a style sublimely philosophical, what may best be described as a certain haze of words imperfectly understood', uses as an example 'the metaphysics and theology of Germany' that are 'exercising a greater influence every day on popular literature. It has been zealously instilled into the minds of many that Germany has something far more profound to supply than anything hitherto extant in our native literature'. All this he at least partly attributed to 'the remark that I have heard highly applauded, that a clear idea is generally a little idea' (the saying is Burke's). Whately believed that not only was there a figure from Britain's native tradition who had earlier taught the lessons that were to be found in the most profound German philosophy, but that, indeed, Bacon offered a greater philosophy than did the Germans. The importance of his thought was disguised by its dissolved presence in German philosophy, but it was important. In particular, his failings as a scientist, the commonest intellectual criticism made of Bacon, should not lead to the assumption of similar shortcomings in his studies of human institutions, for 'rarely, if ever, do we find any such failures in Bacon's speculations on human character and conduct. It was there that his strength lay, and in that department of philosophy it may be safely said that he had few to equal, and none to excel him'. Whately also asserted that 'If Bacon had lived in the present day … certainly he would not have complained of Dialectics as corrupting philosophy.' For the German thought which had a hold in

[35] In his introduction to F. Bacon, *The essays or counsels civil and moral*, ed. H. Morley, London 1882, 11.
[36] 'Preface' to *Bacon's essays: with annotations*, ed. R. Whately, London 1856, pp. iii–xiv.

Britain (such as in the work of Gardiner), of which Bacon was an important progenitor, and which Whately and his fellow Liberal Anglican historians were well acquainted with, was the Idealist/historicist tradition. Gardiner's intellectual respect for Bacon must be seen in the light, not only of his study of the seventeenth century, but also in terms of the ways in which Bacon's ideas were implicated in the thought of more recent philosophers of whose work Gardiner was appreciative.

Gardiner was convinced of the intellectual brilliance of Bacon. For him, the seventeenth-century statesman was a man of ideas. An appreciation of Gardiner's intellectual understanding of the statesman has an impact which goes beyond this general claim, however, for it introduces new meaning into some of the more detailed responses that the historian had to Bacon. For example, it would appear that Gardiner viewed Bacon as the carrier of a certain set of political ideals from an earlier generation. Although Bacon rose to his greatest successes during the early Stuart era, for Gardiner he was a demonstrably Elizabethan politician. Indeed, he believed that Bacon's view of governments was Elizabeth's own, characterised by the historian as one in which the great institutions of the state were parts of an organic whole that operated for the benefit of the country despite their fundamental orientation towards locating final sovereignty in the monarch as head of state.[37] That Bacon's view was an essentially Elizabethan one was the result of his growing into his political role during the late sixteenth century, something that Gardiner felt had not been recognised by historians of the seventeenth century:

> I wish I could dwell at length upon … whether Bacon's constitutional views need to be, to any great extent, explained as the result of self-interest. Dr. Abbott does not seem to be aware how thoroughly they were in harmony with the ideas of the time when Bacon was young enough to be in a receptive condition.[38]

The ideas to which Bacon had been subject, and which he had imbibed, were those of the Elizabethan settlement in Church and State, the keyword of which was 'toleration'. Drawing attention to the statesman's own writings on Elizabeth, ostensibly in order to use the great thinker's defence of the queen to aid him in presenting her reign as the high tidemark of England's greatness, Gardiner brought together Bacon and the last Tudor monarch as the great carriers of English toleration, emphasising the young man's indebtedness to his queen and consequent warmth of feeling towards her and her principles:

37 *HoE* ii. 193.

38 *Academy* xxvii (13 June 1885), 411.

> The best defence of Elizabeth's treatment of the Catholics is to be found in Bacon's tract, *In felicem memoriam Elizabethæ* ... It must, of course, be received with some allowance; but it is remarkable as proceeding from a man who was himself inclined to toleration, and written after all motives for flattering the Queen has ceased to exist.[39]

It was to the Stuarts' dishonour and England's grief that the high principles of that era were not maintained, for James's failure to follow 'the large toleration of Bacon' meant that Elizabeth's successor 'sealed his own fate and the fate of England forever'.[40] According to Gardiner, Bacon's ethical standpoint, born of an earlier reign, was what made the statesman remarkable in Stuart political life.

Although for Gardiner an Elizabethan in principle, Bacon's leading role in the political life of the country coincided with the early years of the reign of the Stuarts in England. In the historian's account of the statesman's life, James I looms large – as indeed one would expect of the monarch under whom Bacon rose to the highest rank in the state's service. Although Gardiner did not hold James I in particularly high esteem – certainly not as high as the esteem in which he held Bacon – he held the first Stuart king of England in much greater regard than he did the subsequent Stuarts. Crucially, his account of James I mirrors, quite remarkably, that of his minister. Thus, if Gardiner's account of Bacon is to be fully understood, it is essential to consider his account of James I.

According to Gardiner, James I was, in comparison with other monarchs, an intellectual: 'His mental powers were of no common order; his memory was good, and his learning, especially on theological points, was by no means contemptible.'[41] Crucially, however, his intellect was directed towards an end to which Gardiner was himself attracted:

> He was intellectually tolerant, anxious to be at peace with those whose opinions differed from his own. He was above all things eager to be a reconciler, to make peace where there had been war before, and to draw those to live in harmony who had hitherto glared at one another in mutual defiance.[42]

Gardiner provided an entertaining and telling example of this bent to James's thought in a biographical article in which he told his readers, in approving terms, of the king's behaviour upon reaching his majority in 1587, recording that he had made sworn enemies walk through the streets of Edinburgh hand in hand as part of the pageant celebrating the event.[43] Such a desire to bring harmony was, according to Gardiner, seen by James as a necessary, if burden-

39 *HoE* i. 12n.
40 *HoE* i. 156–7.
41 *HoE* i. 48.
42 *HoE* i. 48–9.
43 'James VI, king of Scotland, afterwards James I, king of England', *DNB* x. 601.

some, part of his position. During a discussion of the literary-theological products of James's pen, Gardiner wrote of one 'small book, "Meditations on vv.27–29 of the 27th chapter of St. Matthew," [which] is written in a far more melancholy strain [than James's previous texts] … the crown of thorns is spoken of as the pattern of the crown of kings, whose wisdom should be applied to tempering discords into a sweet harmony'.[44] For Gardiner, James's intellectual abilities found an outlet in his promotion of reconciliation.

Gardiner saw this underlying idea in much of James's statesmanship, including his (failed) attempts to bring about peace in Germany, his restatement of the anglican *via media* through his patronage of the English Bible, and his attempts to assert a position between the two contending parties in his home kingdom, the intolerant presbyterian clergy and the armed nobility.[45] One project of James's, however, drew Gardiner's special attention: his plan to bring forward a political union between his English and Scottish kingdoms. Almost immediately upon taking the throne in England and removing his court to London, James began agitating to this end. However, on his presentation of the idea to parliament in April 1604, the king found that his enthusiasm was not shared by the representatives of the English people. Only one politician of the day was notably in favour of such a union, and he, too, was a man drawn to harmony – and to the idea of political union – due to his intellectual principles: Bacon.[46] Although some recent historiography has suggested that support for James's plan may have been forthcoming from a larger number of contemporaries than Gardiner believed,[47] it would certainly appear to be the case that James and Bacon were very much in a minority. Furthermore, it is noteworthy that where support existed for James's policy, recourse was made in argument to a strong intellectual tradition in favour of union. For example, the antiquarian Sir Robert Cotton offered historical evidence both in favour of union and to disprove the warnings of anti-unionists regarding the potential dangers of such a policy, and he showed through detailed etymological enquiry the validity of the title 'King of Great Britain'.[48] Thus, whereas a number of historians have suggested that the policy was solely one of pragmatism, the importance of early modern political theory to James's and Bacon's belief in union has recently been restated.[49] In particular, the theory of the 'body politic,' in which the polity is understood in terms of anatomy, with the head denoting the monarchy,

[44] *DNB* x. 613.

[45] *DNB* x. 599.

[46] *HoE* i. 332.

[47] K. Sharpe, *Sir Robert Cotton, 1586–1631: history and politics in early modern England*, Oxford 1979, 152–4; L. L. Peck, *Northampton: patronage and policy at the court of James I*, London 1982, 186–92.

[48] Sharpe, *Robert Cotton*, 152.

[49] B. P. Levack, *The formation of the British state: England, Scotland, and the union, 1603–1707*, Oxford 1987, 7–8. The most unequivocal rejection of any tradition of an intellectual unionism appears to be M. Lee, *The 'inevitable' union and other essays on early modern*

clearly played a role in the arguments that James himself put forward in his first speech to the English parliament: 'What God hath conioyned then, let no man separate … I am the Head, and it [i.e. 'all the whole Isle'] is my Body … I hope therefore that no man will be so vnreasonable as to think … that I being the Head, should haue a diuided and monstrous Body.'[50] The king and his chief minister were intellectually committed to, and sought to promote, the union of England and Scotland.

Gardiner wrote about another attempted political union in English history in glowing terms – a union which had succeeded. In 1485 the forces of Henry VII had overcome the armies of Richard III at Bosworth, bringing to an end the last civil war to have shaken England prior to the upheavals of the Stuarts, the Wars of the Roses. In the following year, Henry, a scion of the House of Lancaster, married Elizabeth, daughter of Edward IV and thus a member of the House of York. This union of the two Houses was, for Gardiner, a remarkable moment in English history, and he presented it as a crucial turning point in all his writings which deal with the Tudors.[51] Henry was the first Tudor monarch; the second son born to him and Elizabeth became Henry VIII, the founder of the Church of England; their granddaughter, also Elizabeth, presided over the state settlement to which Gardiner looked back with longing; and their daughter Margaret made her own political union – with the crown of Scotland – from which, ultimately, James himself had been born. As if to make clear its significance, the visible sign of that union of York and Lancaster – the Tudor Rose, half-white and half-red – was reproduced in one of Gardiner's school textbooks.[52] For Gardiner, the Tudors represented the idea of union.

In his final assessment of James I, Gardiner brought together the idea of union, the Tudor legacy and the first Stuart king in one striking story:

> Either by the wish of Charles, or by James's own desire, the body of the first of the Scottish line in England was not to lie apart [from the bodies of his predecessors] … The vault in which reposed the remains of Henry VII. and Elizabeth of York was opened, and the occupants of the tomb were thrust aside, to make room for the coffin in which was the body of him who was proud to be their descendant. To unite England and Scotland in peace justly seemed to James to be as great an achievement as to unite the rights of York and Lancaster, and to close the long epoch of civil war.[53]

Scotland, East Linton 2003, although Lee himself recommends Levack's work as the best available account of the project of union.

50 *James VI & I: political writings*, ed. J. P. Sommerville, Cambridge 1994, 136. The theory of the body politic is famously expressed often in Shakespeare's works: for a discussion of its use in *Coriolanus* see chapter 5 below.

51 *Outline of English history*, London 1881, 132; *Student's history*, 345; *The Tudor period*, London 1893, 7–8.

52 *Student's history*, 346.

53 *HoE* v. 316.

This analogy was drawn from James himself, who had spoken in his speech to the English parliament of 'the Vnion which is made in my blood':

> by my descent lineally out of the loynes of Henry the seuenth, is reunited and confirmed in mee the Vnion of the two Princely Roses of the two Houses of LANCASTER and YORKE ... But the Vnion of these two princely Houses, is nothing comparable to the Vnion of two ancient and famous Kingdomes, which is the other inward Peace annexed to my Person.

Unfortunately, of course, whereas Henry and Elizabeth had been able to bring forward a political union from their union in marriage, James had not been able to bring forward a political union from his union of the crowns. According to Gardiner, his policy was too advanced for his time. Being a man of ideas, James could not hope to convince merely practical, and prejudiced, men of the wisdom of his policy, and parliament had rejected it. When he first had raised the idea, in April 1604, James had been baffled by the pragmatic concerns of others:

> He saw the advantages which would accrue to both countries from a complete union, and longed to anticipate the fruits which would eventually spring from the carrying out of the project ... In process of time, such a measure would be heartily welcomed. All that could now be done was to appoint commissioners on either side, who might discuss the whole question, and determine how far it was practicable to remove the barriers by which the two nations were separated.[54]

On raising the matter again, in his speech at the opening of parliament in November 1606, James received two different responses. On the one hand, the innovative nature of his constitutional theories meant that they could not be apprehended by the members. 'On this question [i.e. the union]', wrote Gardiner, 'he was far in advance of the average English opinion ... We can appreciate the prescience of such words now. When they were uttered, they must have raised strange questions in the minds of the hearers.'[55] However, in his speech James had also put forward proposals for opening up trade between the two countries and for naturalising Scots resident in England, to which the response had been far more venomously anti-Scottish:

> Fuller, in his rash, headlong way, said that the Scotch were pedlers rather than merchants ... Sir Christopher Pigott ... poured forth a torrent of abuse against the whole Scottish nation ... No expression of displeasure was heard, and though this silence is attributed in the journals to the astonishment of his hearers, there can be little doubt that they secretly sympathised with the speaker.[56]

54 *HoE* i. 176–7.
55 *HoE* i. 328.
56 *HoE* i. 329–30

James's policy of political union was a product of his intellect and far ahead of its time; paradoxically, it was its intellectual nature which doomed it to failure.

James's desire for political union was also shared by Bacon; and, for Gardiner, all of the latter's ideas shared a similar fate. Drawing attention to Bacon's interest in not just '[t]he union with Scotland', but also 'the civilisation of Ireland, the colonisation of America, the improvement of the law, and abolition of the last remnants of feudal oppression', the historian argued that his ideas were 'so far in advance of the age in which he lived, that even after the lapse of two centuries and a half the descendants of the generation to which they were addressed are still occupied in filling up the outline which was then sketched by the master's hand'.[57] One particular example that Gardiner discussed in detail was Bacon's attempt to define the constitutional role of the judicature in 1617. Repeated clashes had occurred between James and the judges, most notably with Chief Justice Coke, Bacon's leading opponent, with regard to the right and proper position of the monarch in and under (or over) the law, and indeed continued to occur long after 1617. Bacon put forward the principle of the separation of powers, and the division of roles within the state according to competence. In particular, he wished to see political and administrative questions left solely to those with sufficient knowledge and experience to deal with them. An important element in this programme was the removal of the final say on constitutional matters from the hands of the judges, and its placing in the hands of the sovereign. Gardiner noted that this position was far from acceptable to men of his own age – in which 'the victory of parliament' has become a settled matter – but the later solution to the problem was not available to a statesman living at a time when king and parliament were in constant battle and unable to see the issue as deeply as Bacon could. The denial of the judges' role was all that could be attained in his own era, but even this failed to materialise because of his age's blindness to necessity and sense.[58] Although the principles on which they were based were of an earlier age, Bacon's ideas were more than James could follow – more, indeed, than the nation could follow. Bacon was too wise, his plans too radical, for the seventeenth century.[59]

One example of Bacon's brilliance as a political thinker that Gardiner discussed leads the reader to an appreciation of a further important facet of his understanding of the early Stuart statesman's place in history. In 1620, as continental issues impinged greatly on the minds of Englishmen, Bacon attempted to make his king take a position on the difficult matter of the Palatinate, under threat from roman catholic forces during the early stages

57 *HoE* ii. 193–4.
58 *HoE* iii. 2–4.
59 *HoE* ii. 382.

of the Thirty Years War.[60] Many in England wished to see the government act in defence of their fellow protestants on the continent, but a delicate balance needed to be maintained which drew king and parliament together, and indeed the different parties in parliament together. Many tax-payers, and their representatives, were amongst the most voluble supporters of the Palatinate, but were also deeply concerned about the costs of raising an army. The country was divided on religious lines, too, and a decision needed to be reached which would not cause a violent reaction from one party or another. Finally, matters of state and foreign relations had to remain uppermost in the minds of the king's ministers. After much debate, a proclamation was drawn up, on behalf of the Commissioners, by Bacon. Although formally to be as if from the king, it was actually intended, according to Gardiner, 'for the purpose of defining the position which [the Commissioners] hoped that James would take up'.[61] It did indeed state that England would seek to defend the Palatinate, a decision with profound implications for the maintenance of at least political peace in England, but in such a manner, Gardiner believed, that it had the potential to bring all parties together: a proclamation in such 'statesmanlike language', 'so temperate, and yet so firm, [that it] would have served as a rallying point for the whole nation. It would have formed a common ground upon which Pembroke and Abbot could join hands with Digby and Calvert'.[62] Unfortunately, '[t]he proclamation was too good for James', and the chance was lost to create national unity over such a potentially divisive religio-political issue.[63] It was the failure to follow Bacon over these kinds of issues that, Gardiner believed, led England inexorably to the dreadful years of the Great Civil War. The mistakes of the early Stuart period which saw the country tear itself apart in the 1640s could have been avoided – but Bacon was the only man sufficiently wise and statesmanlike to have healed the rifts in the body politic. Where other historians saw his removal from office, and thus from the corrupting influence of the court, as allowing the philosopher the freedom to direct his great mind to purer thoughts, to the eternal blessing of English philosophy, Gardiner believed that, had he been able to stay in office, had his intellect been directed to political ends in his last years, and had his contemporaries been able to comprehend fully the lessons that he taught, the terrible destruction of later years would not have happened. England, led into the future by the greatest man of the present, with principles based in the past, would have been spared the Civil War.

This view of Bacon as the one man with the talents to have saved England is a vital organising principle of Gardiner's conception of the philosopher-statesman, and on a number of occasions he spelled out that analysis for his

60 For an extended analysis of that war, and Gardiner's conception of it see chapter 2 above.

61 *HoE* iii. 378.

62 *HoE* iii. 379.

63 Ibid.

readers. For example, in disagreeing with Spedding's view that Coke had been on the side of right, if not the winning side, in the great constitutional battles of James's reign, he argued that '[t]he Civil War came about, not because Coke's principles prevailed, but because half of Bacon's principles prevailed without the other'.[64] In the midst of the controversy over Bacon's character and actions in the 1880s, Gardiner contrasted the failings of the politicians of the civil war period with the greatness of Bacon thus:

> Study Eliot and Strafford, Pym and Cromwell, and you become aware of a one-sidedness in all of them. It is precisely this one-sidedness which is absent from Bacon. He stands out as the one man, except Turgot, who stood at the beginning of an inevitable revolution with the intelligence which would have enabled him to direct it into peaceful channels.[65]

Again, the historian stresses that he was too far ahead of his age in his thinking to have been able to save England. The brilliant statesman was, whatever his contemporaries were, a brilliant thinker.

For what Gardiner called, when talking of Bacon's thought, 'practical wisdom', he called 'philosophic statesman[ship]' when talking of his political activities.[66] 'He was not one man as a thinker, and another man as a politician', as both his detractors and his supporters had maintained, but a man in whom the synthesis of thought and action was complete. It is crucial for an understanding of Gardiner's conception of Bacon that this is recognised, for to consider his narration of his subject as a political actor to be nothing more than a political understanding of the statesman is to diminish seriously the depth and sophistication of his reading of not just this particular character, but also of his reading of the seventeenth century as a whole. The twentieth-century historian Brian Wormald has recognised this with regard to Gardiner's Bacon studies. In his biography of Bacon, Wormald has discussed Gardiner's writings on his chosen subject in detail.[67] Wormald is no disciple of Gardiner, as any reader of his earlier study of Clarendon knows well. He begins in a similarly critical vein, deploring that Gardiner's histories 'have become, faute de mieux, the authoritative presentation of English events and personalities of the period [in question]'. However, Wormald is of the opinion that 'What [Gardiner] wrote at the start of dealing with [Bacon] was on the right lines', quoting Gardiner with approval: 'It is in Bacon's philosophy that the key to [Bacon's] political life is to be found.'[68] In carrying

64 *HoE* ii. 208–9n.

65 *Academy* xv (3 May 1884), 305.

66 *HoE* iv. 46.

67 B. H. G. Wormald, *Francis Bacon: history, politics and science, 1561–1626*, Cambridge 1993, 21–3.

68 Ibid. 21. The words of Gardiner are to be found at *HoE*, iii. 396. Needless to say, Wormald here contradicts Abbott's complaint that Gardiner paid insufficient attention to philosophy.

out this search, Wormald tells us, Gardiner 'correctly proceeds' in his study of Bacon. The earlier historian recognised that Bacon was, first and foremost, a philosopher, and that the thought of the statesman was essential to understanding his activities and policies. It was to the ideas of an individual or an age that Gardiner turned first, whatever the apparent principal concerns of his writings, such as the actions of members of high political circles.

Gardiner's writings on the politics and the political actors of the seventeenth century were not limited, of course, to those individuals and those theories for which he had respect. If James was, in the main, a worthy monarch in Gardiner's eyes, the contrast is with Charles I; and, if Bacon was for the historian a brilliant advisor, the contrast is with Charles's closest advisors, Buckingham and Laud. In order to understand fully Gardiner's approach to seventeenth-century politics it is necessary to consider also what he had to say about Charles and the men who surrounded him.

According to Gardiner, Charles was, unlike James, characterised by a weak intellect. He was neither a thinker himself, nor a man who sought intelligence in others: 'He was not a man of thought to be attracted by intellectual force.'[69] The general lack of intelligence which the historian perceived in the king was given more specific shape in terms which remind the reader of Gardiner's own conception of the necessary intellectual skills required to understand the world, as taken from the Idealists, when he complained of Charles's 'want of imaginative powers'.[70] Even on those occasions when Gardiner appears to applaud certain characteristics of the king's mind, he ensured that his readers understand that these elements of Charles's psychology were, in fact, deficiencies. For example, after a short passage in which he apparently complimented the king for a willingness and ability to remain committed to an idea or plan in the teeth of opposition – a characteristic for which he had complimented James – Gardiner made clear that it was not due to any intellectual strength: 'The firm conviction of his mind were alike proof against arguments he was unable to understand, and unalterable by the impression of passing events, which slipped by unnoticed.'[71] According to Gardiner, Charles's actions were characterised by his lack of intellect.

Charles's 'firm conviction' was most often observable, the historian believed, in his refusal, throughout his reign, to compromise. The king, Gardiner complained, 'had not the tact to perceive that concession must be made to the feelings of others'.[72] This failing damaged Charles both at home and abroad: during the discussions of the position of the protestants in France which took place between England and its neighbour in February 1626, '[a] foreign Government was to find now, as domestic parties were to

69 *DNB* xx. 75.
70 *HoE* v. 317.
71 *HoE* v. 318.
72 *HoE* vi. 44.

find afterwards, that it was not enough to give way to Charles in some things, unless it was prepared to give way to him in all'.[73] In addition to the portrait that Gardiner produced discursively in his history, he wrote a biographical essay in which these points were discussed in some detail. In it, he explicitly linked Charles's lack of willingness to compromise and his general and specific intellectual weaknesses:

> there was in him no mental growth, no geniality of temperament, leading him to modify his own opinions through intercourse with his fellow men. This want of receptivity in his mind was closely connected with a deficiency of imagination. He could learn nothing from others, because he was never able to understand or sympathise with their standpoint.[74]

Tellingly, Gardiner contrasted these failings with the successes of the last Tudor monarch. While discussing the Stuart king's attempts to enforce the introduction of the Prayer Book in Scotland, Gardiner commented that 'Charles did not know, as Elizabeth had known, how to withdraw from an untenable position'.[75] In Charles's dealings with Scotland, Gardiner perceived the king's policy failures to be the result of his intellectual failings.

The Prayer Book controversy – and his refusal to compromise – was disastrous for Charles, but it was of course in the events which most exercised Gardiner that the ultimate failure of Charles's policies was to be found: in the Great Civil War. Again, the historian laid the blame squarely at the feet of the king, criticising his psychological characteristics and his weakness of mind. In the events which led to war, during the war itself, and after, Charles's conduct was characterised by his failure to compromise and his inability to understand others and the wider intellectual climate:

> wise statesmen – whether monarchical or republican – watch the currents of opinion, and submit to compromises which will enable the national sentiment to make its way without a succession of violent shocks … Charles's fault lay … in his absolute disregard of the conditions of the time, and of the feelings and opinions of every class of his subjects with which he happened to disagree.[76]

Nowhere is this more clear than in the prolonged attempts to find a peaceful settlement following the victory in war of Parliament over the Royalists. Rather than showing wisdom during these needful times, the king behaved in a way which drew particular scorn from Gardiner:

> Charles, if he had been wise, would have closed even now [November 1647, on parliament's attempts to establish presbyterianism in England] with Cromwell

[73] *HoE* vi. 55.
[74] *DNB* iv. 68.
[75] *DNB* iv. 77.
[76] *GCW* iv. 326.

> and the army [by agreeing to the 'Heads of Proposals']. All he thought of was to try to win over the army leaders by offers of peerages and places.[77]

Lacking the intellectual ability to come to a settlement, Charles was drawn into a more base game-playing: 'It is intelligible that Charles should not have been prepared to accede to so wise a settlement [i.e. the 'Heads of Proposals']; but at least he might have been expected not to make the overtures of the army counters in intrigue.'[78] Thus, the king was a man of intrigue, rather than a man of ideas.

The contrast of thought and intrigue as political methods offers the reader an interesting parallel: whereas Charles had tried to counter parliament with intrigues, James had tried to counter parliament with ideas, offering a strong philosophical statement directly to its members in favour of union. It is noteworthy also that Bacon had been acquitted by Gardiner, in the final analysis, of deliberate misconduct, stressing that, rather than being the kind of base individual who indulged in intrigue in his political work, he had been a man who had stepped accidentally over the bounds of acceptable behaviour due to his strong theoretical position. In one passage in his *History*, Gardiner drew an explicit contrast between Bacon and Charles, doing so on this occasion not with regard to their characters but with regard to their constitutional theories. Although lengthy, the passage is worth quoting in full, not just for what it tells us about Gardiner's attitudes towards Bacon, Charles, and their respective approaches to politics, but also for the way in which it encapsulates the historian's appreciation of the political history of England from the 1590s to the 1690s. In the midst of his account of the failures of Charles's second parliament of 1626, Gardiner turned to his final statement on Bacon on the occasion of his death:

> 'Let compounds be dissolved.' The words with which Wotton had closed the epitaph of the great philosopher and statesman who had passed away from his earthly work almost unnoticed amidst the contentions of the session now brought to a close, might fitly be inscribed over the tomb of the constitutional theories which Bacon had striven hard to realise. The king and the House of Commons no longer formed constituent parts of one body. On either side new counsels would prevail. The king would demand to be sole judge of the fitness of his own actions, and to compel the nation to follow him whithersoever he chose to lead. Parliament would grasp at the right of control as well as the right of counsel, and would discover that the responsibility of ministers could only be secured by enforcing the responsibility of kings. At last, after a terrible struggle, teeming alike with heroic examples and deeds of violence, a new harmony would be evolved out of the ruins of the old.[79]

[77] *DNB* iv. 83.
[78] Ibid.
[79] *HoE* vi. 121.

Bacon and all that he had stood for – the Elizabethan state settlement – died at the same moment; the politics of compromise gave way to the politics of tyranny; the great era of thoughtful government was left behind as a new era of forceful government took its place; and the harmony of the older order was lost for a generation or more, until constitutional harmony was restored with the defeat of Charles's son James.[80] For Gardiner, Charles and his system were antipathetic to Bacon and his system.

However, Gardiner did not personify the political parties in as exclusive a manner as this discussion has suggested. Just as Bacon and James I act together in Gardiner's account, jointly embodying the attempt to bring the Tudor era forward into the new Stuart era, so too Charles had his partners in the defeat of their hopes and dreams, and in the construction of a new politics. Two men stand out in the *History* in this regard: William Laud and George Villiers, duke of Buckingham. Gardiner's tying together of individuals in this way brings them so close together that the characteristics explicitly claimed for one may be read into another. For example, there is Gardiner's statement that

> Neither Charles nor Laud, by whose advice in ecclesiastical matters Charles was more than ever guided, had any taste for dogmatic controversy. Laud believed that it only served to distract the clergy from their real work, and he looked with the contempt of a practical man upon endless discussions about problems which it was impossible for the human intellect to solve … Nor had he less contempt for public opinion than he had for abstract thought.[81]

These words are referred to in an index entry for Charles (under the subheading 'has no taste for dogmatic controversy') but there is no matching index entry for Laud. Is the subsequent expansion of the discussion, in which it is apparently stated that Laud held both public opinion and abstract thought in contempt, intended more as a comment on the king than on his archbishop? Most likely, however, and despite Gardiner's own respect for the thought of the archbishop, the characterisation is intended for both Charles and Laud – which underlines the method by which Gardiner melded the individuals into one. Thus, it is no surprise to read a passage contrasting Laud with Bacon: '[s]uch a man' as Charles 'was certain to share Laud's view of the true way of dealing with church controversies – so different from that of Bacon'.[82] The latter sought compromise whereas the king and his archbishop sought to enforce conformity. Given Gardiner's view of Laud's thought and character, it is worth noting that the historian's criticism of Laud is clearly directed at his antagonistic and uncompromising character.

80 See chapter 5, however, for Gardiner's claim that the settlement died with the body of Wentworth rather than Bacon.

81 *HoE* vii. 20.

82 *DNB* iv. 68.

Gardiner contrasted Laud with James and Bacon in the same terms in which he had contrasted Charles with the earlier statesmen.

Nevertheless, Laud had his high intellectualism as a positive trait. Charles's other leading advisor – Buckingham – does not receive such praise from Gardiner. In a short biographical essay, he quoted a contemporary of the favourite,[83] Henry Wotton, who had written that Buckingham was 'by nature little contemplative'.[84] However, Villiers had reached his high position due to the patronage of James, not Charles: it was the contemplative king who had raised him to the peerage. Thus, it was necessary for Gardiner to account for the relationship between the first Stuart king of England and Buckingham. He did so by stressing the relationship between the favourite and Charles, particularly for the period of his greatest power under James, the final years of the elderly king's reign:

> Of Buckingham it might truly be said that he held the government of England in his hands. Whatever wild scheme crossed his brain was accepted with docility by the Prince, as if it had been the highest effort of political and military wisdom; and, when Charles and Buckingham were agreed, James was seldom capable of offering any serious opposition to their impetuous demands.[85]

Similarly, although he took great care to ensure that his readers were well aware of the closeness of Charles's favourite and his archbishop (Laud was Buckingham's confessor, having convinced him to remain in the Church),[86] Gardiner was left with the potential problem of accounting for the period of Bacon's apparent attachment to Buckingham if the contrast was to be maintained. The way in which he did this is telling, arguing that 'Bacon, in tending advice to Villiers on the policy which appeared to him desirable to pursue … probably only did that which scores of less thoughtful persons were doing in the interests of their own advancement.'[87] Bacon and his contemporaries acted in the same way; the difference between the great man and the mass of seekers of patronage was one of principle. The system over which Buckingham presided was one based on the principle of self-interest; Bacon, however, was a more thoughtful person, hoping rather to promote good policy than to gain advancement. Buckingham, like Charles, but unlike Bacon or James, was a man of little intellectual achievement, who, unable to win the day by argument, sought power by underhand means and held that power on the basis of position rather than merit.

83 In a notably dismissive gesture, Gardiner gave Buckingham's occupation as 'court favourite': *DNB* xx. 327.
84 Ibid.
85 *HoE* v. 308.
86 *HoE* iv. 279–81; *DNB* xx. 330.
87 *DNB* xx. 328.

In their edition of selections from the work of Bacon, Percy and Elizabeth Matheson presented Gardiner as the archetypal political historian, interested in the events of the statesman's life and concerned to explore the character and behaviour of the man. On the other hand, they used Macaulay's essay to provide an insight into his philosophy. A similar approach was taken by the editors of the *Dictionary of national biography*, who asked Gardiner to write only the section of political biography for the entry on Bacon. This, indeed, is the prevailing image of Gardiner, as a political historian drawn to the biographical elements of his subjects, even when the subject is a renowned philosopher. Indeed, Gardiner was interested in Bacon as a political actor, and his account of Bacon in those terms was recognised by his contemporaries as an important contribution to the debate over the character of the fallen minister, and since his day he has been considered a leading defender of Bacon's actions. However, the characterisation of Gardiner in such a limited manner as this – as a historian of high politics only – represents a failure properly to engage with his open interest in the history of ideas. Indeed, Bacon is considered by him to be remarkable on the basis of his high intellectualism. His political life is inextricably linked with his philosophy. The importance of ideas to Gardiner's conception of politics is apparent not just in his writings on Bacon, however, for it is James's intellectualism which ultimately acquits him from the denunciations of others – and it is lack of intelligence which finally sentences Charles and Buckingham to his scorn. For Gardiner, the study of the past must be based upon the history of ideas, for it is in the intellectual sphere that men must first be judged.

5

Writing

Gardiner produced a number of different kinds of historiographical discourse. He wrote school textbooks, he was a popular lecturer to university and wider audiences, he was a reviewer of some industry in a number of journals and newspapers, he wrote the histories for which he is famous, and he produced short biographical articles for reference works and, indeed, a full-length biography of Cromwell. If Gardiner as a writer is to be understood, it is necessary to consider the different forms of writing that he practised. Furthermore, Gardiner was always ready to use forms of writing not usually considered historiographical, such as drama, in his work. Therefore, any consideration of Gardiner as a writer must also reach out to such forms of writing and what they say about his own approach to the writing of history. This chapter will seek to do that, using case studies of his theory and practice of biography and historiography and his use of drama in his presentation of Thomas Wentworth.

Gardiner's single-volume study of Cromwell was his only published product 'from a biographical point of view'.[1] This use of the phrase 'point of view' immediately suggests that Gardiner saw biography as conceptually different from historiography. As he went into print as a reviewer, his comments on the biographies of others also provide the student of Gardiner with a great deal of access to his thinking on the role of biography and what should be expected of those who write it.

An attempt to consider Gardiner's approach to historical writing can, then, be made through his own writing on historiographical theory, although it is also necessary to assess whether or how his theoretical position is reflected in his writing practice. Indeed, a comparison of how he treated the figure of Cromwell in the biography and in the *History* can greatly enhance understanding of these important aspects of Gardiner's work.

It is as a military commander that Cromwell is best remembered, and it was in this capacity that he is said to have uttered perhaps the most famous words attributed to him: 'Trust in God, and keep your powder dry.' There is no documentary evidence for this statement, and it is rarely referred to in modern biographies. However, for Gardiner these words were extremely significant, for they displayed the two sides of Cromwell's character which he wished to convey, and to which he continually returned. Nevertheless, it is necessary to discuss the issue of the veracity of the attribution; doing so offers

1 OC, unpaginated preface, fo. 4r.

a window on Gardiner's understanding of the possibilities, and responsibilities, of different genres of historiographical representation.

Gardiner dealt with these words in different ways in his *History*, his biography and in his lectures on Cromwell. In the *Great Civil War*, he tells his readers that 'To trust in God and to keep their powder dry – the popular summary of his requirements – in other words, to combine practical efficiency with enthusiasm, was the secret of the marvellous success of Cromwell's soldiers.'[2] Here, Gardiner uses the words 'popular summary' to push into the background the issue of the possibly fictional nature of the famous phrase. However, he is still happy to use it to describe Cromwell's instructions to his soldiers. 'Trust in God and keep your powder dry' serves here to help Gardiner explain a series of important events in the great military commander's life – his victories in battle. In his biography of Cromwell, Gardiner admits more openly that there is no historical evidence to prove that the general uttered the famous words, but is still anxious to use them: 'Cromwell almost certainly never told his soldiers – in so many words – to trust in God and keep their powder dry. Yet, apocryphal as is the anecdote, it well represents the spirit in which Cromwell's commands were issued.'[3] Here, the issue of historical truthfulness is dealt with in a different way from in the *History*. By parenthetically inserting the comment 'in so many words', the specific phrase is denied while leaving open the possibility of it being a paraphrase of Cromwell's actual words. On this occasion, the words are used for a different purpose, to help Gardiner describe the character of the man. However, in his Ford Lectures, the historian is even more explicit in his disavowal of the historical truth of the words attributed to Cromwell, and yet also much more brazen in his claim to their usefulness in presenting the truth of Cromwell's character:

> There is no reason to suppose that he ever uttered the words traditionally ascribed to him: 'Trust in God and keep your powder dry!' but they represent, more fully perhaps than any phrase which actually passed his lips, the union of religious zeal and practical energy which characterised him.[4]

As with their use in the biography, the issue at hand is the character of Cromwell, but here Gardiner brings to the fore the apparent fictionality of the phrase. This use of supposed events which are not part of 'what actually happened', in order to present a truthful account of the character of a historical person, is essential to Gardiner's method. What are of interest here, however, are the functional differences of genres, that is the different objects of analysis and the differing methods of the presentation and representation of material that are used by Gardiner in the separate genres. In the *History*, the phrase is used to describe events, and in the biography and

[2] *GCW* i. 142.
[3] *OC*, 30.
[4] *CPH*, 27.

the lecture to describe character (to different degrees); and furthermore, whereas the apparent fictionality of the words is pushed to the rear in the *History*, it is brought to the fore (to different degrees) in the biography and the lecture. Gardiner appears to have considered that the different historiographical genres he used had, and should have, distinguishing features which place different expectations on both the writer and the reader.

The example of the diverse presentations of the phrase 'Trust in God and keep your powder dry' is, however, far from unusual. Gardiner did indeed have very definite views on genre, on the different purposes, devices and systems that characterise different methods of exposition on the past. In the preface to the printed edition of the Ford Lectures, he wrote that '[t]hings fit to be spoken are not always fit to be printed, and things fit to be printed are not always fit to be spoken',[5] and it is clear that he said things in these lectures that he elsewhere maintained that historians should not 'say' in history-writing. For example, despite his strong aversion to the use of modern party labels to describe or characterise past political groupings – a universalising, anachronistic device – he freely did just that in the second lecture, likening Cromwell's radical opponents to French revolutionaries.[6] He could do this within the species of historical representation known as 'the lecture', for, in its form and content, it was extraordinarily suited to the discussion of a subject in relation to movements, the 'noblest part[s]' of which are 'invariably universal'.[7] That is, his lectures on *Cromwell's place in history*, as the title of the volume which brought them together suggests, were intended to trace the relationship between Cromwell and not only 'the political and ecclesiastical movements of his time', but also those of all time. A biography, however, is the presentation of the subject's character through that character's actions – in his biography of Cromwell Gardiner wrote that he sought 'a right judgment of Cromwell's character and habits of procedure'[8] – using dramatic elements where necessary in order to display them accurately. Thus, although the lecture and the biography both take the character of individuals as their province, they do so in different ways and in order to display fundamentally different things about those characters. Although they might share much, Gardiner clearly differentiated between spoken and written discourse; and the distinction he made is not just one of mode, nor even just one of methodology, but one of function.

Gardiner's nuanced understanding of genre, however, extended well beyond an appreciation of the differences between spoken and written forms of exposition: he held clear views on the distinguishing features of the historical work, the biographical work and the reference work – that is the modal and functional distinctions that can be recognised within written discourse.

5 *CPH*, unpaginated preface, fo. 3r
6 *CPH*, 41.
7 *CPH*, 1, 4.
8 *CPH*, 123.

In particular, the last is of an entirely different order from the other two genres: different, but assuredly not equal. The *Dictionary of national biography*, to which Gardiner himself was a contributor,[9] may have been 'an excellent work' due to its impartial 'no flowers by request' ethos, but it was little more than a chronicle. Thus, Gardiner congratulated Firth for, in converting his *DNB* article on Oliver Cromwell into a part-biographical, part-historical work, 'educating himself in the art of rising from the mode of recording life as suitable to a dictionary to the mode of recording it suitable for an independent work'.[10] Although he did not expand on what he thought 'the mode of recording life as suitable to a dictionary' was, Gardiner did distinguish between such large-scale, multi-authored books and the 'independent work'.

By 'independent work', Gardiner meant the monograph. He suggested in his review of Firth's book that this class of writing incorporated two distinct genres, historiography and biography, and that they should share page-space, helping and complementing each other in the single work. On one occasion Gardiner argued that David Masson had brilliantly done this in his great seven-volume *Life of Milton* (1871–81): in seeking to provide a context for the work of Milton, Gardiner stated, Masson had inadvertently written the finest history to date of the Civil War.[11] However, elsewhere he criticised the same writer for having provided too much context. As a result of incorporating all the historical detail he had found for his *Life*, the historian complained that 'the poet is almost lost in his surroundings'.[12] Indeed, Gardiner was very concerned at the difficulty of obtaining a good balance between the biographical and the historiographical, and had very high standards with regard to their combination in a single work. Amongst the many reviews that he published of biographies, spread across his thirty-year career as a reviewer, there are countless complaints that the biographer in question has used either too little or too much history, respectively isolating or swamping the subject.

On one occasion only in Gardiner's known review articles is there unequivocal praise for a biographer. While reviewing J. R. Seeley's *Life and times of Stein* (1878), Gardiner says that the title of the biography

[9] Gardiner contributed twenty-five articles (including one as co-author) to the *DNB*, principally on seventeenth-century subjects. He applied himself to the task of writing the articles with his usual dedication, perhaps to the detriment of his well-being: see Gardiner to Sidney Lee, Bodl. Lib., MS Eng misc d. 177, fos 146–50. He was also a contributor of articles to the ninth edition of the *Encyclopædia Britannica* and the 1901 'Revised edition' of *Chambers's cyclopædia of English literature*: see appendix below.

[10] '*Oliver Cromwell and the rule of the Puritans in England*. By Charles Firth' [review], *EHR* xv (Oct. 1900), 803–4: emphasis added.

[11] '*The life of Milton; narrated in connexion with the political, ecclesiastical, and literary history of his time*. By David Masson, M.A., LL.D. Vols. I.–III.' [review], *Academy* v (31 Jan. 1874), 111–13.

[12] '*Milton und seine Zeit*. Von A.Stern. Zweiter Theil, 1649–1674' [review], *Academy* xiv (14 Dec. 1878), 557.

> may raise some apprehensions in those who are familiar with so many unfortunate attempts to portray the life and times of various heroic personages, in which the subject of the biography is almost entirely lost in a mass of details in which he is only indirectly concerned, whilst the details themselves are either left in incoherence or are so grouped as to deprive them of their real historical importance. With Professor Seeley no such danger is incurred. History is kept in due subordination to biography.[13]

However, despite or perhaps because of this, Seeley has also proved himself a great historian, for his

> great merit lies in an unusual combination of biographical and historical power ... [He] has found a pair of eyes to look through, and right good eyes they are. He does not, however, by any means, sink himself in Stein. He gives us sketches, instinct with life, of all personages of importance with whom Stein is brought into contact ... Fortunately, however, the book is more than a biography or a collection of biographies. One of the main differences of the historian is to see each fact as it arises from two entirely different points of view at the same time. He has to keep clearly before him all the consequences of the fact which have since been developed, to see in it simply the seed of fruits garnered in later years for good and for evil, and at the same time to judge the actor as one to whom these consequences were entirely unknown. The power of doing this, combined with the power of tracing events to their true causes, stamps Professor Seeley as an historian as distinguished from the numerous writers about history who are always to be found in profusion.[14]

On the one hand, Seeley had provided portraits of individuals which offered his readers an insight into the character and the actions of certain historical actors, while on the other hand he had been sure to place those lives within the wider landscape of history. Thus he had both written a great biography, and proven himself a great historian. The two were compatible, but rarely successful in combination. That difficulty is born of their differences: the one must attend to the person in his or her own times, and the other must consider the passage of time. Despite his considering them as classed together as 'independent works', biography and historiography are very different creatures in Gardiner's scheme, although the differences that are always implicit are rarely, as here, made explicit in his writings.

He was, indeed, adamant that these two principal forms of telling the past were different in both theory and practice. Their principal difference is their subject. For biography, the subject must be the 'single man in relation to things around him'.[15] This issue of context is crucial to the production of a good biography: '[t]he subject of a biography, if the author's work is to be

13 'Modern history' [review notice], *CR* xxxiv (Feb. 1879), 617.

14 Ibid. 618.

15 'Modern history' [review notice], *CR* xxxiv (Dec. 1878), 196.

attractive, must be the centre of the world in which he moves'[16] but it will fall short of the best if it fails to deal with 'the history of the time … the general course of events … the situation … the background of [the] hero's portrait', even if 'after all, the portrait itself is the main thing'.[17] However, it is not enough just to narrate the actions of the person, providing a context in the process, for '[w]hat interests [the biographer] … is the play and counterplay of character'[18] and 'it is the first canon of biography that the knowledge of a man's aims is the only safe key to the knowledge of what he is'.[19] For such a study, the principal evidence must always be the subject's own words. This was the strength of Carlyle's study of Cromwell, and the reason for considering his work the most important work to date of those that had dealt with the Protector. In order to form 'a judgment on the character and aims of Cromwell', Gardiner argued, 'it is absolutely necessary to take Carlyle's monumental work as a starting point. Every satisfactory effort to understand the character of a man must be based on his own spoken and written words, though it is always possible to throw in further light and shade from other sources'.[20] However, since Carlyle's book had come out, new material had been made available, and it had to be consulted in attempting any advance on the earlier historian's work. Thus, Samuel Church was attacked by Gardiner for having ignored the Clarke papers and thus 'Cromwell's contributions to the Army Debates in 1647, which do more to elucidate the character of the subject of his biography than anything outside Carlyle's pages'.[21] For Gardiner, then, the biography was to be a study of a person's character, brought out by the study of that person's words and actions, and paying due attention to the historical context of the life.

To some degree biography was, for Gardiner, a limited genre, for the biographer 'must make the circumference of his work nearer his centre than the historian'.[22] The latter had a much wider remit, one which included the 'larger and more enduring social and political movements which sweep the course of a nation to one side or another' that the biographer need not, and should not, consider.[23] In attempting to compile a history, even one that is expressly based on biography, '[o]ne would like to find [the historian] looking a little more backwards and forwards, and placing the movements he describes in a wider setting of past and future developments of political and

16 '*Life and times of General Sir Edward Cecil, Viscount Wimbledon*. By Charles Dalton' [review], *Academy* xxviii (24 Oct. 1885), 266.

17 'A later Puritan divine. John Howe. By Robert F. Horton' [unsigned review], *Speaker* xiii (8 Feb. 1896), 170.

18 '*Rupert Prince Palatine*. By Eva Scott' [review], *EHR* xiv (Oct. 1899), 779.

19 'Modern history' [review notice] (Dec. 1878), 195.

20 *GCW* i, p. v.

21 'The Lord Protector. Oliver Cromwell. By S. H. Church' [unsigned review], *Speaker* x (24 Nov. 1895), 578.

22 'The last campaign of Montrose' [unsigned review article], 122–3.

23 '*Rupert Prince Palatinet*' [review], 779.

constitutional action', a project which Gardiner called 'that wide instruction … [which] is the salt of history'.[24] Indeed, whereas the biographer is interested in the facts of the case only, 'History itself is concerned not so much with facts as with the relations between facts'.[25] Those relationships were not just social and political relationships, but ones which Gardiner described (in a phrase somewhat redolent of German historicist discourse) as 'those currents of thought which it is the business of historians to trace out, and which form the true unity of history'.[26] This can arise from the study of historical persons, but 'it is the historian's business to disentangle from the special theories of the actors of history those general tendencies which underlie them, and to trace those tendencies to their special causes'.[27] Perhaps with such a grand notion of what historiography does in contrast to biography, it is no wonder that biographers tended to fall short of Gardiner's high standards when they did attempt such a project. Charles Dalton was one such victim of Gardiner's acute critical eye: he 'is a diligent and truth-loving investigator … and he is free from the lues biographica, to say which is to give him no small praise', the historian tells his readers, but '[u]nluckily, he has attempted not merely to write the life, but also the times, of Sir Edward Cecil', for which he is not qualified and does not have the requisite knowledge.[28] As far as Gardiner was concerned, history is distinct from biography by virtue of its being the study of larger processes, whether social, political or intellectual, than those that lie within biography's purview.

Although biography does then appear to be an inferior discourse compared with historiography, Gardiner insisted that it must attend as closely to the highest ideals of historical study as its senior partner in the narrative presentation of the past. Thus, documentary evidence must be used as the basis of study, and used with the same level of care expected of the trained historian. The work of one admirer of Gardiner was dismissed thus: 'Of manuscript sources … Mr. Morley has evidently no knowledge at all.'[29] Elsewhere, the historian compared the work of two biographers of Archbishop Laud, Charles Simpkinson and William Hutton, complaining that the former's biography 'cannot be taken seriously by historians' due to 'his incapacity for dealing with historical evidence', whereas the latter's 'work is very different', for Hutton 'knows perfectly well how to handle evidence'.[30] However, the nature of biography as a popular mode meant that the amount of documentary evidence needed was less than in the case of history; indeed, it was

[24] 'Oliver Cromwell and the rule of the Puritans in England' [review], 803–4.
[25] 'John Inglesant' [review article], *Fraser's Magazine* n.s. xxv (May 1882), 599.
[26] 'Modern history' [review notice], *CR* xxxv (Apr. 1879), 185.
[27] 'Modern history' [review notice], *CR* xxxvii (June 1880), 1057.
[28] '*Life and times of Sir Edward Cecil*' [review], 266.
[29] 'Mr. John Morley's Cromwell' [review article], *CR* lxxviii (Dec. 1900), 822
[30] '*Life and times of William Laud*. By C. H. Simpkinson. *William Laud*. By W. H. Hutton' [review], *EHR* x (Apr. 1895), 372.

better that it be limited. Eva Scott was lauded by Gardiner for ensuring that there 'is no overburdening of the narrative with documentary evidence' in her study of Charles I's nephew Rupert, and that 'everything of that nature which is introduced strengthens the author's argument instead of distracting the attention of the reader'.[31] Biography must attend to the standards of historical study, but need not concern itself, in exposition, with the evidential detail expected of historiography.

Although Gardiner continually stressed the differences between biography and historiography, there is much to indicate that he saw no radical distinction. It is rather the case that he saw the differences as ones of degree. This can most clearly be seen in the repeated concern to stress the need for historical context in the biography, the background to the portrait. However, it is also the case that he believed that certain historical events could not be understood without attempting a full appreciation of the characters of the actors involved. This is particularly the case for those events which a single individual dominated, such as those of his own chosen period: 'No writer of the history of the Civil War can avoid the difficult task of forming a judgment on the character and aims of Cromwell'.[32] Such biographical concerns must be present, but always in the background, in historiography. Similarly, historiographical concerns must play the same part in biography: one reason for Gardiner's preference for Stern's biography of Milton over Masson's is that in the former the 'history is still there, but it is distinctly relegated to the background'.[33] Gardiner insisted on a certain separateness for the biographer and the historian, but he found it impossible to define a distinct border between their work, and was never able to find a text which alone adequately straddled that border or incorporated both discourses in a fully synthesised manner. This problem becomes an issue for the student of Gardiner when an attempt is made to analyse his use of biography and historiography in practice. A reading of Gardiner's biography of Cromwell, and of those of his historical works that cover Cromwell's career reveals there are certain differences, and certain similarities, some of which are in accordance with his theoretical principles as outlined in his reviews of the work of other historians and biographers, but some of which contravene those principles. A close reading of Gardiner's 'independent works' is therefore essential to an appreciation of his understanding of the modes of historiographical discourse. Readings of Gardiner's histories of the *Great Civil War* and the *Commonwealth and Protectorate*, together with his *Oliver Cromwell* may be used as case studies. The latter two texts are of particular use, for his writing of them overlapped in time, so that any differences must be of stylistic and/or theoretical purpose, rather than representing changes in his approach over

31 '*Rupert Prince Palatine*' [review], 779.

32 GCW i, p. v.

33 '*Milton und seine Zeit*. Zweiter Theil' [review], 557. Gardiner was a correspondent of Stern: *HoE* xi. 64.

time. Just as Gardiner could not find a wholly satisfactory genre distinction in the works of others, so he was unable to fulfil his theories in his own work.

Thus, despite the dissimilarity between the genres in Gardiner's theory, there are striking similarities between the biography and the *History*. This is particularly the case with the narrating of events in Cromwell's life. Nevertheless, in his histories Gardiner often went into much greater detail regarding events than he did in his biography. This is most clearly the case in his accounts of Cromwell's military adventures, which are treated very briefly indeed in the biography. For example, whereas the decisive contribution of Cromwell, and the troop of horse he commanded, to the battle of Naseby in June 1645 takes up the best part of three pages in the *History*, it accounts for barely half of one paragraph in the biography.[34] Even more markedly, the preparations for, and the actual battle of Worcester, in which an English army led by Cromwell defeated an invading Scottish army in September 1651, is described over six pages in the *History*, but merits only two sentences in *Oliver Cromwell*.[35] This must be, at least in part, attributable to his concentration on the character of the subject of the biography rather than his actions. The different central preoccupations of biography and historiography in Gardiner's schema caused him to narrate events very differently in terms of detail.

Despite differences in the amount of detail provided, however, it is noteworthy that the tenor and sense of the reporting of events is often rather similar. This can best be shown by directly comparing how Gardiner presented a particular historical episode in both his *History* and his biography. For example, the descriptions he gives in the *History* and the biography for one extremely important, and much commented-upon, event in Cromwell's life, the dissolution of the Long Parliament in 1653 at his orders, share much detail.[36] In addition to the use of identical original quotes from the sources ('Call them in; call them in'; 'This is not honest, yea it is against morality and common honesty'; 'O Sir Henry Vane! Sir Henry Vane! The Lord deliver me from Sir Henry Vane!'), parallelism is created through the use of pairs of matching noun phrases such as 'brother' and 'a touch of sadness', and similar verb groups such as 'flung/thrown open' and 'tramped in/to'. This example is not an isolated one: although the wording is rarely identical, on many occasions the same events are narrated by Gardiner in remarkably similar ways in the biography and in the *History*.

On one noteworthy occasion, the wording is identical, for Gardiner inserted a long section from one of his histories into the biography. This is the narration of that most controversial of events in Cromwell's life, the execution of the king in January 1649. The words are a discussion of the complex constitutional, legal and moral arguments which surrounded the

34 *GCW* ii. 248–50; *OC*, 62.
35 *C&P* ii. 42–7; *OC*, 195.
36 *C&P* ii. 263; *OC*, 211

trial; they are thus an examination of 'the larger and more enduring social and political movements, which sweep the course of a nation to one side or another' and which are not part of the biographer's task. Rather than paraphrasing his arguments from the histories, or recasting them in other words, as he did elsewhere throughout the biography, on this occasion he presented them as a quotation, placing the arguments in inverted commas, physically marking them on the page and thus lifting them out of the narrative. He presented them as another kind of discourse, which he has had to use: 'I can but repeat here what I have said elsewhere'.[37] He needs the arguments, as background for the biography; but they are not themselves biography. It is important to recognise at this juncture that, although Gardiner did on this occasion incorporate the genre of historiography into a work of biography, he did it in a way which did not dissolve the two forms, but kept them separate, textually distinguished through the use of the device of quotation in order to maintain their conceptual distinction as different genres of historical writing.

What biography was for Gardiner, of course, is the presentation of character. Yet, there is one thing that the histories and the biography, perhaps surprisingly, share in this regard. Although adjectives are used to describe the character of Cromwell's actions, and character traits are often nominalised, the direct application of adjectives to Cromwell's character is very rare indeed. In fact, although there are only four such cases in the *Great Civil War* (practical, impetuous, adventurous, shrewd), there are none at all in the *Commonwealth and Protectorate* and *Oliver Cromwell*. The difference between the earlier history and the later books may represent a change in Gardiner's method, and Gardiner may well have believed that the historian must disavow the direct description of character, but what is interesting is that Gardiner does so in the biography as well. Biography should present the character of the subject, but Gardiner's method of doing so is not that of mere description.

Instead, Gardiner presented character through actions. Here, some major differences between Gardiner's biographical and historiographical treatment of events and actions in Cromwell's life begin to appear. Again, direct comparison of two passages taken respectively from the *History* and *Oliver Cromwell* concerning a pertinent point in Cromwell's life, relating the disagreement Cromwell and Algernon Sidney had on 20 January 1649 over the right of parliament to try a king, may be used to exemplify the point.[38] In the history, the altercation is used to illustrate a shift in the political order; in the biography it is used to illustrate Cromwell's decisiveness and 'vigour', elements of his character. This is particularly clear when the final sentence of each of these passages is compared. Whereas in the

[37] OC, 159. The passage extends over the next four pages. Although he does not actually provide a reference, they are taken from GCW iv. 326–8 (with minor punctuation and spelling changes/errors).

[38] GCW iv. 296; OC, 156–7.

History Gardiner considers the new situation in a strictly legalistic manner, viewing the change as a change in circumstances without any apparent agency having brought it about ('The legal formulas which had fenced the majesty of the King had ceased to be applicable'), in the biography the active involvement of Cromwell in ensuring that a particular project happens is the focus ('Cromwell ... was ready with exhortation and persuasion to complete the work which [the court] had taken in hand'). This contrast between the times and the life is clearly displayed in the different reporting of Cromwell's speech of 15 March 1649 to his men upon accepting the command of the troops due to leave for Ireland. In the history, 'Cromwell's words did but echo the sentiments of the army' whereas in the biography 'these words ... [reveal] the convictions that dominated Cromwell's actions at this period in his life'.[39] In the former, Cromwell is an agent of the army; in the latter he is the active agent in history. The same actions and speeches are used in the histories and the biography to tell the reader different things: about 'forces' and about character.

The issue of forces and character has a further dimension. It is not enough that historiography tells the history of impersonal forces and that biography tells the history of personal character, for there is the much larger issue of which of these is the dominant agent in historical change. Do actors change or limit the world, or does the world change or limit actors? This issue was of enormous importance in nineteenth-century intellectual debate, particularly as it unfolded in literary circles. It was, for instance, the organising question of Carlyle and Thackeray's debates about the role of the hero, usually carried out in private correspondence or at dinner-parties such as those hosted by Charles Dickens.[40] However, the debate was made public, albeit in an implicit way, through the publication of writings not obviously linked to one another. After Carlyle's lecture series on 'Heroes, hero-worship and the heroic in history' was published in 1841, his friend replied with the novel *Vanity Fair: a novel without a hero* in 1848. Whereas Carlyle had argued that there had been men who had changed the world through the force of their personalities, Thackeray presented a narrative of men and women whose lives were buffeted from every side and who, in the final analysis, were subject to the vagaries of forces beyond their control. Thackeray followed up with an openly anti-Carlylean lecture on 'The humourist as man of letters' in 1851.[41] In the middle of the century a battle was raging over who or what could claim dominance in narrative: people or process.

By the end of the century, a consensus in high literary culture was beginning to emerge in favour of the impersonal force. The novelist and poet George Meredith's critique of melodrama – arguably the dominant narrative

39 *C&P* i. 26; *OC*, 172.

40 C. R. Sanders, 'The Carlyles and Thackeray', in C. R. Sanders, *Carlyle's friendships and other studies*, Durham, NC 1977, passim but esp. p. 245.

41 G. N. Ray, *Thackeray: the age of wisdom, 1847–1863*, London 1958, 144–5.

tradition of mid and late nineteenth-century Britain – was based on an analysis of the relationship of character and plot: for him, the characters of melodrama grew out of the plot, whereas he believed the plot should grow out of the characters.[42] Thus, whereas in melodrama the story is finally one about the characters, in Meredith's narration it is the plot which would be presented to the audience as the summation of events. The audiences of melodrama are led to identify with the central hero; audiences of the new narratives would be left in no doubt that what matters is plot. Meredith's friend the literary critic and biographer John Morley was one enthusiastic follower of the new method, and in his *Life of Gladstone* (1903) he presented his hero as representative of his times rather than as the shaper of events. As part of the editorial staff of Macmillan for many years, Morley had an enormous impact upon British historical studies, as did his and Meredith's friend Leslie Stephen as editor of the *Dictionary of national biography*. It is noteworthy that the entries in the *DNB*, biographical as they are in explicit intent, lay enormous stress on the impact of historical conditions upon the individuals discussed: Stephen collected together most of the leading historians of his era for the project, and offered a training in modern historical method to the less-celebrated, younger contributors.[43] The elevation of plot over character in late nineteenth-century literary culture became mirrored in a hierarchy of historical explanation which subordinated the actions of individuals to the influence of wider historical pressures.

This hierarchy of historical explanation is apparent in Gardiner's work. Thus, although '[n]o writer of the history of the Civil War can avoid the difficult task of forming a judgment on the character and aims' of Cromwell, his 'work was accomplished under the conditions to which all human effort is subject'.[44] At his strongest – that is, in the earlier stages of his career – 'as a strong and self-confident swimmer, he was carried onward by the flowing tide' although in 'the latter portion of the Protector's career it was far otherwise', partly as a result of having 'drift[ed] forwards in the direction of that military despotism which neither he nor his comrades wished to establish'.[45] He swam with the tide, but it left him in a place where he did not want to be. Despite his strength of character, his steadfast will and his unique powers, Cromwell could not consciously shape the world of his day: at his weakest, historical forces took control and thrust him aside, but even at his strongest he was merely able to travel along with those forces. For Gardiner, the power of historical conditions governed the individual.

This understanding of historical forces is present also in the work of Fichte. Thomas Carlyle's Cromwell was a hero able to create his times

[42] This view is set forth in his *An essay on comedy and the uses of the comic spirit*, London 1897.

[43] N. Annan, *Leslie Stephen: the godless Victorian*, London 1984, 85–6.

[44] *GCW* i, p. viii; *OC*, 316.

[45] *OC*, 316, 108.

rather than a mere swimmer with the tide, a World–spirit made flesh akin to Hegel's Gustavus Adolphus.[46] Fichte, however, saw the greatness in Man not in the sense propounded by Carlyle or by Hegel, but in his struggle to overcome those forces which he can never master but against which he must strive if he is to hope to accomplish his full realisation of the self. It is the 'Sehnen (longing) and Streben (striving) for the ego's projective activity' which marks the great man,[47] the attempt to assert the noumenal self in the face of the phenomenal world. Gardiner's Cromwell, conditioned by the impact of the hierarchy of historical change, appears to bear the features of the Fichtean hero.

Gardiner had a theory of genre based upon clear differences between both the content and the forms of distinct historiographical discourses. However, despite his attempts to do otherwise, his own examples of historiography and biography often appear rather similar – despite the use of such techniques as quoting his own work from one genre in his work within a different genre. Stylistically, however, the effect appears to have led to the one discourse invading the other. This is most clearly evidenced in the discussion with which this chapter opened: in attempting to provide an account of Gardiner's biographical treatment of Cromwell, it proved necessary to quote from not only *Oliver Cromwell* but also both *The history of the Great Civil War* and *The history of the Commonwealth and Protectorate*. Finally, however, a clear distinction between Gardiner's biographical treatment of Cromwell and the writing on him which appears in the *History* can be drawn. The issue of whether the impersonal force or the character of the individual is what governs historical change is answered in very different ways in the two genres. Perhaps surprisingly, the debate can be traced back into literary, rather than disciplinary, culture. However, the issues can also be understood in Fichtean Idealist terms, as part of the eternal struggle between the noumenal and phenomenal worlds. Necessarily, therefore, Gardiner turns ultimately to the character of Cromwell in his biography. The chapter began with a study of the historian's treatment of the great military and parliamentary leader. Cromwell was, in Gardiner's construction, a man perhaps best described in the words of Rosebery, a man who is likely to have been fully conversant with Gardiner's work. Himself a historian, but also, like Cromwell, a statesman, Rosebery was an avowed admirer of the Protector – one of those nineteenth-century men, indeed, for whom Cromwell was a hero – and it was he who funded the statue of the seventeenth-century despoiler of parliaments that to this day graces the environs of the present Houses of Parliament. At the unveiling of that statue, he lauded his hero as a 'practical mystic'. As a classically dialectical model, it is the most Gardinerian of all possible encomia on Cromwell.

46 See chapter 2 above.

47 This theory was presented in a lecture series on 'The vocation of man', given in 1799–1800, cited in Kelly, *Idealism, politics and history*, 197.

Gardiner's appreciation of historiographical genre, then, is sophisticated, and an understanding of it informs the reader of the ways in which his different books can be read, what can be expected of them, and what he tried to do in each of them. However, his appreciation of the act of writing and the nature of genre was not confined to the more obvious, perhaps more appropriate, genres of historiography. For example, in his writings on the great military leader Wallestein, he used, rather suprisingly perhaps, a non-contemporary play, Schiller's *Wallenstein* cycle. Moreover, the use of Schiller's plays in his historiography was not Gardiner's only insertion of dramatic literature into his work. Indeed, he seems to have been particularly attracted to this literary genre, as the frequent quotations taken from Goethe and Shakespeare suggest.[48] In analysing the importance to Gardiner of drama, what is at issue is not Gardiner's own skills in dramatically recounting the past and his use of the techniques of drama in his presentation of individual characters,[49] but rather his explicit discussion of drama, which raises some extremely important points regarding both his theorisation and his practice of history.

In June 1876 Gardiner read a paper at the 26th meeting of the New Shakspere Society, entitled 'The political element in Massinger'. In August of that year, the paper found a wider audience with publication in the *Contemporary Review*, and it was subsequently also published in the society's *Transactions* for 1875–6, with the addition of a few footnotes by way of response to comments made on the occasion of its original delivery.[50] Ordinarily, a paper of this kind – a sort of hobby-horse of a paper publicising some ideas not particularly central to the main body of the historian's work – would suffer the fate experienced by many of his similar papers and essays, and be forgotten. Gardiner's paper on Massinger, however, was a little different. It turned a historian's eye onto the dramatist Philip Massinger, producing a seemingly quite original account of the politics of his plays, and was thus picked up on by those who took literature, rather than history, as their province.

Gardiner opened his case with these words:

> It will probably be a surprise even to those who are far better acquainted with the history of literature than I can pretend to be, that in many of Massinger's plays we have treatment of the politics of the day so plain and transparent, that any one who possesses only a slight acquaintance with the history of the reigns of the first two Stuarts can read it at a glance. It is quite unintelligible

48 Examples may be found, respectively, in chapters 2 and 3 above.

49 For this see D. M. Fahey, 'Gardiner as dramatist: a commentary', *Journal of Historical Studies* 1 (1967), 351–4.

50 'The political element in Massinger', *CR* xxviii (Aug. 1876), 495–507, and *The New Shakspere Society's Transactions 1875–6* [series I, no. 4], London ?1877, 314–31. As the main body of the latter version is identical to that of the first, but adds the footnoted material, it is this version to which all references below will refer.

> to me that, with the exception of a few cursory words in Mr. Ward's 'History of Dramatic Literature,' no previous inquirer should have stumbled on a fact so obvious.[51]

As Tommy Dunn pointed out in 1957, it takes something more than a 'slight acquaintance' with the history of the period to be able to read the politics in Massinger's play,[52] but nevertheless, Gardiner's complaint seems clear. Students of literature had paid scant attention to the historical context within which the texts were written, and had thus failed to see what, to him, appeared obvious: that Massinger's plays were allegories, or thinly-veiled critiques of the politics of the Caroline period, specifically from the perspective of a Pembrokian opposition party.

As Gardiner himself admitted in a lengthy footnote to the final printed version of the paper, he had somewhat overstated the originality of what he was doing; not only had A. W. Ward made a few comments in his study, but so had a number of other students of Massinger, most notably William Gifford in his famous 1805 edition of the dramatist's works.[53] This has not stopped the likes of Christopher Hill from declaring that 'S. R. Gardiner was as usual the first to spot "The Political Element in Massinger".'[54] Indeed, Gardiner's influence on studies of Massinger's politics often appears to arise from a belief that his was the first account. It is rather more the case, however, as Martin Garrett and Anne Barton have each pointed out, that Gardiner was, if not the first author to write about the politics of Massinger's plays, the first to do so with a sustained, fully-explicated account arising from detailed attention to the content of a number of the plays.[55] Or, rather, that he was the first writer with sufficient authority to get his views on Massinger taken seriously. Thus, although Philip Edwards and Colin Gibson, in the introduction to their 1976 edition of the works of Massinger, pay credit to what they call Thomas Davies's 'anticipatory' work of 1761, they accept the influence of Gardiner's paper, signalling the Victorian's authority as a historian.[56] As a result, all subsequent attempts to discuss the politics of the plays have turned to Gardiner as their starting point, from which they launch their own accounts whether they agree with Gardiner, oppose his conclusions, or wish merely to build upon or offer a gentle corrective to his views.[57]

51 'The political element in Massinger', 314. The earlier work to which Gardiner makes reference is A. W. Ward, *A history of English dramatic literature*, London 1875.

52 T. A. Dunn, *Philip Massinger: the man and the playwright*, Accra–Edinburgh 1957, 172.

53 'Political element in Massinger', n. 2.

54 C. Hill, *Writing and revolution in seventeenth-century England*, Brighton 1985, 68.

55 M. Garrett, 'Introduction', to M. Garrett (ed.), *Massinger: the critical heritage*, London 1991, 37; A. Barton, 'The distinctive voice of Massinger,' *TLS*, 20 May 1977, 623.

56 P. Edwards and C. Gibson, 'General introduction', to *The plays and poems of Philip Massinger*, Oxford 1976, i, p. liii n. 4.

57 See, for instance, A. Gross, 'Contemporary politics in Massinger', *Studies in English Literature* vi (1966), 279–90; P. Edwards, 'The royal pretenders in Massinger and Ford',

However, all of these accounts of Gardiner's theories regarding the politics of Massinger's plays have failed properly to characterise his approach to the dramatist. Seeing Gardiner as a historian of high politics, rather than as a historian of ideas, they have reduced his arguments about Massinger to a simplistic model in which the historian views the dramatist as a mere polemicist on behalf of others. For example, Ira Clark states that he 'finally must agree with [Allen] Gross and [Philip] Edwards rather than with Gardiner ...: regarding Massinger as a political spokesman for the Herberts is straining'.[58] Gardiner, however, had argued that

> [a]s might be expected, Massinger's standpoint is the standpoint of the Herberts. His connection with the younger of the two brothers, the Philip, Earl of Montgomery, who afterwards became Earl of Pembroke, it has hitherto been held that he had no personal dealings. Whether this be so or not, I hope to show that he expressed himself in a way which would have been altogether satisfactory to Pembroke, though this may possibly be accounted for by a wish to please his brother Montgomery.[59]

In other words, Gardiner did not posit Massinger as a spokesman for the Herberts, but as a spokesman for a set of views held by the Herberts. These two stances may on first glance seem similar enough to appear, practically, the same, but they are distinct enough to throw doubt on the particularly reductive arguments of the likes of Edwards and Gibson.

The problem which Gardiner's critics see in a simplistic reading of the allegorical possibilities of Massinger's work – which they characterise the historian's paper as providing – is that it does not readily account for the ambiguities that they see in the plays, and the non-exact nature of any possible parallels. Much of the twentieth-century writing on the dramatist's politics holds that Massinger's criticism of the Caroline court and its members was not so much a direct attack on individuals such as the king and Buckingham, as a more general critique of the culture of the court. As early as 1957 Dunn offered a sophisticated, if rather depoliticised, reading of Massinger's views. 'I am inclined to think,' he wrote, 'that Massinger owed little political allegiance to the cause of the Herberts, or of anyone else for that matter, but criticised what he saw and condemned what he disapproved of, honestly, as was his custom. He looks at politics as a moralist, not as a politician or a partisan.'[60] This, whatever Philips, Edwards and others might think,

Essays and Studies xxvii (1974), 18–36; A. Patterson, *Censorship and interpretation: the conditions of writing and reading in early modern England*, Madison, Wi 1984, 87–99; D. Howard, 'Massinger's political tragedies', in D. Howard (ed.), *Philip Massinger: a critical reassessment*, Cambridge 1985, 135 n. 9; and I. Clark, *The moral art of Philip Massinger*, London 1993, 13, 20, 139–40, 295 n. 41.

58 Clark, *Moral art*, 295 n. 41.

59 'Political element in Massinger', 316.

60 Dunn, *Philip Massinger*, 174.

is the central point of Gardiner's view of Massinger: that his criticism rests on a moral sense and is more universalising than a direct political polemic can offer. In accordance with his more sympathetic reading of Gardiner's paper, Dunn duly draws attention to this by calling on the historian as one of his witnesses:

> But Massinger had something of the Puritan in him, at once fascinated by sin and censorious of it. He shared the interest of his audience; but he recommended a more excellent way. As Professor Cruikshank says (and here I cannot but agree with him), 'unlike some of his literary contemporaries, Massinger wishes to show Virtue triumphant and Vice beaten. Vice is never glorified in his pages, or condoned.' Or as S. R. Gardiner puts it, 'He never descends to paint immoral intention as virtuous because it does not succeed in converting itself into vicious act.'[61]

The quotation from Gardiner comes from the very first paragraph of his paper, and provides the context within which the rest of the paper needs to be read. Gardiner was interested in the morality implicit in Massinger's plays and the possibilities which his critique offers for an account of the characters of the members of the court and their approach to politics.

Gardiner's understanding of Massinger was not that which might be expected of the posited historian of high political activity. Before it is possible to offer a closer reading of his views on this particular dramatist, however, it is necessary to consider the wider issue of Gardiner's understanding of drama. For, it may be argued, the principal problem with all accounts of the Massinger paper that have been written to date is that it has been read in isolation, and never alongside Gardiner's other writings on drama. On at least two other occasions he discussed the possible uses of drama for the historian. Those writings may arguably be put at the centre of a new understanding of Gardiner and his work.

In 1876, while visiting Spain for the purposes of studying at a number of archives, Gardiner wrote a letter to the *Academy* from Valladolid in which he discussed the nature of Sir Thomas Wentworth.[62] In the previous year, he had published the third two-volume instalment of his *History*, in which Wentworth first appeared as a significant player in events, and in the following year he published the fourth instalment, covering the years in which Wentworth rose to prominence as a leader of opinion and men in England. Thus, in 1876, Gardiner was thoroughly immersed in Wentworth's life events; however, his discussion of Wentworth in the *Academy* letter was,

61 Ibid. 201.

62 At his first appearance in Gardiner's *History*, Wentworth is simply Sir Thomas Wentworth. Subsequently, he became Lord Wentworth, Viscount Wentworth and, finally, the earl of Strafford. Gardiner's naming of Wentworth throughout his volumes follows the title he held during the times being narrated; however, for simplicity, I will refer to him throughout this chapter as Wentworth.

somewhat surprisingly, centred not on Wentworth in his own time, but on the parallels between him and the eponymous hero of Shakespeare's *Coriolanus*. In 1884 Gardiner published an essay on another dramatist's work, a play based on the final days of Wentworth, in which he came to conclusions regarding the role of drama that have struck a number of critics as incongruous in a 'scientific' historian. Through a discussion of Gardiner's appreciation of this work – Robert Browning's *Strafford, an historical tragedy* – and of Shakespeare's work – as exemplified in his understanding of *Coriolanus* – the modern reader can begin to make some sense of the historian's instinct for drama and its role in telling the past. Without doing this, it is impossible properly to appreciate Gardiner's paper on Massinger. In so doing, a much richer appreciation can be acquired not just of Gardiner's use of drama, but of his full historiographical practice.

Gardiner opened his letter to the *Academy*[63] with a simple statement of the similarity between Wentworth and Coriolanus, with some slight reservation:

> I do not know whether it has occurred to any one that Shakspere's judgment on Coriolanus throws some light on what he would have thought of Strafford if he had lived thirty years longer. Strafford, indeed, is not exactly Coriolanus, and still less are Brutus and Sicinius like Pym and Hampden. The Roman has more command over himself, more versatility of nature; but in the main the characters are the same.

As the two characters are so similar, 'we may be sure that Shakspere, who admired Coriolanus, would have admired Strafford too'. This, Gardiner opined, was despite certain features that moderns might see as bad in the characters and actions of the two men, for Shakespeare, while acknowledging the errors of Coriolanus, calls finally for 'his great qualities [to] … be remembered'. Shakespeare's Coriolanus and Gardiner's Wentworth are imperfect, but worthy of 'noble memory'.[64]

Wentworth was an important figure for Gardiner. In addition to the letter discussed here, and to the highly detailed accounts of his political activities and descriptions of his character and personal life given in the *History*, Gardiner went into print regarding the statesman on several occasions in the journals and elsewhere, providing the text of a previously unknown speech given at York in 1628 and a detailed defence against Macaulay's 'apostate' charge, as well as offering a number of notices and articles, and discussing his history in several reviews.[65] The effect, however, was not just to widen or

63 'Wentworth and Coriolanus' [correspondence], *Academy* x (15 July 1876), 61–2.

64 *Coriolanus*, V.v.153.

65 See, for example, 'On the alleged apostacy of Wentworth (Lord Strafford)' [unsigned review article], *QR* cxxxvi (Apr. 1874), 434–52; 'Date of the privy councillorship of Lord Wentworth' [notice], *Academy* v (2 May 1874), 489; 'An unpublished speech of Lord Wentworth' [notice], *Academy* vii (5 June 1875), 581–3; 'The Forster MSS in the South

deepen knowledge of the man, but to alter the way he was thought about by historians. Hugh Kearney has remarked that the uniformly hostile accounts of Wentworth proffered in English historiography from Clarendon onwards were countered by Gardiner so effectively that the 'pendulum of English historical opinion was to swing no further against Strafford' from Gardiner's position ever again.[66] Similarly, C. V. Wedgwood credited Gardiner as the first historian 'to take a more sympathetic view' of both Wentworth and his master, Charles I.[67] Needless to say, calling Shakespeare as a witness to Wentworth's character, arguing that Shakespeare would have made the same kind of judgement of the statesman that Gardiner did, would have strengthened the latter's position. It is hard to imagine a more reliable witness to character in the eyes of Victorians than Shakespeare. Whatever the method, however, the result is clear: through a detailed engagement with the life of Wentworth, Gardiner revised his reputation in a positive direction.

Gardiner's sympathetic account of Wentworth was built on his recognition of the Jacobean statesman as a representative of the Elizabethan state. 'Wentworth, whose mind was full of schemes for alteration and reform', Gardiner tells us, 'was an advocate of the constitutional forms which had existed in the days of his youth.'[68] Those forms were clearly those of his early youth: throughout his career, he 'attempted to maintain the Elizabethan constitution'.[69] It was an 'active, wise, and reforming Government [that] was the ideal after which he strove from first to last'[70] and, while those three words – active, wise, reforming – are those that Gardiner used most often to describe Wentworth, they were also for Gardiner the concepts which most faithfully described the Elizabethan state.

Like most of his contemporaries, Gardiner saw the Elizabethan state as the perfection of England, the culmination of the great Tudor settlement figured in the union of Lancaster and York in the marriage of Henry VII and Elizabeth.[71] The Tudor monarchs had themselves faced a far from peaceful kingdom, most noticeably in the tumults of Henry VIII's reign, but that reign had seen great reforming work carried out by the likes of Cranmer.[72] It had

Kensington Museum' [notices], *Academy* xi (2 June 1877), 486–7; xii (28 July 1877), 91; 'Four Letters of Lord Wentworth, afterwards earl of Strafford, with a poem on his illness', in *Camden Miscellany, vol. VIII.* (1883); '"English men of action" – *Lord Strafford*, by H.D. Traill' [review], *Academy* xxxvi (30 Nov. 1889), 349–50; 'Plan of Charles I for the deliverance of Strafford' [notice], *EHR* xii (Jan. 1897), 114–16; and the biographical articles provided for the *DNB* and the *Encyclopaedia Britannica*, 9th edn

66 H. Kearney, *Strafford in Ireland, 1633–41: a study in absolutism*, Manchester 1959, pp. ix–x.

67 C. V. Wedgwood, *Thomas Wentworth, first earl of Strafford, 1593–1641: a revaluation*, London 1961, 12.

68 *HoE* vi. 284.

69 *HoE* ix. 370.

70 *HoE* vi. 337.

71 *Outline of English history*, London 1881, 132.

72 *Study of English history*, London 1881, 115.

also resulted in the birth of the Church of England, an institutional expression of England's national greatness and independence that found its finest statement in the work of the Elizabethan theologian Hooker. When Elizabeth had succeeded to the throne, she too had faced division in England, in part born of the difficulties of her father's reign. Gardiner's writings on the early years of her reign are full of references to the struggle of two oppositional voices, just as his accounts of English historiography castigate the extreme parties of Whig and Tory. In theology, the 'extravagance of discipline appeared as the opponent of the extravagance of individual religion', and in church politics 'the tyranny of ecclesiastical democracy' was as dangerous as 'the tyranny of ecclesiastical monarchy'.[73] As the 'last two reigns had shown the impossibility of governing England by the help of either of the extreme parties … the queen was … well advised in taking up her ground between them'.[74] She did so in many symbolic and institutional ways – the example Gardiner dwelled upon was her Prayer Book – and as a result, although she had 'found England divided and weak, she left it united and strong'.[75] The titles of the chapters that dealt with the Elizabethan era in his textbooks are instructive: 'Elizabeth and the national spirit' at once recalls Fichte, and the sense of synthesis that Gardiner imparts in his narration of Elizabeth and England at the end of the sixteenth century is testament to both his age's understanding of that time and his own personal orientation within the debate. The Elizabethans offered the nineteenth century a model of peace and prosperity based on the ending of factional battles.

The Elizabethan period was important to Gardiner the Stuart historian as the counterpoint to his chosen subject, a time of division and bloodshed. Again, the organisation of his textbooks is illustrative. The frontispiece of the *Outline of English history* shows Arthur Lucas's well-known depiction of Drake's famed reaction to the news of the arrival of the Armada as he played bowls. As the excitement builds around him, the great naval commander takes command of his emotions and remains calm and unhurried. The story of the Armada takes up many more pages than it would seem to deserve, because for Gardiner it displayed all of the elements of the great Elizabethan state. The *Outline*, its author tells us in his preface, is divided into two parts, the first intended for young children and telling of uncomplicated times, the second for older, more advanced students capable of understanding a period in which exciting stories have to make way for the more complex analysis needed to make sense of modern times.[76] The year in which the first part ends and the second part begins is 1603, the year of Elizabeth's death and James I's accession to the English throne. The change from Tudor to Stuart

73 Ibid. 118, 121.
74 Ibid. 113.
75 *Outline*, 192.
76 Ibid. p. vii.

bodes ill, as Gardiner illustrated by quoting from Shakespeare at the close of part one:

> This England never did – nor never shall –
> Lie at the proud foot of a conqueror,
> But when it first did help to wound itself.
> (*King John* V.vii.112–14)

His closing comment on the Elizabethans is thus also a condemnation of the Stuarts.

It is significant that Gardiner chose Shakespeare to close this chapter. Just as the Elizabethan state was the high point of the English state, so was Elizabethan culture the high point of English culture. Gardiner prefaced Shakespeare's words with his own estimation of their worth: 'Great writers and great poets arose at the end of Elizabeth's reign. Shakspere, the greatest of them all, expressed the feeling which taught Englishmen that their well-being lay in the unity among themselves which sprang from their devotion to the queen.'[77] The keyword here, as in all of Gardiner's accounts of the Elizabethan period, is 'unity', for these writers were as imbued with the great English and anglican synthesis as their statesmen were:

> The Elizabethan literature was but the expression of a deep-rooted feeling. Holding out its hand, as in Spenser, to Protestantism, it was in the main, as in Shakspere and the dramatists, neither Catholic nor Protestant. It kept steadily in view the human side of life as opposed to the religious. It appealed to human motives, the love of wealth and prosperity, to the human sense of justice, and power, and beauty, and virtue, not to the asceticism of the monk, or the religious self-restraint of the Puritan.[78]

It has been noted by modern critics that, whereas in his earlier plays Shakespeare used the word 'commonwealth', a word imbued with theological significance, to describe the polity, his later tragedies and the Roman plays invariably use the word 'state' with its secular connotations.[79] The unity Gardiner saw was of the Renaissance, but not of the religious strife of either previous reigns or the decades to come.

There is, however, an apparent problem with the characterisation of Wentworth as the representative of the Elizabethan state in Gardiner's work,

77 Ibid. 194

78 *Study of history*, 127.

79 D. B. Hamilton, *Shakespeare and the politics of Protestant England*, Lexington, KT 1992, 11. This point is discussed in a general sense with regards to *Coriolanus* in the introductions to two collections of modern criticism on the play: J. E. Phillips, 'Introduction', to J. E. Phillips (ed.), *Twentieth-century interpretations of Coriolanus*, Englewood Cliffs, NJ 1970; D. Wheeler, 'Introduction', to D. Wheeler (ed.), *Coriolanus: critical essays*, New York 1995. For a detailed study of the implications of this insight for the understanding of *Coriolanus* see P. K. Meszaros, '"There is a world elsewhere": tragedy and history in *Coriolanus*', *Studies in English Literature* xvi (1976), 273–85.

and his characterisation of Shakespeare as the representative of Elizabethan culture, particularly with reference to *Coriolanus*. As a number of critics have pointed out – often in response to E. M. W. Tillyard's famous invocation of an 'Elizabethan world picture'[80] – Shakespeare's great tragedies, which have been the subject of more critical study than any other of his works, and his Roman plays (which include *Coriolanus*), are Jacobean plays rather than Elizabethan. Similarly, Wentworth was only ten years of age when the family of Stuart took possession of the English throne, and his political life reached its apogee under Charles I. However, Gardiner used Wentworth as an interloper-figure who carried forward a world lost to his contemporaries. It was this Elizabethanism that was, for Gardiner, both Wentworth's greatness and his weakness, guaranteeing his 'noble memory' and inevitably leading to his downfall. There are powerful parallels here with the work of those historically-minded critics of both the nineteenth and twentieth centuries, including very recent critics of the 'new historicist' school, who have seen in Shakespeare's Roman plays the great dramatist's own attempt to come to terms with a fading past: for these critics, Shakespeare's Coriolanus is a man of a lost time, thrust forward into an era that he cannot fully understand, in which his figuring of a different, simpler era is both the guarantor of his 'noble memory' and the source of his inevitable failure. Shakespeare's feelings of uncertainty about his own times are Gardiner's uncertainties of Shakespeare's times.

Shakespeare has long been the subject of historicist study, and it comes as no surprise to find that Gardiner was closely associated with the historicist critics of his own day. In contrast to the attempts to depoliticise Shakespeare and his work, as Samuel Taylor Coleridge and Algernon Swinburne had attempted to do, a number of nineteenth-century critics attempted instead to find Shakespeare's place in his own time, the politics and ideologies his writings carried, and their messages for later times. One such group was that centred around F. J. Furnivall and the New Shakspere Society. Furnivall founded a number of literary societies, usually based on the older English literature, such as the Chaucer, Wyclif and Ballad societies, very few of which survived for long.[81] The New Shakspere Society eventually collapsed as a result of the embarrassment many members felt over Furnivall's extremely vituperative, and increasingly personal, debates with Swinburne, principally carried out in the pages of the *Academy*. Furnivall was at his best as an organiser rather than as a critic, although he had a hand in all aspects of the work that his various societies carried out. His dedication to historical method was apparent very early in his career. In 1847 he joined the London Philological Society, becoming its secretary in 1853 and, in that capacity, became acting

80 E. M. W. Tillyard, *The Elizabethan world-picture*, London 1943.

81 The exception is the Early English Text Society, which continues its work to this day, reprinting much early literature that might otherwise have been lost.

editor of the society's great project, the *New English dictionary* ('founded on historical principles'), in 1861. Despite being appointed simply as 'acting' editor, he held the post for eighteen years, handing over to its most famous editor, James A. H. Murray in 1879. He was also heavily involved in education, particularly in the University Extension Movement, and helped to found the London Working Men's College – at which Gardiner taught early in his own career. Furnivall was also a prolific writer, most notably for the *Academy*, the leading historicist journal of the Victorian era.[82] Unsurprisingly, upon the founding of the New Shakspere Society, he made it clear that German scholarship offered the ideal and the model which the society's work must seek to emulate.[83] Much of the early work of the society rested upon close philological analysis and historicist theory.

Furnivall's own work for the society included a number of editions of late sixteenth-century writings, several of which Gardiner reviewed in the pages of the *Academy* in September 1876. In his reviews, the historian tried to claim the texts for historians rather than literary scholars. He noted that, although he was not fit to judge the value of these texts for the Shakespearean scholar, the society had supported an invaluable exercise for historians and 'that the editor has conferred a great obligation on all who wish to understand what the England of their forefathers was like'.[84] It was earlier that year that Gardiner had presented his paper on Massinger to the society, as if to set the seal on the high regard in which he held it and to cement the relationship between its activities and those of historians. To underline Gardiner's close association with the society and its methods, it is significant that Gardiner always used Furnivall's preferred spelling of the great dramatist's name: Shakspere. At a time when Gardiner was regularly contributing to the *Athenaeum* on Elizabethan and Stuart topics, the controversy over the 'correct' way to spell that name was raging in its pages. The society's viewpoint was expressed by Alexander Ellis, who argued that 'Shakspere' was the only historically accurate spelling, based on philological analysis and close attention to the pronunciation norms of the years of Elizabeth's reign.[85] Two years later, Furnivall felt the need to defend that position in the pages of the *Academy*, asserting that, as the dramatist signed his own name – as close attention to the manuscripts shows – using the same spelling that he and the society did, 'Shakspere, then, is the right spelling of the poet's name'.[86] By always writing 'Shakspere', Gardiner marked his position in the

82 See chapter 1 above.

83 W. Benzie, *Dr F. J. Furnivall: a Victorian scholar adventurer*, Norman, OK 1983, 183.

84 'Shakspere's England' [review], *Academy* x (30 Sept. 1876), 621–2.

85 A. J. Ellis, 'The pronunciation of Shakespeare's name' [correspondence], *Athenæum* 2338 (17 Aug. 1872), 207.

86 F. J. Furnivall, 'The spelling of Shakspere's name' [correspondence], *Academy* v (24 Jan. 1874), 95.

debate, his methodological approach, and his close association with the work of Furnivall.[87]

However, Gardiner's identification of Wentworth with Coriolanus is anomalous for historicist criticism. Accepting the historical implications of *Coriolanus* has been *de rigueur* for historically-minded Shakespeare critics in recent years as well as during the nineteenth century. Just as Gardiner sought to show that Massinger's characters reflected political actors of the dramatist's own times – seeing representations of Buckingham, Middlesex, the Elector Palatine, James I, Charles I, Henrietta Maria, Weston and the Spanish ambassador in *The bondsman* (1623), *The great duke of Florence* (1627), *Believe as you list* (1631) and *The maid of honour* (1631/2?) – so critics have sought to 'locate' the historical basis of the character of Coriolanus. Identifications have included James I,[88] Essex[89] and Raleigh,[90] and contemporary events such as the Oxfordshire corn-riots are widely accepted as being represented in Shakespeare's unruly mobs. In a parallel exercise, Gardiner saw some evidence for identifying Philip, earl of Montgomery (later the earl of Pembroke and Massinger's patron), with Hamlet, drawing upon Clarendon for support.[91] In comparing Coriolanus with Wentworth, however, Gardiner was discussing a historical actor not contemporary with the writing of the play. Coriolanus helps us, as later historians, through providing a window upon Wentworth's character.

A central theme in Gardiner's discussion of Coriolanus and Wentworth is their shared carrying of an older philosophy into new, more democratic times. Thus, '[t]hey both despise the masses for their incapacity for action, their ignorance, and their unsteadiness. They both have a thorough knowledge of all of the conditions of success, except that which depends upon sympathy with inferior natures'.[92] Indeed, Gardiner tells us, 'Coriolanus shares with Strafford a special dislike of popular control over government', an argument which he supported with words from the play:

[87] It is interesting also to note the close relationship between liberalism and historicist criticism: James Joyce, when parodying the work of Edward Dowden – who was not obviously of the historicist school, but whose work is closely allied to it – and in particular the volume called *Shakspere* that he wrote for J. R. Green's *Literature Primers* series, in his *Ulysses* (1922), has Buck Mulligan say, 'William Shakespeare and company, limited. The people's William. For terms apply: E. Dowden.'

[88] Garnett, *Universal Review* (Apr. 1889), cited in *The New Variorum Shakespeare: The tragedie of Coriolanus*, ed. H. H. Furness, Philadelphia, PA 1928.

[89] P. A. Jorgensen, 'Shakespeare's Coriolanus: Elizabethan soldier', *PMLA* lxiv (1949), 221–35, and *Shakespeare's military world*, Berkeley 1956, ch. vi.

[90] A. Brandl, *Shakespeare*, Dresden 1894; M. W. MacCallum, *Shakespeare's Roman plays and their background*, London 1910.

[91] 'Political element in Massinger'.

[92] 'Wentworth and Coriolanus'. All following references to Gardiner's writings will be from this letter unless otherwise noted.

They choose their magistrate,
And such a one as he, who puts his shall,
His popular shall, against a graver bench
Than ever frowned in Greece! By Jove himself,
It makes the Consuls base; and my soul aches
To know, when two authorities are up,
Neither supreme, how soon confusion
May enter 'twixt the gap of both, and take
The one by the other. (*Coriolanus* III.i.103–11)

According to Gardiner, 'Shakspere's citizens are wretched creatures, and his tribunes are all that the most embittered Royalist would have said of Pym and Hampden in the days of the long Parliament' and as a result, when Coriolanus 'attacks the tribunes they reply as the House of Commons would have done':

Sicinius. What is the city but the people?
Citizen. True,
The people are the city.
Brutus. By the consent of all, we were established
The people's magistrates. (*Cor.* III.i.197–200)

Coriolanus' response reminded Gardiner of Wentworth's speech at York in 1628:

That is the way to lay the city flat;
To bring the roof to the foundation,
And bury all, which yet distinctly ranges,
In heaps and piles of ruin. (*Cor.* III.i.202–5)

Unsurprisingly, the people begin to despise Coriolanus, and, egged on by the tribunes, soon wish to cause violence to him:

Sicinius. He shall be thrown down the Tarpeian rock
With vigorous hands; he hath resisted law,
And therefore law shall scorn him further trial
Than the severity of the public power
Which he so sets at nought.
First Citizen. He shall well know
The noble tribunes are the people's mouths,
And we the hands. (*Cor.* III.i.264–70)

Reflecting on Shakespeare's apparent distaste for mob violence, Gardiner argues that the reader 'almost fancies that Shakspere was in spirit in Westminster Hall at the great trial [of Wentworth in 1641], and that his sympathy was altogether on the side of the accused'. However, he continues, 'Shakspere knows better', for although 'Coriolanus was a grand figure …/His nature is too noble for this world' (*Cor.* III.i.253). The judgement is severe, for '[i]n this world to stand apart from others', as Coriolanus has done,

> is to be either a god or a wild beast … There is nothing left for him but to die by the hands of those he has wronged. Then at last his great qualities can be remembered:
>
> 'Though in this city he
> Hath widowed and unchilded many a one,
> Which to this hour bewail the injury,
> Yet he shall have a noble memory' (*Cor.* V.vi.150–3)

Coriolanus could not be judged correctly by his contemporaries, but, with hindsight, his great qualities could be recognised.

This much of Gardiner's understanding of Coriolanus can be appreciated. The references to Wentworth in the letter are few, as Gardiner presumably left his readers to lay that judgement on Wentworth themselves. Indeed, many, if not most, of his readers of this letter would have been able to carry out such an exercise. However, what strikes the reader of Gardiner's history books is more than just the parallels drawn in this letter, for Gardiner's Wentworth is expanded in the histories into a much more complex creature, but one which still retains – and builds upon – the identification with Coriolanus. The *Academy* letter represents but little of Gardiner's overall conception of Wentworth, and puts forward only a few of the parallels that he drew with Coriolanus.

Gardiner's opening point about Coriolanus and Wentworth concerns their shared non-membership of the 'popular party'. In part, this opposition to democracy was due to Wentworth's view of the inevitable results of such systems: division and decay. In the speech given at York in 1628 which Gardiner discovered in the Tanner manuscripts and brought to the notice of other historians in a short article in the *Academy* in June 1875, and which he printed in almost its entirety over several pages in his *History*, Wentworth spoke of his concern that should popular government have its day, 'we would become all head or all members'.[93] The 'hydra' of democracy worries Coriolanus also, for 'The beast/With many heads butts me away' (*Cor.* IV.i.1–2) and, for the sake of the state, the Patricians must 'at once pluck out/The multitudinous tongue: let them not lick/The sweet which is their poison' (*Cor.* III.i.154–6). A state of individuals, all tasting liberty, would be a dangerous thing indeed.

However, it was, according to Gardiner, not just ideological opposition to the claims of the popular party upon which Wentworth's opposition to democracy was based, but also his unwillingness or inability to present himself to the popular party in order to gain their support. 'With Wentworth', Gardiner believed,

> good government was the sole object in view. Everything else was mere machinery. Conscious of his own powers, he was longing for an opportunity

93 *HoE* vii. 25.

> of exercising them for the good of his fellow-countrymen; but, excepting so far as they could serve his ends, he cared nothing for these constitutional forms which counted for so much in the eyes of other men. The law of election existed, one may suppose him to think if not to say, for the purpose of sending Sir Thomas Wentworth to Parliament. He was himself arrogant and overbearing to all who disputed his will. In private he expressed his utmost contempt for his fellow-members, and it is not likely that he had any higher respect for his constituents. He was an outspoken representative of that large class of politicians who hold that ability is the chief requisite for government, and who look with ill-concealed contempt upon the view which bases government upon the popular will.[94]

In *Coriolanus*, according to Sidney Lee in his Shakespeare entry for the *Dictionary of national biography*, Shakespeare 'shows ironical contempt' for the people, whilst castigating the eponymous hero for his 'unchecked pride of caste'.

As he did not believe in the theory of government through the popular will, Wentworth rarely attended to democracy's trappings. He was '[c]areless of popularity and disdain[ed] the arts by which it is acquired', so 'he would not condescend to explain his intentions even to those whom he most wished to benefit'.[95] He 'pushed on, heedless of friend or foe' and when Laud, his friend and colleague in much of his work, warned of the growing whispering campaign against him, and urged him to find a way to court popularity without giving up on the work to which he had set himself ('Come, come, you have been too rough, something too rough./You must return and mend it', as Menenius counsels Coriolanus (*Cor.* III.ii. 25–6)), Wentworth declined: 'It was not in Wentworth's nature to offer a public defence of his conduct',[96] for to do so would see him 'thus stoop to th'herd' (*Cor.* III.ii.32). Unwilling to court popularity, Wentworth found solace in the simpler pleasures of the military life: 'Once in Ireland he would be free of the trammels of courtiers' and amongst the 'trusted soldiery'[97] just as Coriolanus found comfort only amongst fighting men.

Gardiner argued further that not only did Wentworth scorn the arts of popular politics, he did not actually have the necessary skills to succeed in them. He could not play the necessary rhetorical games, for '[w]hatever his heart conceived his mouth would speak'.[98] Menenius, Coriolanus' closest ally sees the younger man's great failing in almost exactly the same terms: 'His heart's his mouth:/What his breast forges, that his tongue must vent' (*Cor.* III.i.255–6). He is 'ill school'd/In bold language' (*Cor.* III.ii.318–19). Coriolanus' discomfiture with language has been noted by critics of all ages,

94 *HoE* v. 350.
95 *HoE* viii. 36.
96 *HoE* viii.184–5, 190.
97 *HoE* ix 183.
98 *HoE* vi.127.

and indeed it may be said that silence is often as important as speech in *Coriolanus*. Thus, Coriolanus' most eloquent moment is a stage direction ('Holds her by the hand silent' at V.iii.182), and he refuses to show his wounds in the market-place ceremony expected of him – a soldier's silence.[99] One critic has noted that during one of the most important passages in the play (*Cor.* V.iii.92–182) the ostensible hero, despite being present, speaks only four lines out of the ninety, something unthinkable for the hero of any of the great Tragedies, or even of any of the other Histories.[100] Similarly, Wentworth is for long periods surprisingly silent for such a central figure in Gardiner's *History*, and the historian drew attention to that silence on several occasions. After his first election, to the parliament of 1614, he apparently did not join in a single debate,[101] and following the speech at York on which Gardiner rested much of his analysis of the statesman's political theories, he virtually disappears from the life of England. For Gardiner, Wentworth is a man of few words.

Without the necessary verbal skills, Wentworth 'left his actions to speak for themselves, and wondered that they were so often misinterpreted'.[102] Gardiner did not at all wonder at this. Wentworth had made the mistake of believing that 'Action is eloquence' (*Cor.* III.ii.76). For the historian, the statesman

> had too little attractive force to overcome the difficulties in his path. He was too self-reliant, too ready to leave his deeds to speak for themselves, too haughty and arrogant towards adversaries, to conciliate opposition, or even to be regarded by those whose cause he supported with that mingled feeling of reverence and familiarity which marks out the true leaders of mankind. He might come to be looked upon as the embodiment of force. Men might quail before his knitted brow and his clear commanding voice. They would not follow him to the death as Gustavus was followed, or hasten to his succour as the freeholders of Bucks hastened to the succour of Hampden.[103]

As a result,

> Wentworth in his strength and Charles in his weakness were alike lonely amidst their generation. They understood not the voices which sounded on every side; they drew no strength from the earth beneath nor from the heaven over their heads. They set before them the task of making men other than they were. What could come of it but failure, disgrace, and ruin?[104]

99 L. Danson, *Tragic alphabet: Shakespeare's drama of language*, New Haven, CT 1974, 142–62.

100 M. Charney, 'The dramatic use of imagery in Shakespeare's *Coriolanus*', *ELH* xxiii (1956), 191.

101 *HoE* ii. 231.

102 *HoE* viii. 37.

103 *HoE* vii. 137–8.

104 *HoE* vii.138.

Derivations of 'lone' are more commonly found in Coriolanus than in any other of Shakespeare's plays,[105] underlining the pathos of the hero's failings, and figuring the statesman's distance from his fellow Romans.

It is from an appreciation of Wentworth's non-membership of any popular party at any time in his career that Gardiner took his main points for refuting the charge of apostasy of which all previous English historians had found Wentworth guilty.[106] Although the charge had long been made, it gained its greatest currency in Macaulay's vicious attack, in his article for the *Edinburgh Review,* on Hallam's *Constitutional history*. Wentworth was, according to the great Whig historian whose version of the past Gardiner sought to destroy, the 'lost Archangel, the Satan of the Apostasy'. Gardiner naturally considered this judgement another example of Macaulay's party-spirit and want of decorum, and, as ever, his rebuttal was couched in terms of the coming, scientific redrawing of historiographical debate that would create a new synthesis free of such violent language: 'The real work which is being done by so many hands will, if we mistake not, be chiefly found in the more charitable view which we are enabled to take of the actors on the stage … There will be fewer gibbetings in history; perhaps, too, fewer canonizations.'[107] In the debate, the voice of John Forster is also to be heard: Gardiner often referred to him alongside Macaulay as the more famous historian's fellow subverter of historical truth for ideological ends. On this occasion, however, Forster's work actually shows a way forward, as he 'was the first writer to let light in upon the darkness' cast by Macaulay, although in the final analysis his 'view of Wentworth's conduct appears to us almost, if not quite, as unsatisfactory as Macaulay's'. Its shortcomings were excused in part by Gardiner as being due to the lack of materials which had since become available.[108] These had, according to Gardiner, not so much given historians new information regarding Wentworth's actions, as allowed them to understand more of his principles. Wentworth was defended from the charge of apostasy by Gardiner, not by arguing that his actions were any different from those previously described, but by showing that Wentworth was never of the popular party in the first place:

> After what has now been said, there will probably be no further attempt to charge Wentworth with apostatising from the popular party. The notion that he had ever been united with Coke and Eliot, either by conviction, as Lord Macaulay thought, or by passion, as Mr. Forster thought, turns out to be a pure delusion.[109]

105 H. Levin, *Shakespeare and the revolution of the times*, New York, NY 1976, 196.

106 This point is discussed both in the *History* and (in greater detail) in a separate journal article dedicated to the question: *HoE* vi. 335–6; 'Alleged apostacy', 434–52.

107 'Alleged apostacy', 434.

108 Ibid. 435–6.

109 Ibid. 451.

Wentworth was consistent in his principles, although it was to lead to his destruction; again, the parallels with Coriolanus are striking.

The characters and principles of Wentworth and Coriolanus were their strengths and their downfalls according to the respective narrators of their lives. Unsurprisingly, then, Gardiner's narration of Wentworth's life in the *History* shares much with the action of the play. This can be seen in both the wider narrative form used to tell the lives of each hero, and in the detailed events of each story. With regard to the first point the apparent double-treachery of Wentworth – first against the popular party early in his career in the judgement of historians and, second, against the nation later in his career in the judgement of his contemporaries – seems to follow the strange pattern delineated by Shakespeare that prevents a genuine sense of tragedy developing in the play.[110] There, in addition to the treachery which is his final downfall, Coriolanus is found guilty of treachery against Rome earlier in the play. This double downfall is the result of a 'double-peaked' narrative of military success, first over the Volscians, then over the Romans, after each of which Coriolanus falls under the accusation of treachery. Similarly, Wentworth's alleged treacheries follow, first his attaining the leadership of the Commons and, second, the role of leading advisor to the king. Gardiner gives the story of Wentworth the same double-peaked shape used by Shakespeare in *Coriolanus*.

However, just as Gardiner questioned the first charge of apostasy for Wentworth, so Shakespeare may be seen as questioning the judgement of the Romans on Coriolanus. In fact, for both of these two statesmen, their final downfall comes at the end of an inexorable move to a tragic end, with the apparent first peak actually allowing the reader to understand the consistency of purpose and principle displayed by both of them. Thus, the narratives offered by Shakespeare and Gardiner share a common narratorial convenience that acts against the apparent and traditionally-recognised forms of the passing of their heroes' careers.

Gardiner took an unusual view of how the breach between Wentworth and the nation occurred. For him, Wentworth's consistency of principle and action could only mean that it was the nation that had broken with him, or rather, what he represented. His great opposition to the war with Spain was thus understood by Gardiner as the statesman's holding on to the great elements of England, as the nation – king and people – committed treachery against the Elizabethan state-settlement: 'In 1624 the tide of affairs seemed to have stranded him for ever. To his mind the king and the nation appeared to have gone mad together. What side was he to choose when all England rushed with one consent into war with Spain?'[111] In this light, the king's 'banishment' of the refusers is actually the nation's rush away from

110 Wheeler, 'Introduction', pp. xvi–xvii.
111 *HoE* vi. 127.

the 'passive' Wentworth.[112] In his refusal to move while being mindful of the movement of the nation, Wentworth offers the challenge, 'I banish you' (*Cor.* III.iii.123).

On the one occasion that Wentworth tried to use the constitutional forms that he had so little respect for, the attempt failed dramatically and caused more harm than good. Rather than use his arbitrary will to break the power of the earl of St Albans and Clanrickard in what Wentworth considered the personal fiefdom that he controlled in southern Ireland, the new Lord Deputy attempted to use the courts to obtain an injunction against him backed by a Galway jury. However, much to Wentworth's chagrin, the jury found in the earl's favour. He immediately had the jury called to account, the sheriff fined £1,000 and the troops called in to enforce the judgement that he had wanted but had failed to obtain:

> The result was far worse than if he had interfered authoritatively with the strong hand of power. By consulting the jury and refusing to be bound by its verdict, he sowed broadcast the seeds of distrust and disaffection. He had bowed in semblance before the majesty of the law, only to turn upon it in anger when it ceased to do his pleasure. The King's authority would be associated more than ever in the eyes of Irishmen with unintelligible, incalculable violence.[113]

This mirrors the lowest moment for Coriolanus, the point at which his fall becomes inevitable. Act III, scene ii tells of the events that follow on from his being convinced by his mother to appear before the citizens and follow the constitutional necessities that would confirm him in his position. The crowd turns against him, and his angry reaction destroys any chance of a peaceful settlement between him and the people. From that point on, the people's distrust of him builds until they have only hate in their hearts and vengeance in mind:

> Being once chaf'd, he cannot
> Be rein'd again to temperance; then he speaks
> What's in his heart, and that is there which looks
> With us to break his neck. (*Cor.* III.iii.27–30.)

As the instance of the Galway judgement shows, when Wentworth failed to obtain what he wanted, in his anger he resorted to threats and to violence, which merely increased the anger against him. Outside his control, the plot moves inexorably against him.

The final, inevitable result of Wentworth's failure to procure support was his impeachment in 1641. The fear that had entered Englishmen's minds was that he was about to bring a foreign army on to English soil in order to

112 *HoE* vi. 158.
113 *HoE* viii. 63.

usurp the nation against which he had already been treacherous,[114] just as Coriolanus brought a foreign army to the gates of a Rome that had banished him. Finally, however, both were destroyed as they knowingly laid down their lives to protect another: in Coriolanus' case his mother; and in Wentworth's case the king, figured as the father of the state in the Elizabethan polity. They entered the lair of their opponents, and played the part of tragic hero: 'With a brave heart, though against his own judgment, the doomed statesman set out from that loved home at Wentworth Woodhouse, which he was never to see again.'[115] Coriolanus, too, turned back from the gates of Rome to his inevitable doom at the hands of the Volscians.

At the end, however, Wentworth's nobility is transparent, while still displaying all his main character points that were at the same time both his strengths and his weaknesses. According to Gardiner, '[n]ever had he seemed more truly great than when he appeared at the bar, like some fierce but noble animal at bay, to combat the united attacks of his accusers, in his own unaided strength'. Similarly,

> *Enter* CORIOLANUS *marching with drum and colours* …
> (*Cor.* V.vi.70 s.d.)

At the bar, Wentworth's behaviour is both haughty and familiar:

> The most consummate actor could not have borne himself better. Strafford was no actor. He spoke out of the fulness of his heart, out of his consciousness of his own integrity, out of his incapacity to understand any serious view of the relations between a Government and a nation other than that upon which he had acted.[116]

The result is judgement, and death, at the hands of the citizens.

At the last, Wentworth 'stands revealed [as] the high-minded, masterful statesman, erring gravely through defect of temper and knowledge'[117] and worthy of the 'noble memory' that Gardiner accords him. As Coriolanus had not had anyone to describe him as 'the noblest Roman of them all', as Antony had done for an earlier Roman hero of Shakespeare's,[118] and would have to rely on posterity, so Gardiner had felt moved to do the same for Wentworth.

Given the close relationship in narrative form between the lives told of Wentworth and Coriolanus by Gardiner and Shakespeare, a close correspondence in their language might also be expected. Shakespeare and Wentworth, as late Elizabethan/early Stuart figures, would have shared much in

114 *HoE* ix. 126–7.
115 *HoE* ix. 221.
116 *HoE* ix. 305.
117 *HoE* ix. 229.
118 *Julius Caesar* V.v. 68.

their understandings of the politics of the state. In particular, the favoured metaphors of the political rhetoric of their time would have been familiar to both. They both expressed their concern at the hydra of the democratic polity, a metaphor so common that Christopher Hill has been able to devote an entire chapter of one of his books to its expression in Renaissance literature.[119] However, the carnal realisation of the modern state was usually expressed in the late sixteenth and early seventeenth centuries in the metaphor of the 'body politic', which appears throughout Shakespeare's work.[120] Its most famous appearance is, however, in *Coriolanus*, when Menenius attempts to explain to the mob, 'the great toe', the Roman polity in terms of belly, head, limbs and organs (*Cor.* I.i.95–154). The speech is taken from the immediate literary source of Shakespeare's tale, North's translation of Plutarch's *Lives*, and indeed the metaphor has a long history and solid classical origins, just as the 'beast with many heads' can be traced back to Horace's 'belua multorum capitum'. Historicist critics have pointed out that the use of such metaphors would have underlined the contemporaneity of Shakespeare's political message for his audience and made it intelligible. Its contemporaneous nature is shown in Wentworth's speech at York, replete as it is with carnal imagery, in which ideas are born and institutions are human. Bodily metaphors for the polity are central to both Shakespeare and Wentworth.

These tropes however, are of a kind: they are metonymic and synecdochic. This is unusual for Shakespeare: all of his other plays rely more on metaphor and simile, although all four figural systems are present to some degree in each of the plays. Metonymy and synecdoche are intimately related, as they both refer to the linguistic relationship of parts and wholes. For this reason, whereas metaphor and simile are figures of completeness and of coming together, metonymy and synecdoche are 'figures of fragmentation and usurpation'[121] or even 'of dismemberment'.[122] Their importance for Coriolanus and Wentworth is immediately obvious, for while the former seeks always to maintain his personal indissoluble wholeness, the latter spends his career attempting to protect the indissoluble Elizabethan body-politic. Coriolanus, of course, fails drastically as he is ripped apart by the Volscian crowd at the end of the play. Wentworth is not dismembered by the crowd that lined the route to watch him to the place of execution, although, when 'the sad procession reached the Tower gates, Balfour advised him to take a coach, lest the people should tear him to pieces': he refused, Gardiner reported, with the words, 'I care not how I die, whether by the hand of the executioner

119 'The many-headed monster': C. Hill, *Change and continuity in seventeenth-century England*, London 1974.

120 Phillips, 'Introduction', 4–7.

121 Danson, *Tragic alphabet*, 124.

122 Z. Jagendorf, '*Coriolanus*: body politic and private parts', *Shakespeare Quarterly* xli (1990), 455–69.

or the madness and fury of the people.'[123] The image offered is akin to that of Coriolanus, refusing to be cowed by the crowd, calling out 'Cut me to pieces' (*Cor.* V.vi.111). Wentworth is not torn to pieces by the crowd, but the method of execution, by axe, sees him cut into two pieces. The sense of fragmentation contained in the figures of metonymy and synecdoche are realised in the bodies of two men whose rhetoric rests upon those figures, but who desired wholeness.

Coriolanus and Wentworth are themselves, however, figures for the authors of the narratives of their lives. As the Roman represents Rome, and his dismemberment the pitting of Roman against Roman, as prefigured in the very opening of the play as the mob runs riot, so Wentworth is for Gardiner the Elizabethan state. And, as the political rhetoric of the early Stuart period finds a place in the work of Gardiner in reported speech, so its tropes are imported into Gardiner's understanding of that period. Wentworth's death, the cleaving of his body, takes place in 1641: Gardiner's *History of the Great Civil War*, his narrative of the years of national fragmentation which saw Englishman pitted against Englishman, starts its story in 1642. As the literal body is broken, so too is that which Wentworth embodies – the Elizabethan state.[124]

If Shakespeare prefigured Wentworth in his writing, what of the figuring of the statesman by Gardiner's contemporary, Robert Browning? In 1836 Browning began to write a play based on the final days of Wentworth which, under the title *Strafford: an historical tragedy*, was performed for the first time in the following year. It is a much-maligned play which even its author considered weak. However, in 1884 a new edition was published by George Bell & Sons, edited by Emily Hickey, with an introductory essay written by Gardiner. In this essay the historian sought to deal with a specific issue: 'how far the author has allowed himself to be bound by his knowledge of the actual course of events, and whether, if he has departed from it, it is possible to trace any principle in the variance'.[125] In answering that question, Gardiner provided a detailed analysis in which Browning's errors are excused and his principles delineated. The result, for Gardiner, is a nuanced appreciation of Wentworth that offers substantial truths about that man. The historian used the dramatist to help him figure the statesman.

Gardiner noted that when 'Mr. Browning wrote "Strafford," Mr. Forster's life of that statesman had just been published. There was an intimate friendship between the poet and the biographer, and Mr. Browning thus found the materials which he needed brought easily within his reach.' Nevertheless, Forster's biography was weak:

123 *HoE* ix. 370.

124 It should be remembered, however, that a similar claim had been made by Gardiner on Bacon's death – that the state settlement died with the man. See chapter 4 above.

125 'Introduction' to R. Browning, *Strafford: an historical tragedy*, ed. E.H. Hickey, London 1884, p. ix.

> Partly from want of sympathy with statesmen of Strafford's type, and partly from the lack of material which has since come to light, Mr. Forster did not succeed in constructing [an adequate] biography. ... He enabled us to see the zeal and energy of his hero, and he showed that the result was the establishment of a tyranny. To exhibit Strafford believing that he was establishing a reign of justice, and that he was even defending the English constitution against its assailants, was beyond his range.[126]

Forster was not capable of producing a fair picture of Wentworth that went beyond what happened to the mind and character of the statesman. The dramatist could do this: 'Is it not too hazardous a conjecture to suppose that Mr. Browning was impelled to write "Strafford," not merely by his admiration for the man, but also from some desire to give a portraiture of him which would have the completeness of an imaginative conception?'[127] This complete portrait is one in which character is adequately delineated. Gardiner believed that Browning's account could provide something which Forster's could not – a fair representation of the complex historical actor, Wentworth.

However, Gardiner's conception of how that can be done is extremely surprising coming from the pen of a scientific, truth-seeking historian. First, the requirement to be accurate with regard to real events, to 'what actually happened', is mere hubris:

> We may be sure ... that it was not by accident that Mr. Browning in writing this play, decisively abandoned all attempt to be historically accurate ... [and] So completely does the drama proceed irrespectively of historical truth, that the critic may dispense with the thankless task of pointing out discrepancies, where the writer plainly meant that there should be discrepancies. He will be better employed in asking what ends those discrepancies were intended to serve, and whether the neglect of truth of fact has resulted in the higher truth of character.[128]

Browning had, in fact, attained this 'higher truth'. 'Every time that I read the play', claimed Gardiner, 'I feel more certain that Mr. Browning has seized the real Strafford, the man of critical brain, of rapid decision, and tender heart, who strove for the good of his nation without sympathy for the generation in which he lived.'[129] Gardiner denied the necessity of the *res gestae*, explained that one genre can offer something 'higher' in its representation of the past than historiography, and showed that the play has correctly found the 'truth' of Wentworth which he had imperfectly presented in his *History*.

However, it is not too clear from this essay whether Gardiner believed that Browning's success was due to the author (compared to Forster) or the

126 Ibid. p. x.
127 Ibid. pp. x–xi.
128 Ibid. pp. xi–xii.
129 Ibid. p. xiii.

genre (compared to a biography). To clarify this matter, it is necessary to turn to the tangled and strange history of the writing of Forster's *Life of Strafford*. In 1890 F. J. Furnivall published an article in the *Pall Mall Gazette* which cast doubt upon the identity of Forster as the author of the *Life*.[130] The 'actual' biographer, Furnivall tells us, was gravely ill as he turned to writing the *Life* which was intended to follow, and act as counterpoint to, his recently-completed *Life of Eliot* (1836). Unable to proceed, he entered into an agreement with his then relatively-unknown friend Robert Browning whereby the latter would use the former's material to write up the book, which would retain Forster's name on the title-page. The biography was completed on these lines and duly published. Browning was the actual author of Forster's *Life*.

This fact was duly acknowledged in an edition of *Browning's prose life of Strafford*, edited by Gardiner's student C. H. Firth, and published in 1892 by the Browning Society, another literary society inspired by Furnivall and co-founded with Emily Hickey – the editor of the 1884 edition of the play. Furnivall indeed had a working relationship with Browning, who was honorary president of the New Shakspere Society. However, a problem arises for the student of Gardiner: the realisation that the authors of the *Life* and *Strafford* are the same man raises questions about his contrasting the two in his essay of 1884. On the face of it, he must have been wrong to say that one of these literary productions was inaccurate due to 'want of sympathy' on the part of its author, while the other gave a more sympathetic portrait out of 'admiration for [Wentworth]', particularly as they were written in the same year. Gardiner's analysis of the differences between the biography and the play, if based on authorial intent and ability, would seem to be misguided.

However, Gardiner's analysis was not based on authorial distinction. In Furnivall's forewords to the 1892 edition, in which he used his idiosyncratic 'historical' spellings, he explains that he has discussed the matter with Gardiner:

> Prof. S. R. Gardiner one day in the British Museum renewd our talk of some years before about this Life … When I first spoke to [Gardiner] about the Life of Strafford, I found that he knew Browning's authorship of almost all of it, and was convinst of the fact from his own knowledge of Forster's work and of history. 'It is not a historian's conception of the character, but a poet's. I am certain that it's not Forster's.' 'Yes, it makes mistakes in facts and dates, but, it has got the man – in the main.' Prof. Gardiner had also seen a letter of Browning's – now no longer extant, he believes – in which Browning claimd his part of the *Life of Strafford*, as he also did in talk with the Professor in like words to those he used to me.[131]

[130] *PMG*, 12 Apr. 1890, 3.

[131] F. J. Furnivall, 'Forewords', in *Robert Browning's prose life of Strafford*, ed. C. H. Firth, London 1892, pp. vii–viii.

So, Gardiner knew of Browning's authorship of the *Life*, although Furnivall gives no clues as to whether he had known when he wrote his introduction to the 1884 edition of the play. However the letter, apparently, was still extant in 1892, for it – or, perhaps, another letter similar to it – was reprinted in 1950. In it, Browning told Emily Hickey, 'tell Professor Gardiner by all means [of the rightful authorship] – with the same entreaty for a discretion in the use of the fact'.[132] Gardiner was discreet – Furnivall states that it is one of the reasons why the great historian of the Stuart period would not write the introduction to the *Prose life*, and handed the task over to Firth,[133] although Furnivall says that it was the historian who had 'urged' him 'to make the fact of Browning's authorship public'.[134] When he wrote his essay comparing the *Life* and *Strafford* in 1884, Gardiner was well aware they were written by the same person.

With this information in hand, that essay, and its author's arguments, can be better understood. Thus, when Gardiner asserts that in 'a passage which rises far above Mr. Forster's ordinary level, the true theory of the identity of Strafford's life is set forth', we can know that he was aware the words to which he was referring were written by one of the great Victorian poets. More important, we can recognise that the 'imaginative conception' that can allow Browning to offer the 'truth' of Wentworth – 'the higher truth of character' – does not refer to Browning's imaginative faculties, but to that truth's realisation in imaginative literature itself. Little wonder then, that the play which denied the charge of apostasy (set forth by 'Vane and others' thus: 'Wentworth? Apostate! Judas! Double-dyed/A Traitor!'[135]), just as Shakespeare's play had for Coriolanus and Gardiner's *History* had for Wentworth, was allowed to have the final word in the historian's account of the statesman:

> Pym … Even thus, I love him now:
> And look for my chief portion in that world
> Where great hearts led astray are turned again,
> (Soon it may be, and, certes, will be soon:
> My mission over, I shall not live long,) –
> Ay, here I know I talk – I dare and must,
> Of England, and her great reward, as all
> I look for there; but in my inmost heart,
> Believe, I think of stealing quite away
> To walk once more with Wentworth – my youth's friend
> Purged from all error, gloriously renewed,
> And Eliot shall not blame us.[136]

132 *New letters of Robert Browning*, ed. C. W. de Vane and K. L. Knickerbocker, New Haven, CT 1950, 76.
133 Furnivall, 'Forewords', p. xi.
134 *PMG*, 12 Apr. 1890, 3.
135 *Strafford* I. i.190–1.
136 Ibid. V. ii.289–300, cited in *HoE* xi. 371–2.

Shakespeare's *Coriolanus*, Browning's *Strafford* and Gardiner's *History* shared narrative structure, tropes, conceptions of historical character and the relation of action and actor.

In the introductory essay which Philip Edwards provided for *The maid of honour* in his and Colin Gibson's joint edition of Massinger's works, he complains about 'the vagueness of the parallels' which may be drawn – and which he credits Gardiner with drawing – between the play and historical events:

> The general situation of a king and a favourite concerned in the matter of intervention in a foreign war is not easily attached to a single historical episode. The impartiality with which Massinger handles the motives and responses of the personalities, the expediency of the proposals, and the principles involved, make the idea that he was conducting political propaganda an absurdity.[137]

However, what Gardiner had said was that '"The Maid of Honour" may be taken as a protest against this mode of regarding the world', that is, the base courtly morality which desired peace and good commerce so as to be free to engage in 'self-indulgence', rather than as an honourable policy which sought 'fruitful works', as represented, implicitly, by Shakespeare – representing the Elizabethan state – and Milton, representing a puritan, anti-courtly ethos.[138] Rather than seeing the *Maid of honour* as a polemic against particular individuals regarding specific events or 'a single historical episode', Gardiner called for a cultural reading of Massinger, that is, a reading which showed him as a critic of the culture of the court. Edwards sees Massinger's focus on 'motives and responses of the personalities ... and the principles involved', and the non-polemical nature of his comments as evidence against Gardiner. However, as can be discerned through the appreciation of the uses to which he put drama, it should be recognised that Gardiner was interested in using the play because of Massinger's focus on motives, responses and principles, and his way of presenting them, for they are the elements which provide access to the characters of the members of Charles's court. *Maid of honour* was, for Gardiner, not a simple political polemic produced on behalf of the Herberts, but rather one contemporary's response to the culture of the Caroline court.

According to Colin Gibson, 'S. R. Gardiner found in [Massinger's] *Believe As You List* a transparent commentary on the fortunes of Frederick, the dispossessed elector palatine and king of Bohemia ... [but] There are too

137 P. Edwards, 'The maid of honour: introduction', in *Plays and poems of Philip Massinger*, i. 105–6.

138 'Political element in Massinger', 329–31. Shakespeare was appealed to through the quotation of lines from *Measure for measure*, and Milton through the use of *Comus*.

many discrepancies for [it] to be read as a sustained political allegory.'[139] However, Gardiner did not need exact historical parallels, as he makes clear with the 'not exact' parallels of the lives of Coriolanus, Brutus and Sicinius with those of Wentworth, Pym and Hampden, nor, indeed, did he require anything approaching an accurate account of 'what really happened', as he made clear in his discussion of Browning's *Strafford*. Instead, he wanted an accurate representation of the character of people and events. Indeed, the parallels he drew between *Believe as you list* and the nature of the Caroline court and its members were between the character of Philexenus and that of Weston, the king's Lord Treasurer (his 'materialism, his utter contempt for the ideal'),[140] between the character of Prusias and that of Charles ('the very heart of the man who was to deliver Strafford up to the block'),[141] and between the character of Flaminius' political theories and the prevalent theories at court (presenting 'Flaminius' message … in that low material form which was so familiar to Charles's courtiers').[142] *Believe as you list* offers the historian an account, not of events, but of characters.

Contrary to Gibson's characterisation of Gardiner's view, the historian did not see *Believe as you list* as a 'transparent commentary' on political events, but as a critical account of the characters of individuals at court, and the nature of the political culture within which the court operated. Furthermore, Massinger's plays were not, finally, to be seen as direct interventions in political debate, but rather as imaginative texts, as refigurations, akin to Browning's refiguration of the events surrounding Wentworth's death. And, as with the case of both *Coriolanus* and *Strafford*, Gardiner's use of Massinger's plays to illustrate the points he was making about character was not reserved solely for their discussion outside of his histories, for they were incorporated into the *History*.[143] Gardiner used drama, in his historiography, to throw light upon the characters of individuals and the nature of events.

Gardiner's assertion of the epistemological value of drama is detailed in exposition, and is reminiscent of the arguments put forward by such writers as Schiller and his friend Wilhelm von Humboldt. The latter had put forward a theory of the political life in his *The limits of the state* (1793), in which he stressed the need to protect the creative elements of life. Two years later, in his *On the aesthetic education of man, in a series of letters* (1795), Schiller went further, arguing that an adequate understanding of social and political man could only be attained with an appreciation of his cultural and aesthetic aspirations. Indeed, it is essential both to promote the aesthetic life of man and to seek to understand politics and society – and political

139 C. Gibson, 'Believe as you list: introduction', in *Plays and poems of Philip Massinger*, iii. 329.

140 'Political element in Massinger', 323.

141 Ibid. 325.

142 Ibid. 324.

143 *HoE* vii. 201–4.

and social actors – by aesthetic means. It is to this practice that Schiller appeals as he assures readers of his *Wallenstein* cycle that his play will offer a fairer representation of his hero's character than any historian has been able to – or can – attain.[144] Gardiner understood this sentiment better than any other historian, for this is his 'higher truth of character', although these sentiments were far from rare in literary circles, for they had passed from German Idealism into British Romantic theory, making their indelible mark upon nineteenth-century British culture.

Gardiner's writings on, and use of, drama in his work and elsewhere show that, in direct contradiction of the image of him as a dry empiricist without any concern for the aesthetics of representation, he fully valued the contribution which imaginative literature could make to understandings of the past. Whatever the source of Gardiner's willingness to use drama as historiography, the image of the research-oriented 'dryasdust' can be dismissed. Gardiner cared about literary representation, and it is time to read him again with new eyes.

144 See chapter 2 above.

Conclusion

> 'Gardiner the antiquarian whose obsession for research crowds out the artistic sensibility exists principally in the imaginations of those admirers too respectful of his eighteen-volume opus to read it.'[1]

Indeed, it may also be said to exist only in the imaginations of those detractors too disrespectful of his work to read it. And, of course, both admirers and detractors, fuelled by their failure to read Gardiner, imagine that his work can be characterised in simple terms – that is, according to the life of the writer.

This book has sought to provide a new way to understand the work of Samuel Rawson Gardiner. Traditional ('contextualist') approaches to historiography have sought to 'discover' in a historian's writings the ideological preoccupations of his or her political, religious or institutional lives. The historian's writings have been ignored in favour of biographical material. Thus, Gardiner has been viewed as the Liberal injecting Gladstonian principles into his analysis of the early Stuart, Civil War, Commonwealth and Protectorate periods,[2] or the ex-Irvingite anglican whose religious sensibilities allowed him to take a unique perspective on the protestant/catholic battles of early modernity,[3] or the scientific historian working in the shadow of the professionalisation and disciplinisation models then currently in vogue in English universities.[4] Such accounts, however, rarely stand up to close scrutiny. For instance, Gardiner's support for Irish home rule predates the commitment to it of Gladstone and the Liberal party; his approach to the different religious parties of the seventeenth century can be ascribed to other influences than his own confessional choices; and his historical work and activities display a life that is a long way from the classic model of the late nineteenth-century 'disciplined' historian. However, an overly 'textualist' approach born of the turn to critical theory evident in much historiographical analysis of recent decades has an equally problematic approach to history-writing, seeking as it does the occlusion of the historian as an acting agent in his or her own writing, and the counter-intuitive (certainly to a historian) failure to recognise the role of context in the production of discourse of all kinds. Context is important, but historiography has all too

1 Fahey, 'Gardiner as dramatist', 351.
2 For the most trenchant variant on this analysis see Adamson, 'Eminent Victorians'.
3 This is most clearly set out in Lang, *Victorians*.
4 This is the perspective assumed in Jann, *Art and science*.

often been reduced to a discourse reflective of a context or contexts privileged by its students.

By treating historiography in general as one of a number of related discourses, none of which is privileged as the primary constitutive discourse, and none of which is rejected as irrelevant to historical literature, it is possible to move beyond the problems of the text/context relationship. In this book, Gardiner's writings have been mined for references to adjacent discourses which can then be discussed in terms of their potential relationship to his published work. In this way, it has been possible to suggest new understandings of what constituted both Gardiner's approach to the historical process and his version of the events of his chosen period.

Gardiner's principal intellectual influences are to be found in German philosophy. This element was not that of a Rankean empiricism, but of an earlier Idealist strain of thought. Recognising this helps to explain the otherwise perplexing opinions that he held on seventeenth-century actors such as Laud, Bacon and Wentworth. It also suggests a source for his sophisticated appreciation of the writing of history, and the ways in which the past can be represented on the page. And, although he was assuredly not the consummate stylist, he was a far more interesting writer than has been assumed by many, particularly those who have relied either on the opinions of historians of the Stuart period, uncomprehending of nineteenth-century thought, or of those of ostensible students of historiography such as Kenyon and Jann who do not appear to have actually read him.

This book, then, concludes with two appeals. First, Gardiner needs to be read with fresh eyes and a clear mind. The reductive methods of the past have led to a reductive vision of his work. This book, it is to be hoped, has opened up new ways to look at Gardiner's work. Nevertheless, it cannot be complete. The subject of the fifth chapter, for instance, is a case study betraying a particular interest; there are a number of other subjects which could be drawn upon in a similar way. A detailed analysis of Gardiner's language – he shows interesting uses of agency deletion, for instance – or of his commentary on some of the more esoteric theological treatises of the time would be valuable. Likewise, there are other seventeenth-century figures about whom Gardiner had much to say – his dramatic personae stretches beyond James, Charles, Cromwell, Laud, Wentworth and Bacon. Moreover, given the material available, a study solely on Gardiner's writings on Cromwell could be attempted. There is also a strong case to be made for leaving aside analysis of his great *History*, volumes of which struggled to sell more than a hundered copies a year, and instead seek out his arguably more influential texts, the school and university extension class histories which sold in their thousands, even tens of thousands, many of which stayed in print well into the twentieth century. Thus, new studies of Gardiner's work are to be welcomed, albeit ones which recognise the need to move beyond traditional, simplistic contextualist approaches.

A second plea is to be made for other Victorian historians. Gardiner is not the only historian to have been calumnied by the contextualist approach, misunderstood by historians not comfortable with the Victorian intellectual milieu, or subject to comment by those who have not bothered to read him. Acton, Creighton (who at least has received recent attention and reassessment from Michael Bentley), Freeman, Froude, Green, Seeley and so many others – the list of extremely interesting historians contemporary with Gardiner who are ready for reinterpretation is lengthy. There is an earlier generation, too – not just the group around Arnold and Milman, but also the likes of Stubbs. Men who were young when Gardiner was writing – not least among whom is Firth, but also Maitland, Pollard and Tout – also offer themselves as fit subjects of study. Historiography is not mere disciplinary navel-gazing, but a vital part of the discipline. If historians cannot study the history of History, what can they do? Crucially, however, that study needs to be carried out in a properly historicist fashion. Historiography needs to be understood as an intellectual discourse worthy of study in its own right, with its own texts and contexts, and in relationship with other intellectual texts and contexts. And, most important, that study must start with a currently unfashionable commitment to close reading.

APPENDIX

The Published Writings of Samuel Rawson Gardiner

In 1903 the Royal Historical Society published *A bibliography of the historical works of Dr. Creighton … Dr. Stubbs … Dr S. R. Gardiner and the late Lord Acton*, edited by W. A. Shaw. The section on Gardiner contains a number of errors and, more important, is incomplete. Its 309 entries have been augmented here with a further 140 items discovered in the course of the compilation of this new bibliography. It is divided into journal contributions, books, contributions to multi-authored works, and other publications; each is arranged chronologically within its subdivisions. Needless to say, further items are undoubtedly to be found, especially as further research on journals with anonymous contributors continues. Furthermore, other, more ephemeral pieces – such as newspaper correspondences – are likely to turn up. The author will be most grateful to hear from any readers who can augment this bibliography.

Journal contributions

Contributions to the *Academy*

[journal title omitted from review titles]

'Ritter's History of the German Union. [*Geschichte der deutschen Union von den Vorbereitungen des Bundes bis zum Tode Kaiser Rudolfs II. (1598–1612). Von Moritz Ritter*]' [review], iv (15 Oct. 1873), 392–3

'*Religion and allegiance; two sermons preached before the king*. By Roger Mainwaring' [review], v (3 Jan. 1874), 4–5

'Oliver Cromwell's first parliamentary speech' [correspondence], v (17 Jan. 1874), 65

[untitled notice – reply to correspondence from James Collier published in same issue concerning earlier review in the *Academy* of Spencer's *Descriptive sociology*], v (24 Jan. 1874), 93–4

'*The life of Milton; narrated in connexion with the political, ecclesiastical, and literary history of his time*. By David Masson, M.A., LL.D. Vols. I.–III.' [review], v (31 Jan. 1874), 111–13

[untitled reply to James Collier's correspondence in same issue concerning notice of 24 Jan.], v (7 Feb. 1874), 146

'*Life and death of John of Barneveld, Advocate of Holland: with a view of the primary causes and movements of the Thirty Years' War*. By John Lothrop Motley, D.C.L., LL.D' [review, 'first notice'], v (14 Feb. 1874), 161–3

'*Life and death of John of Barneveld, Advocate of Holland; with a view of the primary causes and movements of the Thirty Years' War*. By John Lothrop Motley, D.C.L., LL.D' [review, 'second notice'], v (21 Feb. 1874), 192–4

'*Biographical and critical essays*. Third series. By A Hayward, Esq., Q.C.' [review], v (7 Mar. 1874), 250–1

'Date of privy councillorship of Lord Wentworth' [notice], v (2 May 1874), 489

'An unpublished memoir by Richelieu' [notice], v (23 May 1874), 563–5

'*Historical courses for schools*. Edited by E.A. Freeman, D.C.L. 1. *General sketch of history*. By the Editor. 2. *History of England*. By Edith Thompson. 3. *History of Scotland*. By Margaret Macarthur. 4. *History of Italy*. By John Hunt. 5. *History of Germany*. By James Sime, M.A.' [review], vi (25 July 1874), 93–4

'*The history of France from the earliest times to the year* 1789. Related for the rising generation by M. Guizot. Translated by Robert Black, M.A. Vols. I.–III.' [review], vi (22 Aug. 1874), 197–8

'*The letters and the life of Francis Bacon*. By James Spedding. Vol. VII.' [review], vi (10 Oct. 1874), 393–4

'A *short history of the English people*. By J. R. Green, M.A.' [review], vi (5 Dec. 1874), 601–2

'*The Paston letters*. Edited by James Gairdner. Vol. II.' [review], vii (23 Jan. 1875), 81–2

'A *history of England, principally in the seventeenth century*. By Leopold von Ranke. In six volumes' [review], vii (20 Mar. 1875), 285–6

'George Herbert's presentation to Bemerton' [notice], vii (3 Apr. 1875), 349

'*Jules Michelet*. Par Gabriel Monod' [review], vii (17 Apr. 1875), 395–6

'George Herbert at Cambridge' [notice], vii (24 Apr. 1875), 425

'An unpublished speech of Lord Wentworth' [notice], vii (5 June 1875), 581–3

'On Wentworth's unpublished speech' [correspondence], vii (12 June 1875), 610–11

'*Calendar of the state papers relating to Ireland, 1608–1610*. Edited by the Rev. C.W. Russell, D.D., and J. P. Prendergast, Esq. Rolls Series' [review], vii (26 June 1875), 654–5

'*Italian Alps: sketches in the mountains of Ticino, Lombardy, the Trentino, and Venetia*. By Douglas W. Freshfield. *Beauty-spots of the continent*. By H. Baden Pritchard' [review], viii (10 July 1875), 29–30

'*L'Histoire de France*. Par M. Guizot. Tome IV.' [review], viii (28 Aug. 1875), 214

'The late Dean Hook' [obituary], viii (30 Oct. 1875), 453–4

'Hook's lives of Laud and Juxon. *Lives of the archbishops of Canterbury*. By W. F. Hook, D.D. Vol. XI.' [review], viii (6 Nov. 1875), 467–8

'Gleanings from the Venetian archives (1628–1637)' [notice], viii (20 Nov. 1875), 527–8

'Gleanings from the Venetian archives (1628–1637). (*Concluded from page* 528)' [notice], viii (27 Nov. 1875), 553–4

'Mr. Green and Mr. Rowley' [correspondence], viii (11 Dec. 1875), 604–5

'*The autobiography of Mrs. Alice Thornton*. [Edited by C. Jackson]' [review], ix (1 Jan. 1876), 4–5

'Earl Stanhope' [obituary], ix (1 Jan. 1876), 9–10

'Mr. John Forster' [obituary], ix (5 Feb. 1876), 122

'*Tyrol and the Tyrolese: the people and their land in their social, sporting, and mountaineering aspects*. By W.A. Baillie Grohman' [review], ix (5 Feb. 1876), 117–18

'*The Paston letters*. Edited by James Gairdner. Vol. III.' [review], ix (4 Mar. 1876), 209

'*English history for the use of public schools*. By the Rev. J. F. Bright. Period II, personal monarchy' [review], ix (27 May 1876), 504–5

'Panzoni at the court of Charles I.' [notice], x (1 July 1876), 10–11

'Wentworth and Coriolanus' [correspondence], x (15 July 1876), 61–2

'*Marie de Medicis dans les Pays-Bas*, 1631–1638. Par P. Henrard [*Annales de l'Académie d'Archéologie de France. 3e Série, T.1*]' [review], x (30 Sept. 1876), 333–4

'*Life of William, earl of Shelburne*. By Lord Edmond Fitzmaurice. Vol. III., 1776–1805' [review], x (9 Dec. 1876), 558–9

'*Shakespere's England*. 1. *Harrison's description of England*. Part I. Edited by F. J. Furnivall. 2. *Tell-trothes New Yeares gift, and the passionate Morrice*, 1593; *John Lane's Tom Tell-trothes message*, 1600; *Thomas Powell's Tom of all trades; The glass of godly loue (by J. Rogers?)*. Edited by F. J. Furnivall. 3. *W. Stafford's compendious or briefe examination of certayne ordinary complaints of divers of our countrymen in these our dayes*, 1581. With an Introduction by F. D. Matthew. Edited by F. J. Furnivall. *P. Stubbes's anatomy of abuses in England*, 1583. Part I. Edited by F. J. Furnivall' [review], x (30 Dec. 1876), 621–2

'*Milton und seine Zeit*. Von A. Stern. Erster Theil, 1608–1649' [review], xi (24 Feb. 1877), 156–7

'The Forster MSS. In the South Kensington Museum. I.' [notice], xi (2 June 1877), 486–7

'The late Mr. J. L. Motley' [obituary], xi (9 June 1877), 509–10

'*Bacon and Essex*. By Edwin Abbott, D.D.' [review], xi (23 June 1877), 547–8

'The Forster MSS. In the South Kensington Museum. II.' [notice], xii (28 July 1877), 91

'*Calendar of state papers relating to Ireland of the reign of James I.*, 1611–1614. Edited by the Rev. C.W. Russell, D.D., and J. P. Prendergast' [review], xii (15 Sept. 1877), 261–2

'*Henriette-Marie de France, reine d'Angleterre*. Études historique par le comte de Baillon, suivie de ses lettres inédites' [review], xii (13 Oct. 1877), 356–8

'*Histoire politique et diplomatique de Pierre-Paul Rubens*. Par M. Gachard' [review], xii (17 Nov. 1877), 46

'*Geschichte des Dreissigjährigen Krieges*. Von Anton Gindely. Zweiter Band' [review], xiii (23 Feb. 1878), 162–3

'*The life of Milton, narrated in connexion with the political, ecclesiastical, and literary history of his time*. By David Masson. Vols. IV. And V.' [review], xiii (30 Mar. 1878), 276–7

'*The chief actors in the puritan revolution*. By Peter Bayne' [review], xiii (18 May 1878), 430–1

'*Geschichte des Dreissigjährigen Krieges*. Von Anton Gindely. Dritter Band' [review], xiv (14 Sept. 1878), 257

'*Calendar of state papers, colonial series: East Indies, China, and Japan*, 1622–1624; *preserved in Her Majesty's Public Record Office and elsewhere*. Edited by W. Noel Sainsbury' [review], xiv (26 Oct. 1878), 398–9

'*Milton und seine Zeit*. Von A. Stern. Zweiter Theil. 1649–1674' [review], xiv (14 Dec. 1878), 557–8

'*John Lothrop Motley: a memoir*. By Oliver Wendell Holmes' [review], xiv (21 Dec. 1878), 578

'*History of the English people*. By J. R. Green, M.A. Vol. III.' [review], xv (3 May 1879), 381

'Identity of Strode of the Long Parliament with the imprisoned member of 1629' [correspondence], xv (28 June 1879), 565

'*Milton*. By Mark Pattison, B.D. ["English Men of Letters." Edited by J. Morley]' [review], xvi (6 Dec. 1879), 401

'Viscount Scudamore' [correspondence], xvi (13 Dec. 1879), 430

'A *contemporary history of affairs in Ireland from 1641 to 1652*. Edited by J.T. Gilbert' [review], xvii (17 Jan. 1880), 40

'*Εικων Βασιλικη*. A new edition, with a preface by C. M. Phillimore' [review], xvii (28 Feb. 1880), 152–3

'Mr. Marsh and the "Eikon Basilikè"' [correspondence], xvii (3 Apr. 1880), 252

'*Εικων Βασιλικη*. A reprint of the edition of 1648. By E. J. L. Scott' [review], xvii (17 Apr. 1880), 282

'A *contemporary history of affairs in Ireland from 1641 to 1652*. Edited by J. T. Gilbert, F.S.A., M.R.I.A. Vol. II.' [review], xvii (22 May 1880), 379

'*History of the English people*. By J. R. Green. Vol. IV.' [review], xviii (10 July 1880), 19

'The Hamilton papers' [correspondence], xviii (25 Sept. 1880), 223

'A *history of our own times*. By Justin McCarthy, M.P. Vols. III. and IV.' [review], xviii (9 Oct. 1880), 251–2

'*Calendar of state papers, domestic series*. 1640. Edited by W. D. Hamilton, F.S.A. Rolls Series' [review], xix (29 Jan. 1881), 74–5

'*Calendar of state papers relating to Ireland in the reign of James I – 1615–1625*. Edited by the Rev. C. M. Russell, D.D., and J. P. Prendergast, Esq.' [review], xix (14 May 1881), 347

'*St. Giles's lectures. first series – the Scottish Church*' [review], xix (18 June 1881), 445–6

'*Danmarks y dre politiske Historie (1635–45)*. Af J. A. Fridericia' [review], xx (9 July 1881), 25

'Gindely's history of the Thirty Years' War. *Geschichte des Dreissigjähren Krieges*. Von Anton Gindely. Vierter Band' [review], xx (6 Aug. 1881), 101

'Hallam's account of the Triennial Act of 1641' [correspondence], xx (8 Oct. 1881), 277

'Amerigo Salvetti' [correspondence], xx (24 Dec. 1881), 476

'*The first and second battles of Newbury and the siege of Donington Castle during the Civil War*. By Walter Money, F.S.A.' [review], xx (31 Dec. 1881), 484

'Jews in England in 1643' [correspondence], xxi (4 Mar. 1882), 158–9

'*Evenings with a reviewer;* or, Macaulay and Bacon. By James Spedding. With a prefatory notice by G. S. Venables' [review], xxi (18 Mar. 1882), 187

'A *guide to modern English history*. By W. Cory. Part II., 1830–1835' [review], xxii (21 Oct. 1882), 288–9

'"English men of letters." *Macaulay*. By J. Cotter Morison' [review], xxii (16 Dec. 1882), 425–6

'"Hobbes" in Clough's "Bothie"' [correspondence], xxii (30 Dec. 1882), 471

'A new diary of the Long Parliament' [correspondence], xxiii (27 Jan. 1883), 62

'*Calendar of state papers. domestic series, 1640–1641.* Edited by W. D. Hamilton' [review], xxiii (24 Feb. 1883), 126–7

'J. R. Green' [obituary], xxiii (17 Mar. 1883), 186–7

'*Rise of constitutional government in England.* By C. Ransome' [review], xxiii (19 May 1883), 340–1

'Two books About Cromwell. *Calendar of state papers. domestic series, 1655–1656.* Edited by M. A. Everett Green. *Cromwell in Ireland.* By the Rev. Denis Murphy' [review], xxiii (9 June 1883), 394–5

'*Bacon.* By Dean Church' [review], xv (3 May 1884), 305

'*Ireland in the seventeenth century; or, the Irish massacres of 1641–1642.* By Mary Hickson. With a preface by J. A. Froude' [review], xvi (26 July 1884), 53

'Ireland in the seventeenth century' [correspondence], xvi (23 Aug. 1884), 121

'*Vingt Années de république parlementaire au dix-septième siècle.* Jean de Witt. Par M. A. Lefèvre Pontalis' [review], xvi (6 Sept. 1884), 145

'Ireland in the seventeenth century' [correspondence], xvi (13 Sept. 1884), 169

'*The office of the historical professor:* an inaugural lecture. By E. A. Freeman' [review], xvi (13 Dec. 1884), 386

'Death of Cromwell's son' [correspondence], xxvii (14 Mar. 1885), 188

'Death of Cromwell's son' [correspondence], xxvii (28 Mar. 1885), 224–5

'The Squire papers' [correspondence], xxvii (5 Apr. 1885), 261

'The Squire papers' [correspondence], xxvii (2 May 1885), 313

'*Francis Bacon: an account of his life and works.* By Edwin A. Abbott' [review], xxvii (13 June 1885), 411–12

'*History of the Irish confederation and the war in Ireland.* Vol. III. 1643–1644. Edited by J.T. Gilbert' [review], xxviii (18 July 1885), 36

'*Life and times of General Sir Edward Cecil, Viscount Wimbledon.* By Charles Dalton' [review], xxviii (24 Oct. 1885), 266–7

'Historical gift-books' (*With the king at Oxford.* By A. J. Church; *Border lances:* a romance of the northern Marches in the reign of Edward III. By the author of "Belt and spur"; *The lion of the north:* a tale of the times of Gustavus Adolphus. By G. A.Henty; *The champion of Odin*; or, Viking life in the days of old. By J. Frederick Hodgetts; *The dragon and the raven*; or, The days of King Alfred. By G. A. Henty; *No. XIII.*; or, The story of the last Vestal. By Emma

Marshall; *Gytha's message*, a tale of Saxon England. By Emma Leslie; *Stirring stories*. By James Macaulay)' [review, unsigned], xxviii (28 Nov. 1885), 355

'"With the king at Oxford"' [correspondence], xxviii (12 Dec. 1885), 394

'*Ireland under the Tudors*. By R. Bagwell. In 2 vols' [review], xxviii (26 Dec. 1885), 419

'*A life of Joseph Hall, D.D., bishop of Exeter and Norwich*. By the Rev. Geo. Lewis' [review], xxix (17 Apr. 1886), 267

'Leopold von Ranke' [obituary], xxix (29 May 1886), 380–1

'"English worthies." – *Raleigh*. By Edmund Gosse' [review], xxx (14 Aug. 1886), 97

'*Clarendon's history of the rebellion:* Book VI. Edited by T. Arnold' [review], xxx (4 Sept. 1886), 145

'Clarendon's history, Book VI.' [correspondence], xxx (2 Oct. 1886), 226

'*Seventeen lectures on the study of mediaeval and modern history and kindred subjects, delivered at Oxford under statutory obligation*. By W. Stubbs, bishop of Chester' [review], xxx (13 Nov. 1886), 319–20

'*Calendar of state papers, domestic series, 1641–1643*. Preserved in H. M. Public Record Office. Edited by W.W. Hamilton' [review], xxxii (27 Aug. 1887), 127

'*William Laud, sometime archbishop of Canterbury: a study*. By Arthur Christopher Benson' [review], xxxii (19 Nov. 1887), 332

'*History of the Irish confederation and the war in Ireland*. Edited by John T. Gilbert. Vol. IV.' [review], xxxiii (17 Mar. 1888), 180–1

'*Oliver Cromwell*. By Frederic Harrison' [review], xxxiv (28 July 1888), 48–9

'"Calendar of state papers." *Domestic series of the reign of Charles I., 1644*. Edited by W. D. Hamilton' [review], xxxiv (29 Dec. 1888), 411

'The finances of the Long Parliament. *Calendar of the proceedings of the Committee for Advance of Money*, 1642–1656. Edited by Mary Anne Everett Green' [review], xxxvi (27 July 1889), 47

'"English men of action." – *Lord Strafford*. By H. D. Traill' [review], xxxvi (30 Nov. 1889), 349–50

'*The life of Lady Arabella Stuart*. By E. T. Bradley' [review], xxxvii (11 Jan. 1890), 20

'*Memorials of the Civil War in Cheshire*. Edited by James Hall for the Record Society for the Publication of Original Documents relating to Lancashire and Cheshire' [review], xxxviii (9 Aug. 1890), 104–5

'Presbyterianism and the Long Parliament. *Minutes of the Manchester Presbyterian Classis*. Edited by William S. [*sic*] Shaw. Part I.' [review], xxxix (17 Jan. 1891), 55

'*Calendar of state papers. Domestic series of the reign of Charles I, 1645–1647.* Edited by W. D. Hamilton' [review], xli (5 Mar. 1892), 224–5

Contributions to the *Athenæum*
[journal title omitted from review titles]

'*The condition of Catholics under James I. Father Gerard's narrative of the Gunpowder plot.* Edited, with his Life, by John Morris, priest of the Society of Jesus' [unsigned review], 2297 (4 Nov. 1871), 587–9

[unsigned, untitled notice on 'the "Cheque-book of the Chapel Royal," edited by Dr. Rimbault' (for the Camden Society)], 2301 (2 Dec. 1871), 724

[unsigned, untitled notice on 'the letters of A. Valaresso'], 2303 (16 Dec. 1871), 796

[unsigned, untitled notice on 'documents illustrating the impeachment of the duke of Buckingham in 1626'], 2315 (9 Mar. 1872), 308

[unsigned, untitled notice on forthcoming Camden Society publications], 2316 (16 Mar. 1872), 337

'*The life and times of Margaret of Anjou, queen of England and of France, René "the Good," king of Sicily, Naples, and Jerusalem. With memoirs of the house of Anjou.* By Mary Ann Hookham' [unsigned review], 2320 (13 Apr. 1872), 455–6

'*The letters and life of Francis Bacon.* By James Spedding. Vol. VI.' [unsigned review], 2337 (10 Aug. 1872), 173–4

'*A calendar of the papers of the Tresham family, of the reigns of Elizabeth and James I., preserved at Rushton Hall, Northamptonshire*' [unsigned notice], 2343 (21 Sept. 1872), 365

'*Calendar of the Clarendon state papers preserved in the Bodleian Library.* Vol. I., to January, 1649. Edited by the Rev. O. Ogle, M.A., and W. H. Bliss, B.C.L., under the direction of the Rev. H. O. Coxe, M.A.' [unsigned review], 2345 (5 Oct. 1872), 423–4

'The Thirty Years' War' [notice], 2347 (19 Oct. 1872), 499

'The true story of the ships lent by Charles I. to serve against the French Protestants' [notice], 2355 (14 Dec. 1872), 768–9

'*A list of the Roman Catholics in the county of York in 1604.* Edited by Edward Peacock' [unsigned review], 2359 (11 Jan. 1873), 48–9

[untitled notice on 'the elegy, written by William Basse, upon the death of Henry prince of Wales'], 2379 (31 May 1873), 693

[unsigned, untitled notice on planned publication of 'the diary of Sir Bulstrode Whitelocke'], 2385 (12 July 1873), 49 [unsigned, untitled notice on the tracts in 'Mr. Golding's library'], 2388 (2 Aug. 1873), 145

[unsigned, untitled notice on '*Derry and Enniskillen in the year* 1689: *the story of some famous battle-fields in Ulster*. By Prof. Thomas Witherow'], 2414 (31 Jan. 1874), 159

[unsigned, untitled notice on forthcoming Camden Society publications], 2416 (14 Feb. 1874), 227

[unsigned, untitled notice on forthcoming Camden Society publications], 2433 (13 June 1874), 795

[unsigned, untitled notice on forthcoming Camden Society publications], 2456 (21 Nov. 1874), 680

[unsigned, untitled notice on forthcoming Camden Society publications], 2464 (16 Jan. 1875), 86

[unsigned, untitled notice on forthcoming Camden Society publications], 2485 (12 June 1875), 787

[unsigned, untitled notice on forthcoming Camden Society publications], 2520 (12 Feb. 1876), 235

[unsigned, untitled notice on forthcoming Camden Society publications], 2524 (11 Mar. 1876), 364

[untitled notice on 'Vane's notes'], 2537 (10 June 1876), 797

[unsigned, untitled notice on forthcoming Camden Society publications], 2555 (14 Oct. 1876), 498

[unsigned, untitled notice on forthcoming Camden Society publications], 2565 (23 Dec. 1876), 836

[unsigned, untitled notice on forthcoming Camden Society publications], 2573 (17 Feb. 1877), 226

[unsigned, untitled notice on forthcoming Camden Society publications], 2612 (17 Nov. 1877), 631

'The Camden Society' [unsigned notice], 2689 (10 May 1879), 601

[unsigned, untitled notice on the Camden Society], 2793 (7 May 1881), 624

[unsigned, untitled notice on the Camden Society], 2846 (13 May 1882), 603

[unsigned, untitled notice on forthcoming Camden Society publications], 2874 (25 Nov. 1882), 700

[unsigned, untitled notice on discovery of a letter from the earl of Manchester], 2894 (14 Apr. 1883), 478

[unsigned, untitled notice on forthcoming issue of the 'Cabinet edition' of Gardiner's *History of England*], 2894 (14 Apr. 1883), 478 [unsigned, untitled notice on the Camden Society], 2926 (24 Nov. 1883), 67

[unsigned, untitled notice on the Camden Society], 3367 (7 May 1892), 602

[unsigned, untitled notice on the Camden Society], 3374 (25 June 1892), 825

'Algernon Sydney's correspondence' [correspondence], 3554 (7 Dec. 1895), 792

[untitled notice on forthcoming publication of vol. 2 of Gardiner's *History of the Commonwealth and Protectorate* and preparation of *Cromwell's place in history*], 3611 (9 Jan. 1897), 50

'Cromwell's speeches' [notice], 3620 (13 Mar. 1897), 347–8

'Speaker Lenthall' [correspondence], 3638 (17 July 1897), 97

'The alleged bigamy of Thomas Percy, the conspirator' [notice], 3646 (11 Sept. 1897), 352

[untitled notice on 'Thomas Winter's long narrative of Gunpowder plot'], 3656 (20 Nov. 1897), 711

'The alleged forgery of Winter's narrative of the Gunpowder plot' [correspondence], 3658 (4 Dec. 1897), 785–7

'Charles I. and Lord Glamorgan' [notice], 3670 (26 Feb. 1898), 278–9

'The assassination plot of 1654' [notice], 3681 (14 May 1898), 631–2

'Henshaw's plot against the Protector' [notice], 3685 (11 June 1898), 758

'Thomas Winter's confession' [notice], 3698 (10 Sept. 1898), 352–3

'The date of the "New Atlantis"' [correspondence], 3772 (10 Feb. 1900), 176

'The date of Pepys's marriage' [notice], 3791 (23 June 1900), 786

Contributions to the *English Historical Review*
[journal title omitted from review titles]

'An early tract on liberty of conscience' [notice], i (Jan. 1886), 144–6

'*Memoirs of the life of Colonel Hutchinson*. By his widow, Lucy. Revised with additional notes by C. N. [*sic*] Firth' [review], i (Jan. 1886), 173–4

'*The first and second battles of Newbury*. By Walter Money, F.S.A. 2nd edition' [review], i (Apr. 1886), 386–9

'The Squire papers' [notice], i (July 1886), 517–21

'*The life of William Cavendish, duke of Newcastle*. By Margaret, duchess of Newcastle. Edited by C. H. Firth, M.A.' [review], ii (Jan. 1887), 172–3

'A scheme of toleration propounded at Uxbridge in 1645' [notice], ii (Apr. 1887), 340–2

'Charles I and the earl of Glamorgan' [article], ii (Oct. 1887), 687–708

'Collections by Isaak Walton for the Life of John Hales of Eton' [notice], ii (Oct. 1887), 746–52

'Note on Charles I and the earl of Glamorgan' [notice], iii (Jan. 1888), 125–6

'Two declarations of Garnet relating to the Gunpowder plot' [notice], iii (July 1888), 510–19

'Sir Anthony Ashley Cooper, and the relief of Taunton' [notice], iv (July 1889), 521–5

'*Errata in No.* 23, *Vol. VI*' [notice, signed 'Ed. E.H.R.'], vi (Oct. 1891), 815

'*The Interregnum: studies of the Commonwealth*. By F. A. Inderwick, Q.C.' [review], vi (Oct. 1891), 785–6

'*The manuscripts of his grace the duke of Portland*. Vol. I. Hist. Manuscripts Commission Thirteenth Report. Appendix. Part I.' [review], vii (Jan. 1892), 176–7

'*History of the Irish confederation*. Edited by John T. Gilbert, F.S.A., M.R.I.A. *A Jacobite narrative of the war in Ireland*. 1688–1690. Edited by John T. Gilbert, F.S.A., M.R.I.A.' [review], vii (Apr. 1892), 368

'The storm of Maidstone by Fairfax 1648' [reply notice], vii (July 1892), 536

'*Sir Walter Raleigh*. By William Stebbing' [review], vii (July 1892), 571–3

'*Minutes of the Manchester Presbyterian Classis*. Edited by W. A. Shaw' [review], vii (Oct. 1892), 786–7

'*Queen Elizabeth*. By E. S. Beesly' [review], vii (Oct. 1892), 776–7

'*The table talk of John Selden*. Edited by S. H. Reynolds' [review], viii (Jan. 1893), 161

'Draft by Sir Edward Hyde of a declaration to be issued by Charles II. in 1649' [notice], viii (Apr. 1893), 300–7

'*The political value of history*. By W. E. H. Lecky' [review], viii (Apr. 1893), 394–5

'Member of Parliament' [notice], viii (July 1893), 525

'*The memoirs of James, marquis of Montrose*. By the Rev. George Wishart, D.D., Translated, with an introduction, notes, appendices, and the original Latin, by the Rev. O. Murdoch and H. F. Morland Simpson' [review], viii (July 1893), 581–3

'*The worship of the Church of Scotland during the Covenanting period*, 1638–1661. By G.W. Sprott, D.D.' [review], viii (Oct. 1893), 779

[untitled review of 'Green's *Short history of the English people*'; signed 'S.R.G.'], ix (Jan. 1894), 189–90

'*Studies of travel: I; Italy*. By E. A. Freeman' [review], ix (Jan. 1894), 182–3

'*Manuscripts of the duke of Portland*. Vol. II. Historical Manuscripts Commission. Thirteenth report. Appendix. Part II.' [review], ix (Apr. 1894), 380–1

'Lord Mordaunt's resignation in 1668' [reply notice, signed 'Editor'], ix (Oct. 1894), 819

[untitled, unsigned review notice of '*The manuscripts of the earl of Lonsdale*, Historical Manuscripts Commission, Thirteenth report, Appendix, part vii.'], ix (Oct. 1894), 818

'An alleged notebook of John Pym' [notice], x (Jan. 1895), 105–6

'*Life and times of William Laud*. By C. H. Simpkinson. *William Laud*. By W. H. Hutton' [review], x (Apr. 1895), 372–3

'*The growth of British policy*. By Sir J. R. Seeley' [review], xi (Jan. 1896), 159–61

'*A lecture on the study of history*. By Lord Acton' [review], xi (Jan. 1896), 121–3

'*Social England*. By various writers. Edited by H. D. Traill, D.C.L. Vol. IV. 'From the accession of James I to the death of Anne' [review], xi (Apr. 1896), 378–9

'Cromwell and Mazarin in 1652' [article], xi (July 1896), 479–509

[untitled review of T. Hodgkin, *George Fox*, signed 'S.R.G.'], xi (Oct. 1896), 811–12

[untitled review of J. F. Taylor, *Owen Roe O'Neill*, signed 'S.R.G'], xi (Oct. 1896), 811

'Plan of Charles I for the deliverance of Strafford' [notice], xii (Jan. 1897), 114–16

'*The theory of the divine right of kings*. By J. N. Figgis. 'Cambridge historical essays,' No. 9' [review], xii (Jan. 1897), 171–2

[untitled, unsigned review notice of '*Diary of Sir Archibald Werriston*'], xii (July 1897), 575

[untitled, unsigned review notice of J.W. Gordon, *Monopolies by patents*], xii (Oct. 1897), 813

'*Introduction aux études historiques*. Par C.V. Langlois et C. Seignobois' [review], xiii (Apr. 1898), 327–9

'Alleged fighting in line in the First Dutch War' [notice], xiii (July 1898), 533

'*Cromwell's Scotch campaigns*, 1650–51. By W. S. Douglas' [review], xiii (Oct. 1898), 790–1

'*The history of English democratic ideas in the seventeenth century*. By G. P. Gooch' [review], xiii (Oct. 1898), 784–5 [untitled notice on the papers of Father Henry Garnett, S.J., signed 'S.R.G.'], xiii (Oct. 1898), 816

'Blake at Leghorn' [notice], xiv (Jan. 1899), 109–11

'*Cromwell as a soldier*. By Lieut.-Col. T. S. Baldock, P.S.C.' [review], xiv (July 1899), 569–71

[untitled review of S. F. von Bischoffshausen, *Die Politik des Protectors Oliver Cromwell in der Auffasung und Thätigkeit seines Ministers des Staatssecretärs John Thurloe … Im Anhang: die Briefe John Thurloes an Bulstrode Whitelocke und sein Bericht über die Cromwell'sche Politik für Edward Hyde*, signed 'S.R.G.'], xiv (July 1899), 608

[untitled review of E. Rodocanachi, *Les Derniers Temps du siege de La Rochelle, 1628. Relation du nonce apostolique*, signed 'S.R.G.'], xiv (July 1899), 607–8

'*Rupert Prince Palatine*. By Eva Scott' [review], xiv (Oct. 1899), 779–80

'The transplantation to Connaught' [article], xiv (Oct. 1899), 700–34

[untitled review of '*Life of Richard Badiley*, by Spalding'], xv (Jan. 1900), 196–7

'*The life and campaigns of Alexander Leslie, first earl of Leven*. By Charles Sanford Terry' [review], xv (Apr. 1900), 376–7

'*The United Kingdom: a political history*. By Goldwin Smith, D.C.L.' [review], xv (Apr. 1900), 348–50

'*Oliver Cromwell and the rule of the puritans in England*. By Charles Firth' [review], xv (Oct. 1900), 803–7

[untitled review of 'the first volume of *La libertà religiosa* [by] Professor Ruffini', signed 'S.R.G.'], xvi (Jan. 1901), 199

'*The Protestant interest in Cromwell's foreign relations*. By Jacob N. Bowman. *Sverige och England* 1655–*Aug*. 1657. Af Fil. Lic. J. Levin Carlbom. *Friherre Frans Paul von Lisola*. Af Fil. Lic. J. Levin Carlbom' [review], xvi (Jan. 1901), 166–8

Contributions to *Notes and Queries*
[journal title omitted from review titles]

'The sessions of parliament in 1610' [notice], ii (17 Mar. 1860), 191–3

'James I. and the recusants' [notice], ii (28 Apr. 1860), 317–21

'Speeches of Bacon and Yelverton in the debate on impositions' [notice], ii (19 May 1860), 382–3

'James I. and the recusants' [notice], ii (30 June 1860), 497–9

'James I. and the recusants' [notice], ii (4 Aug. 1860), 81–5

'King's prerogative in impositions' [notice], ii (11 Aug. 1860), 111–15

'James I. and the recusants' [notice], ii (24 Nov. 1860), 413–15

'Count Gondomar's "Transactions"' [notice], iv (12 Nov. 1870), 421

'Gondomar's "Transactions"' [notice], iv (17 Dec. 1870), 535–6

'Facts and fictions about the duke of Buckingham's mother' [notice], iv (3 June 1871), 469–71

'Facts and fictions about the duke of Buckingham's mother' [notice], iv (24 June 1871), 544

'Sir Rob. Killigrew: Burlamachi' [notice], iv (24 June 1871), 550

'Sir Fulke Greville, Lord Brooke' [notice], iv (29 July 1871), 88–9

'Sir Fulke Greville, Lord Brooke' [notice], iv (16 Sept. 1871), 234

'Three letters written by Charles I when prince of Wales, on the subject of his marriage' [notice], iv (6 Jan. 1872), 6–8

'Notes by Sir James Bagg on the parliament of 1626' [notice], iv (26 Oct. 1872), 325–6

'Historical stumbling-blocks' [notice], iv (19 July 1873), 50

'Milton's Bishop Mountain' [notice], iv (6 Dec. 1873), 453

'Bishop Hall's "Satires"' [notice], v (3 July 1875), 16

'"The shepherd's paradise"' [notice], v (29 Apr. 1876), 351–2

'Wager of battle: appeal for murder' [notice] vi (16 Oct. 1880), 312

'An English mission to Spain in 1638' [notice], vi (23 Oct. 1880), 332–3

'Nineteenth century criticism of "Lycidas"' [notice], vi (23 Apr. 1881), 329–30

'The Camden Society' [notice], vi (4 June 1881), 444–5

'Rushworth's collections' [notice], vi (29 Apr. 1882), 325–6

'Mr. Gardiner's "Fall of the monarchy of Charles I."' [notice], vi (30 Dec. 1882), 538–9

'A French despatch, 1606' [notice], vi (24 Mar. 1883), 232

'Touching for scrofula' [notice], vi (16 June 1883), 474

'Toleration' [notice], vi (24 Nov. 1883), 410

'Signatures to the Solemn League and Covenant' [notice], vi (17 May 1884), 396–7

'Solemn League and Covenant' [notice], vi (14 June 1884), 476

'Was Cromwell ever a foot soldier?' [notice], vi (14 Feb. 1885), 127

'A judge censured in the Star Chamber' [notice], vi (24 Oct. 1885), 328

'Warrant of Charles I. to the earl of Glamorgan' [notice], vii (5 Mar. 1887), 188

'Hugh Peters' [notice], vii (12 Nov. 1887), 394–5

'Tresham' [notice], vii (28 July 1888), 76

'Peace of 1642' [notice], vii (13 Oct. 1888), 295

'Grangerizing' [notice], vii (19 July 1890), 52

'Crucifix in the banana fruit' [notice], vii (5 Dec. 1891), 453

'Hamilton's "Calendar of state papers"' [notice], viii (22 Sept. 1894), 231

'Cromwell in Wales' [notice], viii (16 Mar. 1895), 215–16

'The man of Ghent' [notice], viii (16 Jan. 1897), 50

'George Herbert' [notice], viii (6 Mar. 1897), 192

'Portraits of General Desborough and Lady Claypole' [notice], ix (3 Dec. 1898), 448

'Liddell and Scott' [notice], ix (24 June 1899), 493

'Green ribbons at a funeral' [notice], ix (15 July 1899), 55

'Elizabeth Alkin' [notice], ix (19 May 1900), 400–1

'"The devil walking through Athlone"' [notice], ix (7 July 1900), 14

'Desborough portrait and relics' [notice], ix (11 Jan. 1902), 30

Contributions to other journals

'Spanish and Venetian diplomacy in England in the reign of James I.' (G. A. Bergenroth [ed.], *Calendar of letters, despatches, and state papers, relating to the negotiations between England and Spain, preserved in the archives of Simancas and elsewhere* [vol. I.]; R. Brown [ed.], *Calendar of state papers and MSS. relating to English affairs, existing in the archives and collections of Venice, and in other libraries of northern Italy* [vol. I.]) [review article], *FR* iii (15 Dec. 1865), 344–51

'The case against Sir Walter Raleigh' [article], *FR* n.s. i (1 May 1867), 602–14

'On certain letters of Diego Sarmiento de Acuña, count of Gondomar, giving an account of the affair of the earl of Somerset as a public man' ('Read March 22nd, 1866') [article], *Archæologia* xli (1867), 151–86

'On four letters from Lord Bacon to Christian IV. King of Denmark, together with observations on the part taken by him in the grants of monopolies made by James I.' ('Read February 7, 1867') [article], *Archæologia* xli (1867), 219–69

'*Zur Geschichte vom Religionsfrieden bis zum dreissigjährigen Krieg*. Von. L. von Ranke' [unsigned review], *NBR* li (Oct. 1869), 239–40

'*The letters and life of Francis Bacon* (*sic*). By James Spedding. Vols. III. And IV.' [unsigned review], *NBR* li (Oct. 1869), 235–7

'*Geschichte Wallensteins*. Von L. von Ranke' [unsigned review], *NBR* li (Jan. 1870), 551–3

'*Gustaf Adolf*. Von G. Droysen' [unsigned review], *NBR* li (Jan. 1870), 550–1

'*Cinco cartas de D. Diego Sarmiento de Acuña, primer conde de Gondomar*. Publícalas la Sociedad de Bibliofilos' [unsigned review], *NBR* lii (Apr. 1870), 253–4

'*The life and letters of Francis Bacon*. By James Spedding. Vol. V.' [unsigned review], *NBR* lii (Apr. 1870), 251–3

'James I. and Lord Digby; A reply to Mr. Spedding' [article], *Fraser's Magazine* n.s. iii (May 1871), 571–83

'On the alleged apostacy of Wentworth (Lord Strafford) (*Shorthand notes taken in the House of Commons by Edward Nicholas in the first session of the third parliament of Charles* I. MS. State papers. Domestic, Charles I. Vol. 97; *A diary of proceedings in the parliament which began on Monday, the* 17th *of March*, 1628. Harleian MSS., 4771; *Official notes of the debates in the House of Lords in 1628*. By Henry Elsing the younger. MS. In possession of Colonel Carew, of Crowcombe Court; *Sir John Eliot; a biography*. By John Forster. Second edition)' [unsigned review article], *QR* cxxxvi (Apr. 1874), 434–52

'Angleterre. Travaux sur le XVIe et le XVIIe siècle' (M. A. E. Green [ed.], *Calendar of state papers, domestic series [1649–50]*; J. A. Froude, *The English in Ireland in the eighteenth century*; J. S. Brewer [ed.], *Calendar of state papers for the reign of Henry VIII [1524]*; J. Bruce and D. Masson [eds], *The quarrel between the earl of Manchester and Oliver Cromwell: an episode of the English Civil War. Unpublished documents relating thereto collected by J. Bruce, with fragments of a historical preface by* Mr. *Bruce, annotated and completed by D. Masson*; J. G. Nichols [ed.], *The autobiography of Anne, Lady Halkett*; J. G. Nichols [ed.], 'Two sermons [on Psalm cxii.1 and Matt. xviii.3] preached by the boy bishop at St. Paul's, temp. Henry VIII., and at Gloucester, temp. Mary', in *Camden Miscellany Vol. VII*; W. H. D. Longstaffe [ed.], *Heraldic visitation of the Northern counties in 1530 .... with an appendix of other heraldic documents relating to the North of England*; J. J. Cartwright [ed.], *The memoirs of Sir John Reresby, 1634–1689*; J. M. Graham [ed.], *Annals and correspondence of the viscount and first and second earls of Stair*; E. Thompson, *History of England*; E. A. Freeman, *History of Europe*; C. A. Fyffe, *History of Greece*; M. Creighton, *History of Rome*; J. R. Green, *A short history of the English people*; W. Warburton, *Edward the Third*; J. Gairdner, *The houses of Lancaster and York, with the conquest and loss of France*; J. Gairdner [ed.], *The Paston letters*; M. Bright (ed.), *The diary and correspondence of Samuel Pepys*, vol. I) [review notice], *RH* i (Jan. 1876), 287–98

'Un Mémoire inédit de Richelieu' [notice], *RH* i (Jan. 1876), 228–38

'The political element in Massinger' [article], *CR* xxviii (Aug. 1876), 495–507

'Angleterre. Travaux relatifs au moyen-âge et aux temps modernes' (E. A. Freeman, *The history of the Norman conquest of England, its causes and its results*, vol.v; W. Stubbs, *The constitutional history of England, in its origin and development*; F. W. Wyon, *The history of Great Britain during the reign of Queen Anne*; H. R. F. Bourne, *The life of John Locke*; F. Fitzmaurice, *The life of William, earl of Shelburne*, vols i, ii; G. O. Trevelyan, *The life and letters of Lord Macaulay*; E. Ashley, *The life of J. H. Temple, Viscount Palmerston [1846–1865]*; D. le Marchant, *Memoir of John Charles, Viscount Althorp, third Earl Spencer*; F. Bright, *English history, for the use of public schools*, vols i, ii; M. Creighton, *The age of Elizabeth*; S. R. Gardiner, *The first two Stuarts and the Puritan Revolution*; E. E. Hale, *The fall of the Stuarts and western Europe from 1678 to 1697*; J. M. Ludlow, *The war of American Independence*; J. C. Robertson [ed.], *Materials for the history of Thomas Becket, archbishop of Canterbury*, vol.i; E. Magnusson [ed.], *Thomas Saga Erkibyskups*, vol i; T. D. Hardy [ed.], *Registrum Palatinum Dunelmense: The register of Richard de Kellawe, Lord Palatine and bishop of Durham, 1311–1316*, vol. iii; J. Stevenson [ed.], *Rodulphi de Coggeshale Chronicon Anglicanum*; E. M. Thompson [ed.], *Letters of Humphrey Prideaux, sometime dean of Norwich, to John Ellis, 1674–1722*; A.J. Horwood [ed.], *The common-place book of John Milton*; E.T. Rogers [ed.], *A complete collection of the protests of the Lords*; M. Hertslet, *The map of Europe by treaties, showing the various political and territorial changes which have taken place since the general peace of 1815*) [review notice], *RH* ii (Oct. 1876), 575–95

'Die Franzœsische Heirath. Frankreich und England 1624 und 1625, von Dr. J. Goll' [review], *RH* ii (Oct. 1876), 624–5

'Grande Bretagne. Temps modernes' (J. A. Symonds, *Renaissance in Italy*, I: 'The revival of learning'; P. de Gayangos [ed.], *Calendar of state papers preserved in the archives of Simancas and elsewhere*; F. S. Stoney [ed.], *A memoir of the life and times of the right honourable Sir Ralph Sadleir, compiled from state papers*; J.W. Burton [ed.], *The register of the privy council of Scotland*, I: *1545–1569*; J. Morris [ed.], *The troubles of our Catholic forefathers, related by themselves*, vol. iii; E. A. Abbott, *Bacon and Essex: a sketch of Bacon's earlier life*; C.W. Russell and J. P. Prendergast [eds], *Calendar of the state papers relating to Ireland and of the reign of James I*, IV: *(1611–1614)*; S. R. Gardiner [ed.], *Documents relating to the proceedings against William Prynne in 1634 and 1637, with a biographical fragment by the late John Bruce*; *The acts of the parliament of Scotland, published by the authority of the Lords Commissioners of the Treasury*; M. A. E. Green (ed.), *Calendar of state papers. domestic series, 1651*; E. E. Morris, *The age of Anne*; L. Stephen, *History of English thought in the eighteenth century*; E. Fitzmaurice, *Life of William, earl of Shelburne*, vols iii, iv; D. M. Wallace, *Russia*) [review notice], *RH* v (Apr. 1877), 368–83

'Grande Bretagne. Temps modernes' (P. Bayne, *The chief actors in the Puritan Revolution*; D. Masson, *The life of Milton, narrated in connexion with political, ecclesiatical and literary history of his time*, vols iv, v; W. E. H. Lecky, *A history of England in the eighteenth century*, vols i, ii; A. R. Wellesley [ed.], *Despatches*, *correspondence and memoranda of Field Marshal Arthur, duke of Wellington. Edited by his son, the Duke of Wellington*, VII; *Mémoires du comte Horace de Viel-Castel sur le régne de Napoleon III, 1851–1864*; W. D. Hamilton [ed.], *A chronicle of England during the reigns of the Tudors from 1485 to 1559, by Charles Wriothesley*, vol. ii; N. Pocock [ed.], *A treatise on the pretended divorce between Henry VIII. and Catharine of Aragon. By Nicholas Harpsfield. Now first printed from a collation of four manuscripts*; W. D. Hamilton [ed.], *Calendar of state papers. Domestic series of the reign of Charles I, 1639–1640*; M. A. E. Green [ed.], *Calendar of state papers. Domestic series, 1651–1652*; *Calendar of state papers. Colonial series: East India, China and Japan, 1622–1624*; M. C. M. Simpson [ed.], *Conversations with M.Thiers, M.Guizot and other distinguished persons during the second empire, by the late N. W. Senior*) [review notice], *RH* viii (Oct. 1878), 376–85

'Modern history' (P. Baynes, *Chief actors in the puritan revolution*; D. Masson, *Life of Milton, narrated in connexion with the political, ecclesiastical, and literary history of his time*, vols iv, v; *Additional despatches of the duke of Wellington*, vol. vii; M. A. Legrette, *Louis XIV. et Strasbourg*; W. E. H. Lecky, *History of England in the eighteenth century*) [review notice, '*Under the direction of* Professor S. Rawson Gardiner'], *CR* xxxiii (Oct. 1878), 626–9

'Modern history' (J. B. Mozley, *Essays historical and theological*; A. Stern, *Milton und seine Zeit*; A. H. A. Hamilton, *Quarter sessions from Queen Elizabeth to Queen Anne: illustrations from local government and history*; S. Walpole, *A history of England from the conclusion of the Great War in 1815*; H. Martineau, *History of England, A.D. 1800–1815*; Ld Teignmouth, *Reminiscences of many years*) [review notice, '*Under the direction of* Professor S. Rawson Gardiner'], *CR* xxxiv (Dec. 1878), 195–7

'Modern history' (J. R. Seeley, *Life and times of Stein; or Germany and Prussia in the Napoleonic age*; R. Davenport-Hill and P. Davenport-Hill, *The recorder of Birmingham: a memoir of Matthew Davenport Hill, with selections from his correspondence*; J. T. Bunce, *History of the corporation of Birmingham*; J. A. Robertson, *A course of lectures on the government, constitution, and laws of Scotland*; M. E. Green, *Calendar of state papers, domestic series, December 1652–June 1653*; W. D. Hamilton, *Calendars of the domestic papers of the reign of Charles I*; E. M. Thompson [ed.], *Correspondence of the family of Hatton*) [review notice, '*Under the direction of* Professor S. Rawson Gardiner'], *CR* xxxiv (Feb. 1879), 617–20

'Angleterre. Temps modernes' (T. Martin, *The life of H.R.H. the prince consort*, vol. iv; J. McCarthy, *A history of our own times, from the accession of Queen Victoria to the Berlin Congress*; J. R. Green, *History of the English people*, vol. iii; P. Foley [ed.], *Records of the English provinces of the Society of Jesus*; A. Jessop, *One generation of a Norfolk house: a contribution to Elizabethan history*; S. Walpole, *A history of England from the conclusion of the Great War in 1815*, vols i, ii; C. J. Abbey and J. H. Overton, *The English Church in the eighteenth century*; L. J. Trotter, *Warren Hastings: a biography*; R. Davenport-Hill and P. Davenport-Hill, *The recorder of Birmingham: a memoir of Matthew Davenport Hill, with selections from his correspondence*; E. M. Thompson [ed.], *Correspondence of the family of Hatton, being chiefly letters addressed to Christopher, first Viscount Hatton. A.D. 1601–1704*; S. R. Gardiner [ed.], *Notes of the debates in the House of Lords. Officially taken by Henry Elsing, clerk of the parliaments, A.D. 1624 and 1626*; M. A. E. Green, *Calendar of state papers. Domestic series, 1652–1653*) [review notice], *RH* xi (Apr. 1879), 393–9

'Modern history' (J. McCarthy, *History of our own times*; L. J. Trotter, *Warren Hastings: a biography*) [review notice, '*Under the direction of* Professor S. R. Gardiner'], *CR* xxxv (Apr. 1879), 184–6

'Modern history' (J. R. Green, *History of the English people*, vol. iii; T. Martin, *Life of his royal highness the prince consort*, vol. iv; A. Jessop, *One generation of a Norfolk house: a contribution to Elizabethan history*; J. Simon, *The government of M. Thiers, from 8th February, 1871 to 24th May, 1873*; J. V. A. de Broglie, *The king's secret: being the secret correspondence of Louis XV. with his diplomatic agents, from 1752 to 1774*) [review notice, '*Under the direction of* Professor Gardiner'], *CR* xxxv (July 1879), 760–2

'Modern history' (J. H. Burton, *A history of the reign of Queen Anne*; G. S. Godkin, *Life of Victor Emmanuel II, first king of Italy*; J. Webb [ed. T. W. Webb], *Memorials of the Civil War between King Charles I. and the parliament of England as it affected Herefordshire and the adjacent counties*; J. Macdonell [ed. A. H. Macdonell], *France since the First Empire*; J. Geddes, *The history of the administration of John de Witt, Grand Pensionary of Holland*) [review notice, '*Under the direction of* Professor S. R. Gardiner'], *CR* xxxvii (Mar. 1880), 529–32

'Modern history' (D. Masson, *Life of Milton, narrated in connexion with the political, ecclesiastical, and literary history of his time*, vol. vi; W. Cory, *Guide to modern English history*, part I: 1815–1830; T. Martin, *The life of his royal highness the prince consort*, vol. v; T. P. Taswell-Langmead, *English constitutional history*; S. Amos, *Fifty years of the English constitution*; J.W. Willis Bund, *Selection of cases from the state trials*, I: *Trials for treason, 1327–1660*) [review notice, '*Under the direction of* Professor S. R. Gardiner'], *CR* xxxvii (June 1880), 1054–9

'Angleterre. Temps modernes' (J. H. Burton, *A history of the reign of Queen Anne*; A. R. Wellesley [ed.], *Despatches, correspondence and memoranda of Field Marshal Arthur, duke of Wellington. Edited by his son, the duke of Wellington*, vol. viii; S. Walpole, *A history of England from the conclusion of the Great War in 1815*, vol. iii; D. Masson, *Life of Milton, narrated in connexion with the political, ecclesiastical, and literary history of his time*, vol. vi; J. R. Green, *A history of the English people*, vol. iv; J. W. Willis Bund, *Selection of cases from the state trials*, I: *Trials for treason, 1327–1660*; S. Amos, *Fifty years of the English constitution, 1830–1880*; A. Jessop [ed.], *Œconomy of the fleete*; M. S.

Simpson [ed.], *Documents illustrating the history of St Paul's Cathedral*; S. R. Gardiner [ed.], *The Hamilton papers, being selections from original letters in the possession of his grace the duke of Hamilton and Brandon, relating to the years 1638–1650*) [review notice], *RH* xv (Jan. 1881), 162–8

'John Inglesant' (J. H. Shorthouse, *John Inglesant. A romance*) [review article], *Fraser's Magazine* n.s. xxv (May 1882), 599–605

'Oxford professors and Oxford tutors' [correspondence, co-signed with E. S. Beesley, W. Hunt, M. Creighton and T. F. Tout], *CR* lvii (Feb. 1890), 183–4

'More state papers. Calendar of state papers, domestic series, of the reign of Charles I., 1644–1645. Edited by W. D. Hamilton, F.S.A. Rolls Series. Calendar of the proceedings of the Committee for Compounding, etc., 1643–1660. Part II. Edited by M. A. Everett Green. Rolls Series' [unsigned review], *Speaker* ii (23 Aug. 1890), 220–1

'A Cromwellian record. The Clarke papers, vol. I. Edited by C. H. Firth for the Camden Society' [unsigned review], *Speaker* iv (25 July 1891), 115

'Early home rulers in Ireland. History of the Irish confederation and the war in Ireland. Edited by John T. Gilbert' [unsigned review], *Speaker* iv (13 Dec. 1891), 717–18

'Montrose. By Mowbray Morris. "English Men of Action"' [unsigned review], *Speaker* v (19 Mar. 1892), 359

'Royalist letters: 1645–7. Calendar of state papers. Domestic series of the reign of Charles I. 1645–1647. Edited by W. D. Hamilton, under the direction of the Master of the Rolls' [unsigned review], *Speaker* v (23 Apr. 1892), 509

'James Howell's "letters". The familiar letters of James Howell. Edited, Annotated, and Indexed by Joseph Jacobs' [unsigned review], *Speaker* vi (27 Aug. 1892), 265

'A misleading history. History of the English parliament: together with an account of the parliaments of Scotland and Ireland. By G. Barnett Smith' [unsigned review], *Speaker* vii (11 Mar. 1893), 285–6

'The last campaign of Montrose. *The memoirs of James marquis of Montrose, 1639–1650*. By the Rev. George Wishart, D.D.. Translated, with introduction, notes, appendices, and the original letters. (Part II. now first published.) By the Rev. Alexander D. Murdoch and H. F. Morland Simpson' [unsigned review article], *ER* clxxix (Jan. 1894), 122–57

'An English republican. The memoirs of Edmund Ludlow. Edited by C. H. Firth' [unsigned review], *Speaker* x (15 Sept. 1894), 302–3

'Seventeenth century memoirs. *The memoirs of Edmund Ludlow*. Edited by C. H. Firth' [review], *ILN*, 29 Sept. 1894, 406

'The Lord Protector. Oliver Cromwell. By S. H. Church' [unsigned review], *Speaker* x (24 Nov. 1894), 578

'New light on the Commonwealth. The Clarke papers Vol. II. Edited by C. H. Firth' [unsigned review], *Speaker* xi (27 Apr. 1895), 469

'A later Puritan divine. John Howe. By Robert F. Horton' [unsigned review], *Speaker* [supplement] xiii (8 Feb. 1896), 169–70

'A new book by Carlyle. Sketches of James I. and Charles.' (T. Carlyle [ed. A. Carlyle], *Historical sketches of notable persons and events in the reigns of James I and Charles I*)' [review, unsigned], *DN*, 28 Nov. 1898, 7

'The peace crusade' [correspondence], *The Times*, 14 Feb. 1899, 10

'Cromwell's constitutional aims' [article], *CR* lxxvii (Jan. 1900), 133–42

'Mr. John Morley's Cromwell' [review article], *CR* lxxviii (Dec. 1900), 821–34

Books

Published works and textbooks

History of England from the accession of James I. to the disgrace of chief justice Coke, 1603–1616, London 1863

Prince Charles and the Spanish marriage, 1617–1623, London 1869

The first two Stuarts and the puritan revolution, 1603–1660 ('Epochs of Modern History'), London 1874

The Thirty Years War, 1618–1648 ('Epochs of Modern History'), London 1874

A history of England under the duke of Buckingham and Charles I., 1624–1628, London 1875

The personal government of Charles I.: a history of England from the assassination of the duke of Buckingham to the declaration of the judges on ship-money, 1628–1637, London 1877

Historical biographies ('English History Reading Books'), London 1881

(with J. B. Mullinger) *Introduction to the study of English history*, London 1881

Outline of English history, B.C. 55 – A.D. 1880 ('English History Reading Books'), London 1881, with subsequent editions (bringing the narrative up to date), 1887, 1896, 1901

The fall of the monarchy of Charles I., 1637–1649, London 1882

Illustrated English history, London 1883; rev. edn, London 1902

History of England, from the accession of James I. to the outbreak of the civil war ('Cabinet edition'), London 1883–4

History of the Great Civil War, 1642–1649, London 1886–91

An easy history of England ('Longman's New Historical Readers'), London 1887–8

A student's history of England, London 1890–1

A school atlas of English history: a companion atlas to the 'Student's history of England', London 1891

History of the Great Civil War, 1642–1649 ('Cabinet edition'), London 1893

The Tudor period ('Longmans "Ship" Historical Readers'), London 1893

The Hanoverian period ('Longmans "Ship" Historical Readers'), London 1894

The Stuart period ('Longmans "Ship" Historical Readers'), London 1894

History of the Commonwealth and Protectorate, 1649–1660, London 1895–1902

What gunpowder plot was: a reply to Father Gerard, London 1897

Cromwell's place in history. Founded on six lectures delivered in the University of Oxford, London 1898

Oliver Cromwell, London 1899

History of the Commonwealth and Protectorate, 1649–1660, III: *1654–1656: supplementary chapter*, London 1903

History of the Commonwealth and Protectorate, 1649–1660: with a supplementary chapter ('Cabinet edition'), London 1903

Editions of documentary material

Parliamentary debates in 1610 (Camden 1st ser. lxxxi, 1862)

'Documents relating to Sir Walter Raleigh's last voyage', in *Camden Miscellany, Vol. V* (Camden 1st ser. lxxxvii, 1864), 7–13

'Letter of the Council to Sir Thomas Lake, relating to the proceedings of Sir Edward Coke at Oatlands', in *Camden Miscellany, Vol. V* (Camden 1st ser. lxxxvii, 1864), 3–6

Letters and other documents illustrating the relations between England and Germany at the commencement of the Thirty Years' War: from the outbreak of the revolution in Bohemia to the election of the emperor Ferdinand II. (Camden 1st ser. xc, 1865)

Letters and other documents illustrating the relations between England and Germany at the commencement of the Thirty Years' War: Second series: from the election of the emperor Ferdinand II. to the close of the conferences at Mühlhausen (Camden 1st ser. xcviii, 1868)

El hecho de los tratados del matrimonio pretendido por el principe de Gales con la serenissima infante de España Maria, tomado desde sus prinipios para maior demonstración de la verdad, y ajustado con los papeles originales desde consta por el maestro F. Francisco de Jesus, predicador del rey nuestro señor. Narrative of the Spanish marriage treaty (Camden 1st ser. ci, 1869)

Notes of the debates in the House of Lords, officially taken by Henry Elsing, clerk of the parliaments, A.D.1621 (Camden 1st ser. ciii, 1870)

'The earl of Bristol's defence of his negotiations in Spain', in *Camden Miscellany Vol. VI* (Camden 1st ser. civ, 1871), i–xxxix, 1–56

The Fortescue papers; consisting chiefly of letters relating to state affairs, collected by John Packer, secretary to George Villiers, duke of Buckingham (Camden 2nd ser. i, 1871)

Debates in the House of Commons in 1625 (Camden 2nd ser. vi, 1873)

'Letters relating to the mission of Sir Thomas Roe to Gustavus Adolphus, 1629–1630', in *Camden Miscellany Vol. VII* (Camden 2nd ser. xiv, 1875)

'Notes of the judgement delivered by Sir George Croke in the case of ship-money', in *Camden Miscellany Vol. VII* (Camden 2nd ser. xiv, 1875), 1–17

'Speech of Sir Robert Heath, attorney-general, in the case of Alexander Leighton, in the Star Chamber, Jun. 4, 1630', in *Camden Miscellany Vol. VII* (Camden 2nd ser. xiv, 1875)

Documents relating to the proceedings against William Prynne in 1634 and 1637 (Camden 2nd ser. xviii, 1877)

The Hamilton papers; being selections from original letters in the possession of his grace the duke of Hamilton and Brandon, relating to the years 1638–50 (Camden 2nd ser. xxvii, 1880)

Notes of the debates in the House of Lords, officially taken by Henry Elsing, clerk of the parliaments, A.D.1624 and 1626 (Camden 2nd ser. xxiv, 1880)

'Four letters of Lord Wentworth, afterwards earl of Strafford, with a poem on his illness', in *Camden Miscellany Vol. VIII.* (Camden 2nd ser. xxxi, 1883), 1–9

'A letter from the earl of Manchester to the House of Lords, giving an opinion on the conduct of Oliver Cromwell', in *Camden Miscellany Vol. VIII* (Camden 2nd ser. xxxi, 1883), 1–3

Reports of cases in the Courts of Star Chamber and High Commission (Camden 2nd ser. xxxix, 1886)

The constitutional documents of the puritan revolution, 1628–1660, Oxford 1889; 2nd edn, 'revised and enlarged' [*1625–1660*], Oxford 1899; 3rd 'revised' edn, Oxford 1906

Documents illustrating the impeachment of the duke of Buckingham in 1626 (Camden 2nd ser. xlv, 1889)

'Letters and papers illustrating the relations between Charles the second and Scotland in 1650' (Scottish Historical Society xvii, 1894)

'Hamilton papers: addenda', in *Camden Miscellany Vol. IX.* (Camden 2nd ser. liii, 1895), 1–42

Letters and papers relating to the first Dutch war, 1652–1654. Vol. I. (Navy Records Society xiii, 1899)

Letters and papers relating to the first Dutch war, 1652–1654. Vol. II. (Navy Records Society vol xvii, 1900)

'Prince Rupert at Lisbon', in *Camden Miscellany Vol. X.* (Camden 3rd ser. iv, 1902), **00–00**

Letters and papers relating to the first Dutch war, 1652–1654. Vol. III. (completed by C. T. Atkinson) (Navy Records Society xxx, 1906)

Contributions to multi-authored works

Contributions to the *Dictionary of national biography*, ed. L. Stephen and S. Lee, London 1885–1903, repr. Oxford 1921–2

Aston, Walter, Baron Aston of Forfar (vol. i. 213 in London edition; i. 685 in Oxford edition)

Bacon, Francis [pt I] (ii. 328–49; i. 800–21)

Carr, Robert, earl of Somerset … or Ker (ix. 172–6; iii. 1081–5)

Cary, Lucius, second Viscount Falkland (ix. 246–51; iii. 1155–60)

Charles I (x. 67–84; iv. 67–84)

Chichester, Arthur, Lord Chichester of Belfast (x. 232–5; iv. 232–5)

Conn (Conæus), George (xii. 20–1; iv. 945–6)

Dering, Sir Edward (xiv. 395–6; v. 845–6)

Devereux, Robert, third earl of Essex (xiv. 440–3; v. 890–3)

Digby, John, first earl of Bristol (xv. 56–60; v. 961–5)

Eliot, Sir John (xvii. 186–9; vi. 604–7)

Graham, James, fifth earl and first marquis of Montrose (xxii. 316–19; viii. 316–19)

Hamilton, James, third marquis and first duke of Hamilton …[and] second earl of Cambridge (xxiv. 179–83; viii. 1063–7)

Hay, James, first earl of Carlisle, first Viscount Doncaster, and first Baron Hay (xxv. 265–7; ix. 265–7)

Henrietta Maria (xxv. 429–36; ix. 429–36)

James VI, king of Scotland, afterwards James I, king of England (xxix. 161–81; x. 598–618)

Laud, William (xxxii. 185–94; xi. 626–35)

Macdonald/Macdonnell, Alexander/Alaster (xxxv. 25–6; xii. 469–70)

O'Neill, Owen Roe (xlii. 201–4; xiv. 1095–8)

Pym, John (xlvii. 75–83; xvi. 518–26)

Stuart, Arabella (ii. 53; i. 525)

Villiers, George, first duke of Buckingham (lviii. 327–37; xx. 327–36)

Wentworth, Thomas, first earl of Strafford (lx. 268–83; xx. 1179–94)

Williams, John, archbishop of York (lxi. 414–20; xxi. 414–20)

Yelverton, Sir Henry (lxiii. 316–18; xxi. 1231–3)

Contributions to the *Encyclopædia Britannica* (9th edn), ed. T. S. Baynes and W. R. Smith, Edinburgh 1875–89

Buckingham, George Villiers, duke of (iv. 417–19)

England, History (1603–1874) (viii. 343–67)

George I (x. 420–1)

George II (x. 421–3)

George III (x. 423–7)

George IV (x. 427–9)

Hampden, John (xi. 428–9)

Henrietta Maria [unsigned] (xi. 655)

Laud, William (xiv. 346–7)

Montrose, James Graham, marquis of (xvi. 795–6)

Northampton, Henry Howard, earl of [unsigned] (xvii. 558)

Northampton, Spencer Crompton, earl of [unsigned] (xvii. 558)

Prynne, William [with Osmund Airy] (xx. 25–8)

Pym, John (xx. 120–2)

Raleigh, Sir Walter (xx. 262–4)

Sports, The Book of, or … the Declaration of Sports [unsigned] (xxii. 431)

Strafford, Thomas Wentworth, earl of (xxii. 584–6)

Whig and Tory [unsigned] (xxiv. 540)

Whitelocke, Bulstrode [unsigned] (xxiv. 552–3)

Contributions to other multi-authored projects

'The puritan movement', in D. Patrick and others (eds), *Chambers's cyclopædia of English literature*, 'revised edition', Edinburgh 1901, i. 542–6

'Britain under James I', in A. W. Ward, G. W. Prothero and S. Leathes (eds), *The Cambridge modern history*, III: *The wars of religion*, London 1904, 549–78

Other published writings

Thiersch, H. W. J., *Christian family life*, trans. J. R. Gardiner [i.e. S. R. Gardiner], London 1856

'Report of the Council of the Camden Society ... 1871' [signed by 'Samuel R. Gardiner, Director & William J. Thoms, Hon. Sec.', and appended to Camden 2nd ser. iii, 1872]

'Report of the Council of the Camden Society ... 1872' [signed by 'Samuel Rawson Gardiner, Director & William J. Thoms, Hon. Secretary.', and appended to Camden 2nd ser. v, 1873]

'Report of the Council of the Camden Society ... 1873' [signed by 'Samuel Rawson Gardiner, Director & Alfred Kingston, Hon. Secretary', and appended to Camden 2nd ser. ix, 1874]

'Report of the Council of the Camden Society ... 1874' [signed by 'Samuel Rawson Gardiner, Director & Alfred Kingston, Hon. Secretary', and appended to Camden 2nd ser. x, 1874]

[Additions to the introduction, and corrections] (by 'The Director' [Gardiner]), in J.G. Nichols (ed.), *The autobiography of Anne Lady Halkett* (Camden 2nd ser. xiii, 1875)

'Report of the Council of the Camden Society ...1875' [signed by 'Samuel Rawson Gardiner, Director & Alfred Kingston, Hon. Secretary', and appended to Camden 2nd ser. xv, 1875]

'Report of the Council of the Camden Society ...1876' [signed by 'Samuel Rawson Gardiner, Director & Alfred Kingston, Hon. Secretary', and appended to Camden 2nd ser. xvii, 1876]

'The political element in Massinger', in *The New Shakspere Society's Transactions 1875–6*, 1st ser. iv, n.d. but ?1877, 314–31

'Report of the Council of the Camden Society ... 1877' [signed by 'Samuel Rawson Gardiner, Director & Alfred Kingston, Hon. Secretary', and appended to Camden 2nd ser. xix, 1877]

'Report of the Council of the Camden Society ... 1878' [signed by 'Samuel Rawson Gardiner, Director & Alfred Kingston, Hon. Secretary', and appended to Camden 2nd ser. xxii, 1878]

'Report of the Council of the Camden Society … 1880' [signed by 'Samuel Rawson Gardiner, Director & Alfred Kingston, Hon. Secretary', and appended to Camden 2nd ser. xxvi, 1880]

'Report of the Council of the Camden Society …1882' [signed by 'Samuel Rawson Gardiner, Director & Alfred Kingston, Hon. Secretary', and appended to Camden 2nd ser. xxx, 1882]

'Report of the Council of the Camden Society … 1883' [signed by 'Samuel Rawson Gardiner, Director & Alfred Kingston, Hon. Secretary', and appended to Camden 2nd ser. xxxi, 1883]

'Introduction' to R. Browning, *Strafford: a tragedy*, ed. E. H. Hickey, London 1884

'Report of the Council of the Camden Society …1885' [signed by 'Samuel Rawson Gardiner, Director', and appended to Camden 2nd ser. xxxvii, 1884]

'Report of the Council of the Camden Society … 1886' [signed by 'Samuel Rawson Gardiner, Director & James Gairdner, Secretary', and appended to Camden 2nd ser. xxxix, 1886]

'Report of the Council of the Camden Society … 1887' [signed by 'Samuel Rawson Gardiner, Director & James Gairdner, Secretary', and appended to Camden 2nd ser. xlii, 1888]

'Report of the Council of the Camden Society … 1888' [signed by 'Samuel Rawson Gardiner, Director & James Gairdner, Secretary', and appended to Camden 2nd ser. xliii, 1888]

'Report of the Council of the Camden Society …1889' [signed by 'Samuel Rawson Gardiner, Director & James Gairdner, Secretary', and appended to Camden 2nd ser. xlvi, 1889]

[untitled contribution] to A. Herbert (ed.), *The sacrifice of education to examination*, London 1889, 77–8

'Report of the Council of the Camden Society … 1890' [signed by 'Samuel R. Gardiner, Director & James Gairdner, Secretary', and appended to Camden 2nd ser. xlviii, 1891]

'Report of the Council of the Camden Society … 1891' [signed by 'Samuel R. Gardiner, Director & James Gairdner, Secretary', and appended to Camden 2nd ser. xlix, 1891]

'Introductory note', in F. P. Verney, *Memoirs of the Verney family during the Civil War*, London 1892

'Report of the Council of the Camden Society … 1892' [signed by 'Samuel R. Gardiner, Director & James Gairdner, Secretary', and appended to Camden 2nd ser. li, 1892]

'Report of the Council of the Camden Society … 1893' [signed by 'Samuel R. Gardiner, Director & James Gairdner, Secretary', and appended to Camden 2nd ser. lii, 1894]

'Report of the Council of the Camden Society … 1894' [signed by 'Samuel R. Gardiner, Director & James Gairdner, Secretary', and appended to Camden 2nd ser. lii, 1894]

'Report of the Council of the Camden Society … 1895' [signed by 'Samuel R. Gardiner, Director & James Gairdner, Secretary', and appended to Camden 2nd ser. lvi, 1896]

Bibliography

Unpublished primary sources

Calgary University Library
MS Add. 333/83.30

Cambridge, King's College
MSS Browning

Cambridge University Library
MS Add. 6443/159–61
MS Add. 7348/10/113
MS Add. 8119(2)/G13–29
MS Add. 8119(6)/W1146
MS Add. 8406/37–8, 60
MS Add. 8916/A84/111, 115
MS Add. 8916/A85/1, 3
MS Add. 8954/40

London, British Library
MSS Add. 31111–12, 31998–2004, 34486 (transcripts), 35252
MS Add. 44512
MS Add. 45747
MS Add. 45880
MS Add. 48341
MS Add. 50957

London, Caird Library, National Maritime Museum
LGH/9–11
MS 81/143

London, King's College London
KA/IC/G48 (bundle of papers regarding Gardiner)

London Metropolitan Archives
LMA/4266/A/043

London, University College, London
Royal Historical Society papers

London, University of London
MS 903/1B/8
MS 924/638/(i)–(xxiv)
MS 924/936
MS 924/937

Oxford, All Souls College
MSS Anson

Oxford, Bodleian Library
Don. e. 207, fos 41–9
MS Firth d.4, 6, e.3 (notes, transcripts)
MSS Autogr. e.10, fo. 120
MSS Bryce 68, fos 54–89; 213, fos 108–12
MSS Eng Hist d.4–15, e.59–84 (notes, transcripts)
MSS Eng lett d.100, fos 246–7
MSS Eng lett d.456, fos 139–47
MSS Eng misc. d.177, fos 146–50
MSS Fisher 58, fos 60–1

Oxford, Christ Church College
Dean and chapter records, D&C, i.b.10

Oxford, Merton College
MS 1.5a College Register 1877–1914
MCPh/A13/4 photograph of Gardiner

Philadelphia, University of Pennsylvania
MS Lea

Reading University Library
Longman archives

San Marino, California, Huntington Library
FU 306–7
HM 43314

Contemporary books and articles

Abbott, E. A., *Bacon and Essex*, London 1877
—— *Francis Bacon: an account of his life and works*, London 1885
Acton, Lord, *A lecture on the study of history*, London 1895
Adamson, R., *Fichte*, Edinburgh 1881
Appleton, J. H. and A. H. Sayce, *Dr. Appleton: his life and literary relics*, London 1881
Bacon, F., *Bacon's essays: with annotations*, ed. R. Whateley, London 1856
—— *The essays or counsels civil and moral*, ed. H. Morley, London 1882

—— *Francis Bacon: selections: with essays by Macaulay & S. R. Gardiner*, ed. P. E. Matheson and E. F. Matheson, London 1926

Brandl, A., *Shakespeare*, Dresden 1894

Browning, R., *Strafford: an historical tragedy*, ed. E. Hickey, London 1884

—— *Robert Browning's prose life of Strafford*, ed. C. H. Firth, London 1892

—— *New letters of Robert Browning*, ed. C. W. de Vane and K. L. Knickerbocker, New Haven, Ct 1950

Bury, J. B., *The science of history*, Cambridge 1903

Church, R. W., *Bacon*, London 1884

Coleridge, S. T., *Collected works of Samuel Taylor Coleridge*, ed. J. C. C. Mays, Princeton, NJ 1971–2001

Craik, H., *The life of Edward earl of Clarendon, lord high chancellor of England*, London 1911

Davidson, R. T. and W. Benham, *Life of Archibald Campbell Tait, archbishop of Canterbury*, London 1891

Davies, C. M., *Unorthodox London: or, phases of religious life in the metropolis*, 2nd edn, London 1876

Dilthey, W., *Selected writings*, ed. H. P. Rickman, Cambridge 1976

Dowden, E., *Puritan and Anglican: studies in literature*, London 1900

Fichte, J. G., *Addresses to the German nation* (1812–13), trans. R. F. Jones and G. H. Turnball, ed. G. A. Kelly, New York 1968

—— *Introductions to the Wissenschaftslehre and other writings (1797–1800)*, ed. and trans. D. Breazeale, Indianapolis, In 1994

Firth, C. H., 'Two Oxford historians: 2. Samuel Rawson Gardiner', *QR* cxcv (1902), 547–66

—— *A plea for the historical teaching of history*, Oxford 1904

—— 'Samuel Rawson Gardiner' [obituary], *Proceedings of the British Academy, 1903–4*, 294–301

—— 'Samuel Rawson Gardiner', in S. Lee (ed), *The dictionary of national biography: supplement, 1901–1911*, Oxford 1912

—— *Modern history at Oxford, 1841–1918*, Oxford 1920

Fletcher, C. R. L., *Gustavus Adolphus and the struggle of Protestantism for existence*, London 1890

Fowler, T., *Bacon*, London 1881

Furnivall, F. J., 'The spelling of Shakspere's name', *Academy* v (24 Jan. 1874), 95

—— 'Forewords', in *Robert Browning's prose life of Strafford*, ed. C. H. Firth, London 1892

Gardiner, B. M., *The French revolution, 1789–1795*, London 1882

Gladstone, W. E., *The State in its relations with the Church*, London 1841

—— *Diaries*, ed. M. R. D. Foot and H. C. G. Matthew, Oxford 1968–94

Grant, A. J., *English historians*, London 1906

Green, J. R., *Letters of John Richard Green*, ed. L. Stephen, London 1901

Hegel, G. W. F., *The philosophy of right* (1821), trans. T. M. Knox, Oxford 1952

—— *Lectures on the history of philosophy*, trans. E. S. Haldane and F. H. Simpson, London 1896

Hook, W. F., *Lives of the archbishops of Canterbury*, London 1860–75

Hooker, R., *The works of that learned and judicious divine, Mr. Richard Hooker*, ed. J. Keble, London 1836

—— *The works of that learned and judicious divine, Mr. Richard Hooker*, ed. R. W. Church and F. Paget, London 1888

James VI and I, *James VI and I: political writings*, ed. J. P. Somerville, Cambridge 1994

Jones, W., *Biographical sketch of the reverend Edward Irving*, London 1835

Kant, I., *The conflict of the faculties* (1798), trans. M. J. Gregor, London 1992

—— *Political writings*, ed. H. Reiss, Cambridge 1970

Leak, J. J., *King and hero*, London 1891

MacCallum, M. W., *Shakespeare's Roman plays and their background*, London 1910

Mackintosh, J., J. Forster and T. P. Courtenay, *Lives of eminent British statesmen*, London 1831–9

Massinger, P., *The plays and poems of Philip Massinger* ed. P. Edwards and C. Gibson, Oxford 1976

Masson, D., *The life of Milton, narrated in connexion with the political, ecclesiaitical, and literary history of his time*, London 1859–94

Mehring, F., 'Einem Anhange über den historischen Materialismus', in *Die Lessing-Legende*, Stuttgart 1893

—— *Aus dem literarischen Nachlass von Karl Marx, Friedrich Engels, und Ferdinand Lassalle*, Stuttgart 1902

—— *Karl Marx, Geschichte seines Lebens*, Leipzig 1918

Meredith, G., *An essay on comedy and the uses of the comic spirit*, London 1897

Morley, J., *Oliver Cromwell*, London 1900

Nichol, J., *Carlyle*, London 1892

Oliphant, M. O., *The life of Edward Irving, minister of the national Scotch Church, London: illustrated by his journals and correspondence*, London 1862

Prothero, R. E., *The life and correspondence of Arthur Penrhyn Stanley, D.D., late dean of Westminster*, London 1893

Schiller, F. von, *'The robbers' and 'Wallenstein'* (1780, 1798–9), trans. F. J. Lamport, Harmondsworth 1979

—— *On the aesthetic education of man* (1794), trans. E. M. Wilkinson and L. A. Willoughby, Oxford 1967

Shakespeare, W., *The New Variorum Shakespeare: The tragedie of Coriolanus*, ed. H. H. Furness, Philadelphia, PA 1928

—— *Coriolanus*, ed. P. Brockhurst, London 1976

Shaw, W. A. (ed.), *A bibliography of the historical works of Dr. Creighton … Dr. Stubbs … Dr. S. R. Gardiner and the late Lord Acton*, London 1903

Spedding, J., *The life and letters of Francis Bacon*, London 1861–72

Stubbs, W., *Seventeen lectures on the study of medieval and modern history and kindred subjects*, Oxford 1887

Swinborne, F. P., *Gustavus Adolphus: an historical poem and romance of the Thirty Years' War*, London 1884

Thiersch, Josias, *Über Christliches Familienleben*, ?Munich 1854

Traill, H. D., *Lord Strafford*, London 1889

Secondary sources

Adamson, J. S. A., 'Eminent Victorians: S. R. Gardiner and the Liberal as hero', *HJ* xxxiii (1990), 641–57

Amigoni, D., *Victorian biography: intellectuals and the ordering of discourse*, Hemel Hempstead 1993

Annan, N., *Leslie Stephen: the godless Victorian*, London 1984

Arx, J. P. von, *Progress and pessimism: religion, politics, and history in late nineteenth-century Britain*, Cambridge MA 1985

Asch, R. G., *The Thirty Years' War: the Holy Roman Empire and Europe, 1618–1648*, Basingstoke 1997

Ashley, M., 'Introduction', to S. R. Gardiner, *Oliver Cromwell*, repr. edn, New York, NY 1962

Ashton, R., *The German idea: four English writers and the reception of German thought, 1800–1860*, Cambridge 1980

Ausubel, H., J. B. Brebner and E. M. Hunt, *Some modern historians of Britain*, New York, NY 1951

Bahners, P., '"A place among the English classics": Ranke's *History of the popes* and its British readers', in B. Stuchtey and P. Wende (eds), *British and German historiography, 1750–1950: traditions, perceptions, and transfers*, Oxford 2000

Baillie, A. V. and H. Bolitho (eds), *A Victorian dean: a memoir of Arthur Stanley, dean of Westminster*, London 1930

Barnett, S. A., *Canon Barnett: his life, work, and friends*, 2nd edn, London 1919

Barton, A., 'The distinctive voice of Massinger', *TLS*, 20 May 1997, 623

Beiser, F. C., *Enlightenment, revolution and romanticism: the genesis of modern German political thought, 1790–1800*, Cambridge, MA 1992

—— *German Idealism: the struggle against subjectivism, 1781–1801*, Cambridge, MA 2002

Bentley, J., *Ritualism and politics in Victorian Britain: the attempt to legislate for belief*, Oxford 1978

Benzie, W., *Dr F. J. Furnivall: a Victorian scholar adventurer*, Norman, OK 1983

Bevir, M., *The logic of the history of ideas*, Cambridge 1999

Blaas, P. B. M., *Continuity and anachronism: parliamentary and constitutional development in Whig historiography and the anti-Whig reaction between 1890 and 1930*, The Hague 1978

Breazeale, D., 'Circles and grounds in the Jena *Wissenschaftslehre*', in D. Breazeale and T. Rockmore (eds), *Fichte: historical contexts/contemporary controversies*, Atlantic Highlands, NJ 1994

Brock, M. G. and M. C. Curthoys, *The history of the University of Oxford*, VII: *Nineteenth-century Oxford*, II, Oxford 2000

Burns, A., 'Introduction', to W. J. Coneybeare, 'Church parties', in S. Taylor (ed.), *From Cranmer to Davidson: a Church of England miscellany*, Woodbridge 1999

Burrow, J. W., *A Liberal descent: Victorian historians and the English past*, Cambridge 1981

Butterfield, H., *The Whig interpretation of history*, Cambridge 1931

—— *Man on his past: the study of the history of historical scholarship*, Cambridge 1955

Charney, M., 'The dramatic use of imagery in Shakespeare's *Coriolanus*', *ELH* xxiii (1956), 183–93

Clark, I., *The moral art of Philip Massinger*, London 1993

Coates, W. H., 'An analysis of major conflicts in seventeenth-century England', in W.A. Aiken and B. D. Henning (eds), *Conflict in Stuart England*, London 1960

Crowther, J. G., *Francis Bacon: the first statesman of science*, London 1960

Cust, R., *The forced loan and English politics, 1626–1628*, Oxford 1987

—— and A. Hughes (eds), *The English Civil War*, London 1997

D'Entrèves, A. P., *The medieval contribution to political thought*, New York, NY 1959

Danson, L., *Tragic alphabet: Shakespeare's drama of language*, New Haven, CT 1974

Darby, G., *The Thirty Years' War*, London 2001

Drummond, A. L., *Edward Irving and his circle*, London ?1934

Dunn, T. A., *Philip Massinger: the man and the playwright*, Accra–Edinburgh 1957

Eccleshall, R., *Order and reason in politics: theories of absolute and limited monarchy in early modern England*, Oxford 1978

Edwards, P., 'The royal pretenders in Massinger and Ford', *Essays and Studies* xxvii (1974), 18–36

Elton, G., *Studies in Tudor and Stuart politics and government*, III: *Papers and reviews, 1973–1981*, Cambridge 1983

Fahey, D. M., 'Gardiner as dramatist: a commentary', *Journal of Historical Studies* i (1967), 351–54

Feyerabend, P., *Against method*, 3rd edn, London 1975

Finlayson, M. G., *Historians, Puritanism, and the English revolution: the religious factor in English politics before and after the interregnum*, Toronto1983

Firth, C. H., *Modern history in Oxford, 1841–1918*, Oxford 1920

Fisher, H. A. L., *Pages from the past*, Oxford 1930

Fletcher, A., *The outbreak of the English Civil War*, London 1985

Forbes, D., *The Liberal Anglican idea of history*, Cambridge 1952

—— 'Introduction', to G. W. F. Hegel, *Lectures on the philosophy of world history: introduction: reason in history*, trans. H. B. Nisbet, Cambridge 1975

Garrett, M., 'Introduction', in M. Garrett (ed.), *Massinger: the critical heritage*, London 1991

Gordon, P. and J. White, *Philosophers as social reformers: the influence of Idealism on British educational thought and practice*, London 1979

Gross, A., 'Contemporary politics in Massinger', *Studies in English Literature* vi (1966), 279–90

Hale, J. R., *The evolution of British historiography: from Bacon to Namier*, London 1967

Hamilton, D. B., *Shakespeare and the politics of protestant England*, Lexington, KT 1992

Hill, C., *Change and continuity in seventeenth-century England*, London 1974

—— *Writing and revolution in seventeenth-century England*, Brighton 1985

—— 'Introduction', to S. R. Gardiner, *History of the Great Civil War*, repr. edn, London 1987

Hirst, F. W., *In the golden days*, London 1947

Holstun, J., *Ehud's dagger: class struggle in the English revolution*, London 2000

Howard, D., 'Massinger's political tragedies', in D. Howard (ed.), *Philip Massinger: a critical reassessment*, Cambridge 1985

Howell, R., 'Who needs another Cromwell? The nineteenth-century image of Oliver Cromwell', in Richardson, *Images of Oliver Cromwell*, 96–107

Hunt, E. M., 'Samuel Rawson Gardiner', in H. Ausubel, J. B. Brebner and E. M. Hunt (eds), *Some modern historians of Britain*, New York 1951

Iggers, G. G., *The German conception of history: the national tradition of historical thought from Herder to the Present*, rev. edn, Middletown, CT 1983

Jagendorf, Z., '*Coriolanus*: body politic and private parts', *Shakespeare Quarterly* xli (1990), 455–69

Jann, R., *The art and science of Victorian historiography*, Columbus, OH 1985

Johnson, R., 'The story so far: and other transformations', in D. Punter (ed.), *Introduction to contemporary cultural studies*, London 1986

Jones, H. and J. H. Muirhead, *The life and philosophy of Edward Caird*, Glasgow 1921

Jorgensen, P. A., 'Shakespeare's Coriolanus: Elizabethan soldier', *PMLA* lxiv (1949), 221–35

—— *Shakespeare's military world*, Berkeley, CA 1956

Kearney, H., *Strafford in Ireland, 1633–41: a study in absolutism*, Manchester 1959

Kelley, D. M., *Fortunes of history: historical inquiry from Herder to Huizinga*, New Haven, CT 2003

Kelly, G. A., *Idealism, politics and history: sources of Hegelian thought*, Cambridge 1969

Kenyon, J. P., *The history men: the historical profession in England since the renaissance*, London 1983

La Vopa, A. J., *Fichte: the self and the calling of philosophy, 1762–1799*, Cambridge 2001

Lamont, W., *Puritanism and historical controversy*, London 1996

Lang, T., *The Victorians and the Stuart heritage: interpretations of a discordant past*, Cambridge 1995

Lee, M., *The 'inevitable' union and other essays on early modern Scotland*, East Linton 2003

Levack, B. P., *The formation of the British state: England, Scotland, and the union, 1603–1707*, Oxford 1987

Levin, H., *Shakespeare and the revolution of the times*, New York, NY 1976

Limm, P., *The Thirty Years War*, Harlow 1984

MacGillivray, R., *Restoration historians and the English Civil War*, The Hague 1974

MacLachlan, A., *The rise and fall of revolutionary England: an essay on the fabrication of seventeenth-century history*, Basingstoke 1996

Marsh, P. T., *The Victorian Church in decline: Archbishop Tait and the Church of England, 1868–1882*, London 1969

Mathews, N., *Francis Bacon: the history of a character assassination*, New Haven, CT 1996

Merritt, J. F. (ed.), *The political world of Thomas Wentworth, earl of Strafford, 1621–1641*, Cambridge 1996

Meszaros, P. K., '"There is a world elsewhere": tragedy and history in *Coriolanus*', *Studies in English Literature* xvi (1976), 273–85

Meyer, M., 'Between theory, method, and politics: positioning of the approaches to CDA', in R. Wodak and M. Meyer (eds), *Methods of critical discourse analysis*, London 2001

Mueller, G. E., 'The Hegel legend of "thesis-antithesis-synthesis"', *Journal of the History of Ideas* xix (June 1958), 411–14

Munz, P., *The place of Hooker in the history of thought*, London 1952

Nockles, P., *The Oxford Movement in context: Anglican High Churchmanship, 1760-1857*, Cambridge 1994

Norbrook, D., *Poetry and politics in the English renaissance*, rev. edn, Cambridge 2002

Oredsson, S., *Gustav Adolf, Sverige och trettioåriga kriget: historieskrivning och kult*, Lund 1992

Parker, C., *The English historical tradition since 1850*, Edinburgh 1990

—— *The English idea of history from Coleridge to Collingwood*, Aldershot 2000

Parker, G., *The Thirty Years' War*, London 1984

Patterson, A., *Censorship and interpretation: the conditions of writing and reading in early modern England*, Madison, WI 1984

Peck, L. L., *Northampton: patronage and policy at the court of James I*, London 1982

Phillips, J. E., 'Introduction', to J. E. Phillips (ed.), *Twentieth-century interpretations of Coriolanus*, Englewood Cliffs, NJ 1970

Pocock, J. G. A., *Politics, language and time: essays on political thought and history*, Chicago 1971

Polišenský, J. V., 'The Thirty Years' War and the crises and revolutions in seventeenth-century Europe', *Past and Present* xxxix (1968), 34–43

—— *The Thirty Years' War*, trans. R. Evans, London 1974

Rabb, T. K., 'Reflections on the comparison between historians and scientists', in H. Kozicki (ed.), *Developments in modern historiography*, New York, NY 1993, 63–78

—— (ed.), *The Thirty Years' War: problems of motive, extent, and effect*, Boston, MA 1964

Ray, G. N., *Thackeray: the age of wisdom, 1847–1863*, London 1958

Richardson, R. C., 'Cromwell and the inter-war European dictators', in Richardson, *Images of Oliver Cromwell*, 108–23

—— *The debate on the English revolution*, 3rd edn, Manchester 1998

—— (ed.), *Images of Oliver Cromwell: essays for and by Roger Howell Jr*, Manchester 1993

Ringmar, E., *Identity, interest and action: a cultural explanation of Sweden's intervention in the Thirty Years' War*, Cambridge 1996

Roberts, M., *Gustavus Adolphus: a history of Sweden, 1611–1632*, London 1953–8

—— *Gustavus Adolphus*, 2nd edn, Harlow 1992

Rossi, P., *Francis Bacon: from magic to science* (1957), trans. S. Rabinovich, London 1968

Russell, C., *Parliaments and English politics, 1621–1629*, Oxford 1979

—— *Unrevolutionary England, 1603–1642*, London 1990

—— (ed.), *The origins of the English Civil War*, London 1973

Sanders, C. R., 'The Carlyles and Thackeray', in his *Carlyle's friendships*, 226–66

—— *Carlyle's friendships and other studies*, Durham, NC 1977

Scollon, R., *Mediated discourse as social interaction: a study of news discourse*, Harlow 1998

Sharpe, K., *Sir Robert Cotton, 1586–1631: history and politics in early modern England*, Oxford 1979
—— *The personal rule of Charles I*, New Haven, CT 1992
Skinner, Q., *Visions of politics*, I: *Regarding method*, Cambridge 2002
Steinberg, S. H., *The 'Thirty Years War' and the conflict for European hegemony, 1600–1660*, London 1966
Strachey, L., *Portraits in miniature and other essays*, London 1931
Sutherland, N. M., 'The origins of the Thirty Years War and the structure of European politics', *EHR* cvii (1992), 587–625
Sutton, C., *The German tradition in philosophy*, London 1974
Sykes, N., 'Richard Hooker', in F. J. C. Hearnshaw (ed.), *The social and political ideas of some great thinkers of the sixteenth and seventeenth centuries: a series of lectures delivered at King's College University of London during the session 1925–6*, London 1926
Tillyard, E. M. W., *The Elizabethan world-picture*, London 1943
Turner, P., *English literature, 1832–1890, excluding the novel*, Oxford 1989
Tyacke, N., 'An unnoticed work by Samuel Rawson Gardiner', *Bulletin of the Institute of Historical Research* xlvii (Nov. 1974), 244–5
—— *Aspects of English Protestantism* c. *1530–1700*, Manchester 2001
Usher, R. G., *A critical study of the historical method of Samuel Rawson Gardiner with an excursus on the historical conception of the puritan revolution from Clarendon to Gardiner*, St Louis, WA 1915
Ward, A. W., *A history of English dramatic literature*, London 1875
—— 'Historians, biographers, and political orators', in A. W. Ward and A. R. Waller (eds), *The Cambridge history of English literature*, XIV: *The nineteenth century*, III, Cambridge 1916
Wedgwood, C. V., *Thomas Wentworth, first earl of Strafford, 1593–1641: a revaluation*, London 1961
Wheeler, D., 'Introduction', in D. Wheeler (ed.), *Coriolanus: critical essays*, New York, NY 1995
White, H., *Metahistory: the historical imagination in nineteenth-century Europe*, Baltimore, MD 1973
Wormald, B. H. G., *Clarendon: politics, historiography, and religion, 1640–1660*, Cambridge 1964
—— *Francis Bacon: history, politics and science, 1561–1626*, Cambridge 1993
Yates, N., *Anglican ritualism in Victorian Britain, 1830–1910*, Oxford 1999

Unpublished secondary sources

Noonkester, M. C., 'Liberalism in imperialism: S. R. Gardiner confronts English hegemony in Ireland', unpubl. paper, Southern Conference on British Studies, Forth Worth, TX, 5 Nov. 1999
Scollon, R. and S. W. Scollon, 'Nexus analysis: expanding the circumference of discourse analysis', unpubl. paper, PARC Forum, Paolo Alto, CA, 12 Dec. 2002

Index